WI   N

THE DOMESTIC ASSAULT OF WOMEN

Psychological and Criminal Justice Perspectives

DONALD G. DUTTON

University of British Columbia

Allyn and Bacon, Inc.

Boston   London   Sydney   Toronto

To my father,
W. George Dutton,
a gentle and generous man

Per ardua ad libram

Series Editor: Karen Hanson
Developmental Editor: Alicia Reilly
Production Administrator: Annette Joseph
Production Coordinator: Susan Freese
Editorial-Production Service: Cynthia Hartnett
Cover Administrator/Designer: Linda K. Dickinson

Library of Congress Cataloging-in-Publication Data

Dutton, Donald G., 1943–
  The domestic assault of women.

  Bibliography: p. 193
  Includes index.
  1. Wife abuse – Psychological aspects.
2. Wife abuse – Investigation.   3. Abused
wives.   I. Title.
HV6626.D87   1988   362.8'3   87-19309
ISBN 0-205-11323-0

Printed in the United States of America
10 9 8 7 6 5 4 3 2 1   92 91 90 89 88 87

Credits: Section 1.5, D. G. Dutton, An ecologically nested theory of male violence towards intimates, *International Journal of Women's Studies* (Oct.–Nov. 1985), reprinted with permission of Eden Press. Figure 1.3, M. Straus, A general systems theory approach to a theory of
violence between family members, *Social Science Information, 12*(3), 105–125, used with permission. Table 2.1 & Figure 2.3, A. Bandura, The social learning perspective: Mechanisms of
aggression, in H. Toch (Ed.), *The psychology of crime and criminal justice* (New York: Holt,
Rinehart, and Winston, 1979), used with permission. Section 3.3, D. G. Dutton, Wife
assaulters' explanations for assault: The neutralization of self-punishment, *Canadian Journal of
Behavioural Science, 18*(4), 381–390, copyright © Canadian Psychological Association,
reprinted with permission. Section 4.5, D. G. Dutton, Traumatic bonding: The development
of emotional attachments in battered women and other relationships of intermittent abuse,
Victimology: An International Journal, 6(1981) 2–4: 139; © 1983, Victimology Inc. Other
credits are cited in the text.

Contents

Preface

My interest in the domestic assault of women as a social problem and psychological phenomenon began in 1974 when I took on the task of advising local authorities on how social sciences could contribute to police training. The area of their work that caused police the greatest consternation and for which they were most ill prepared was domestic disturbances, which frequently involve husband-wife violence. For two years I attended "domestics" with the Vancouver police and eventually developed a training program to help them with intervention practices.

It became evident to me as a result of this work that police intervention strategies were shaped by policy and practice in other areas of the criminal justice system. If judges, for example, were consistently lenient with men convicted of wife assault, prosecutors would invest less effort in wife assault cases, and the police, in turn, would see little point in arresting for wife assault. It seemed to me that if a more effective criminal justice response to wife assault were to come about, it would require a sentencing option for judges that represented a compromise between incarceration and a slap on the wrist.

Many men who came before the courts for assaulting their wives were still in a relationship with the victim, and the judges were loath to remove the man's wage-earning capacity by incarcerating him. The alternative sentence—merely putting the man on probation—appeared to offer little protection to the wife, especially as probation officers' caseloads swelled during tight fiscal times, diminishing their per-client contact. What appeared to be required was a type of therapeutic milieu that did not require the man to relinquish his job but which nevertheless afforded him the opportunity to learn nonviolent means of marital conflict resolution.

In 1978 I undertook an internship in group therapy at Cold Mountain Institute on Cortes Island, British Columbia. Fascinated by the potential therapeutic power of group process, I began to serve as a therapist in a then fledgling treatment group for wife assaulters. This group experience continues to provide an important source for me for insights about male violence in intimate relationships.

Since I was initially trained as an experimental social scientist with an interest in the relationship between individuals and social systems—and a perspective of developing scientific laws or principles that hold true across individual cases—the clinical material I was hearing in the treatment groups began to be translated into experimental hypotheses. I remain convinced that, as Kurt Lewin once said, "Nothing is so practical as a good theory," and by implication, that theory, empirical research, and social policy should continually and mutually inform and challenge each other. For example, some implications of research on wife assault appear to carry policy suggestions: arrest seems to have the greatest impact on recidivism reduction (as we shall see in Chapter 5 of this book), and court-mandated treatment appears to be effective (as we shall see in Chapter 6).

Social-psychological theories of aggression, especially social learning theory, appear to be applicable both to treatment and research with wife assaulters. Chapter 2 of this book represents, as far as I know, the first systematic attempt to apply such analysis to an empirically based understanding of the wife assaulter. On the other hand, the deindividuated rage states of some individuals suggest that we should not rely too heavily on purely cognitive formulations of aggression. Forcing psychological theory to eschew lab experiments on college sophomores cannot help but improve that theory's ecological validity and sophistication.

One way we have attempted to expand the data base in our research has been to undertake the laborious task of using convicted wife assaulters as our subject population. As a result of these studies, we have been able to contrast wife assaulters with matched control groups of males and have discovered that the distinguishing features are not attitudes to women or strongly patriarchal perspectives per se but rather an exaggerated emotional reaction to the perception of loss of the female (even if they have acted to drive her away), coupled with poor verbal conflict-resolution skills. This work is reported in Chapter 3.

As a consequence of interviewing the wives of men in our treatment group, of supervising a doctoral dissertation on the cognitive consequences of wife assault, and of participating in two research projects with my colleague Susan Painter, I began to develop a sense of the trauma experienced by battered women. As a rejoinder to simplistic notions that battered women were merely masochistic, we developed traumatic bonding theory, which examines the social forces acting on victims of spouse assault to entrap them in battering relationships. This theory and research is reported in Chapter 4.

Beginning with a definition of wife assault, Chapter 1 presents a brief social-legal history and a review of the main theoretical perspectives on the problem. Chapter 2 systematically applies social learning theory to wife assault and ends with a test case. Chapter 3 presents some empirical studies that compare wife assaulters with appropriate control groups in order to ascertain how they might, as a group, differ from other males. Chapter 4 switches to the psychology of the victims of wife assault and tries to explain the psychological prison created by incremental violence. As a result of this exploration, it is hoped that the reader will gain insight into the difficulty battered women have in exiting abusive relationships.

Chapter 5 examines the criminal justice response to wife assault from its initial reporting to the authorities, to their attendance, arrest, and the outcome in court. A logical outcome of a conviction, it is argued, is mandatory treatment that can teach assaulters alternative behaviors for dealing with violence and alter their interpretation of the causes of their violence. This interpretation often serves to regulate or maintain the violence. These issues are dealt with in Chapter 6. Chapter 7 examines the effects of wife assault on children present in the home and then examines global changes in incidence of wife assault over time. This chapter derives an optimistic conclusion about future incidence rates from pessimistic premises based on population demographics.

Acknowledgments

I would like to acknowledge several people for contributions to my thinking in this book: Kurt Lewin and Solomon Asch, my intellectual godfathers in social psychology; John Arrowood, for launching me and providing continuing support; John Hogarth, for intriguing me with the connection between law and psychology; Dale Trimble, for developing the Assaultive Husbands Project with me; Bruce Levens, for our studies on the police response to family crisis; Anne Ganley, for her pioneering work in treatment of wife assaulters and her ideas about the psychology of the wife assaulter; Murray Straus, without whom we would know considerably less about wife assault; Susan Painter, for numerous brainstorming sessions on the psychology of the victims of wife assault; Jim Browning, for extended intellectual support; and Liz McCririck, for word processing help over and above the call of duty.

Katy Strachan has challenged my thinking at several junctures in this book, and has been an essential catalyst for changing my mind set on numerous ideas, as well as providing considerable editorial help. Barbara McGregor has tempered my most egregious overstatements. I would also like to thank the Social Sciences and Humanities Research Council of Canada for supporting my efforts to write this book.

Finally, I would like to acknowledge Allyn and Bacon's reviewers, who evaluated this text at various stages: Ehor O. Boyanowsky (Simon Fraser University); Mark K. Covey (University of Idaho); Peter Jaffe (Family Court Clinic, London, Ontario), Karil S. Klingbeil (Harborview Medical Center, Seattle); and Kirk R. Williams (University of New Hampshire).

CHAPTER 1

Explanations of Wife Assault

> *How vast is the number of men, in any great country, who are a little higher than brutes. . . . This never prevents them from being able, through the laws of marriage, to obtain a victim. . . . The vilest malefactor has some wretched woman tied to him against whom he can commit any atrocity except killing her—and even that he can do without too much danger of legal penalty.*
>
> —John Stuart Mill, *The Subjection of Women* (1869, p. 62)

Wife assault refers to any physical act of aggression by a man against a woman with whom he is in an intimate (i.e., sexual-emotional) relationship. Researchers (e.g., Schulman, 1979; Straus, 1979) typically define *severe assault* as actions with a relatively high likelihood of causing injury to the victim. Hence, kicking, biting, hitting with a fist or object, beating, or using a weapon against a victim are all actions regarded as severe assault. These actions are likely to carry medical consequences for the victim, and they are actions that in practice are considered grounds for arrest. Other assaultive acts (e.g., slapping, pushing, shoving, grabbing, throwing objects at the victim) are less likely to invoke medical or criminal justice consequences.

Some might object that this classification system ignores the effects of the actions it classifies. Shoving someone down a flight of stairs, for example, may have more serious consequences than hitting the person with a rolled-up newspaper. However, since we will be making use of research that has followed this convention of classifying violent acts (i.e., the Straus *Conflict Tactics Scale*), and because we wish to connect our understanding of the psychology of such actions to the criminal justice policy used to reduce their likelihood of recurring, we will use this definition of wife assault throughout this book.

A second objection to limiting the study of violence toward wives to discrete physical actions is that these actions are only part of what is experienced in wife assault. Physical assault may be accompanied by verbal abuse, psychological abuse, and threats or acts of destruction toward children, pets, and personal property. This constellation of destructive actions more fully represents a continuum of coercive control and therefore, some would argue, constitutes the proper subject matter for a psychology of interpersonal violence. This argument is an important one, and we will return to it at various times in this book. But since our level of explanation for wife assault is related to social intervention, it is primarily interested in focusing on behaviors that society agrees are unacceptable and that require the intervention of agents from outside the family.

While some disagreement exists over how society should control wife assault, there is little agreement whatsoever over social intervention into family conflict. Some people are revulsed by patriarchal-authoritarian family systems; others believe them to be desirable. Whatever our philosophical and political beliefs may tell us about the pathological nature of power imbalances and coercion in social systems, it is rare that social agents become involved in altering the use of coercion in families unless that coercion involves physical force or threats of physical force (see also Steiner, 1981). By concentrating our explanation on physical assault, we can develop an explanation that will have the greatest utility for intervention into family dysfunction. At the same time, we must remain aware that wife assault may have a common psychological substratum with other less dramatic coercive actions.

Our definition of wife assasult, then, is chosen with a view to intervention, and the questions we will pose about the causes of wife assault will bear on the strategies a society might invoke to reduce its incidence.

1.1   INCIDENCE OF WIFE ASSAULT: THE MAGNITUDE OF THE PROBLEM

The distinction between use and effects of violence made in the last section has implications for the importance we attach to the incidence of various types of violence. As Straus (1980) points out, the national "speed limit" on marital violence is that it must be severe enough to cause an injury requiring medical treatment for police intervention to lead to arrest. The distinction between the Violence Index and the Severe Violence Index on the Straus *Conflict Tactics Scale (CTS)* reflects this attitude: actions such as slapping or shoving are less likely to produce injury than are punching, beating, or using a weapon. Exceptions exist, of course, as in our example of shoving someone down a staircase, but in general the *Conflict Tactics Scale* ranks actions with potentially more physically injurious effects. Similarly, although slapping or pushing someone is technically an assault, in practice, police in most jurisdictions would not arrest unless an action corresponding to the Severe Violence Index had occurred. Accordingly, in reviewing the incidence of wife assault, we will focus on these more serious actions that have greatest potential for injury.

Estimating the incidence of wife assault is difficult because the event occurs in private. Two general measures of wife assault are of interest, for somewhat different reasons. The first measure is an actual estimate of the frequency and incidence of wife assault in a general population. This is obtained by a victim survey that interviews a representative sample drawn from a general population about any experiences they have had with being victimized by violence. Five such surveys have been completed. They are:

- the National Crime Survey of victimization based on interviews conducted from 1973 to 1976 with 136,000 people across the United States (U.S. Department of Justice, 1980)
- a nationally representative sample of 2,143 interviewed in 1974 by Response Analysis Corporation (Straus, Gelles, & Steinmetz, 1980)
- a survey of spousal violence against women in the state of Kentucky that interviewed 1,793 women (Schulman, 1979)
- the Canadian Urban Victimization Survey of 61,000 people in seven Canadian cities (Solicitor General of Canada, 1985)
- a second national survey completed by Straus and Gelles (1985, 1986)

The second general measure is the proportion of a social service agency's client population that has been generated by family violence. Stark, Flitcraft, and Frazier (1979) determined what proportion of clients for urban hospital emergency services were assaulted women, and Levens and Dutton (1980) determined what proportion of clients for police service were the result of domestic disputes. Contrasting these two types of data suggests that although a small percentage of all assaulted women make use of hospital or police service, they still constitute a sizable proportion of the entire hospital or police client population. This finding underscores the seriousness of wife assault and the considerable aftermath costs associated with it. We turn our attention first to the victim surveys.

1.1.1 Surveys of Incidence

Both the often-cited Straus survey (Straus, Gelles, & Steinmetz, 1980) and the Kentucky survey (Schulman, 1979) used the Straus *Conflict Tactics Scale* as a measure of the type of actions used to resolve family conflicts. This common measure enables some direct comparison between the two surveys. The National Crime Survey (NCS) and the Canadian Urban Victimization Survey (CUVS) used different questions and definitions that make comparisons of data more difficult.

Both the Straus and the Kentucky surveys, for example, use Straus's definition of severe assault as anything from item O on the Straus *Conflict Tactics Scale* (kicked, bit, or hit you with a fist) to item S (used a knife or fired a gun) as shown in Figure 1.1. Using this definition, the victimization rates for husband-to-wife violence on the two surveys were 8.7% (Schulman) and 12.6% (Straus et al.). Corresponding rates, using the more inclusive measure of any violent husband-wife acts (including slapping, pushing, shoving) were 21% (Schulman) and 27.8% (Straus). These rates refer to the use of violence at any time in the marriage. In Chapter 7 we will examine the results of the 1985 U.S. national survey (Straus & Gelles, 1985, 1986) that indicated a decrease in incidence of wife assault from the 1975 data.

The Kentucky survey reported single versus repeat assault in its data, specifically asking respondents the number of times they had been assaulted in the past 12 months. These data bear on an issue we will consider in more detail in Chapter 2: wife assault as a repeated, self-sustaining habit. Table 1.1 shows the percentage of women in the Schulman survey reporting single or repeated victimizations in the prior 12 months. These data indicate that assaults are likely to be repeated in about 63% of cases where they occur once.

If we combine this estimate with the incidence estimates for severe violence ever occurring in a marriage obtained by Straus and Schulman (12.6% and 8.9%, respectively), we obtain the estimate that severe repeated violence occurs in about 6.8% of all marriages. It is these incidents that represent the major challenges to the criminal justice system, since single assaults are unlikely to be prevented via police intervention. As we will see in Chapter 5, police typically respond after an assault has occurred. Hence, police intervention should be most effective in preventing future assaults in repeat assaulters. An understanding of the repeat assasulter will require analysis not only of the circumstances of the initial assault but also of the mechanisms that sustain an assaultive habit.

Table 1.2 indicates the seriousness of assaults reported in crime and conflict-resolution surveys. The Canadian Urban Victimization Survey (Solicitor General of Canada, 1985) generated a subsample of 10,100 incidents of wife assault. Six percent of these were series assaults (five or more) by the same offender. Forty-five percent were reported to police either by the woman or a third party.

TABLE 1.1   Percentage of women reporting single, repeated victimization in prior year (*n* = 1,793) on Schulman (1979) survey

	Single	Repeated	Total	Probability Action Repeated
Violence items (L-N)	2.0	3.40	5.4	63%
Severe violence items (O-S)	.6	1.04	2.0	63%
Comparable Estimates from Straus et al. (1980) (for 1975)				
Violence items (L-N)			9.00	66%
Severe violence items (O-S)			2.24	66%

FIGURE 1.1 Straus *Conflict Tactics Scale*

1. No matter how well a couple gets along, there are times when they disagree on major decisions, get annoyed about something the other person does, or just have spats or fights because they're in a bad mood or tired or for some other reasons. They also use different ways of trying to settle their differences. I'm going to read a list of some things that you and your (spouse/partner) might have done when you had a dispute, and would first like you to tell me for each one how often you did it in the past year.

Frequency of:	You 1 2 5 10 20+20 Ever?	Partner 1 2 5 10 20 +20 Ever?
a. Discusses the issue calmly.	1 2 3 4 5 6 X	1 2 3 4 5 6 X
b. Got information to back up (your/his) side of things.	1 2 3 4 5 6 X	1 2 3 4 5 6 X
c. Brought in or tried to bring in someone to help settle things.	1 2 3 4 5 6 X	1 2 3 4 5 6 X
d. Argued heatedly but short of yelling.	1 2 3 4 5 6 X	1 2 3 4 5 6 X
e. Insulted, yelled, or swore at other one.	1 2 3 4 5 6 X	1 2 3 4 5 6 X
f. Sulked and/or refused to talk about it.	1 2 3 4 5 6 X	1 2 3 4 5 6 X
g. Stomped out of the room or house (or yard).	1 2 3 4 5 6 X	1 2 3 4 5 6 X
h. Cried.	1 2 3 4 5 6 X	1 2 3 4 5 6 X
i. Did or said something to spite the other one.	1 2 3 4 5 6 X	1 2 3 4 5 6 X
j. Threatened to hit or throw something at the other one.	1 2 3 4 5 6 X	1 2 3 4 5 6 X
k. Threw or smashed or hit or kicked something.	1 2 3 4 5 6 X	1 2 3 4 5 6 X
l. Threw something at the other one.	1 2 3 4 5 6 X	1 2 3 4 5 6 X
m. Pushed, grabbed, or shoved the other one.	1 2 3 4 5 6 X	1 2 3 4 5 6 X
n. Slapped the other one.	1 2 3 4 5 6 X	1 2 3 4 5 6 X
o. Kicked, bit, or hit with a fist.	1 2 3 4 5 6 X	1 2 3 4 5 6 X
p. Hit or tried to hit with something.	1 2 3 4 5 6 X	1 2 3 4 5 6 X
q. Beat up the other one.	1 2 3 4 5 6 X	1 2 3 4 5 6 X
r. Threatened with a knife or gun.	1 2 3 4 5 6 X	1 2 3 4 5 6 X
s. Used a knife or gun.	1 2 3 4 5 6 X	1 2 3 4 5 6 X
t. Other _____	1 2 3 4 5 6 X	1 2 3 4 5 6 X

TABLE 1.2 Seriousness of assaults reported by crime victim and conflict-resolution surveys

	NCS	CUVS	Schulman	Straus et al.
Weapon used	29.7	34.0	0.6	0.5
Gun	11.3	4.0		
Knife	10.6			
Physical attack occurred	66.6	52.0		
Injury as result	56.8	61.0		
Medical care required	23.7	27.0	15.0	
Hospital care required	14.3			
Time lost from work (>1 day)	21.	52.0		

Fifty-one percent of the women were injured, 27% required medical treatment, and 52% percent lost time from their job. The 6% series assault rate is very close to the 6.8% rate generated by the Straus and Schulman studies.

The National Crime Survey (NCS) in the United States used a stratified multicluster sample design. The U.S. Bureau of Census selected a rotating sample of 72,000 households that were representative of the entire population (U.S. Dept. of Justice, 1980). Of these, 60,000 yielded interviews. Sample households were interviewed every six months until seven interviews had been completed in each household. At each interview, respondents were asked to recall incidents of crime that occurred during the previous six months.

As with the CUVS, the NCS was not specifically designed to answer certain questions that are especially important to family violence research. Spouse or ex-spouse was a single category used to define the victim's relationship to the offender, so no reliable distinction could be made between assaults that occurred while the victim was married to the offender and those that occurred after separation (Gaquin, 1977). The NCS survey revealed that 32% of assaults by a spouse/ex-spouse were repeated three or more times, but the survey did not ask questions about victim reactions that may have accounted for repeater/nonrepeater differences.

For a total of 1,058,500 victimizations recorded by the NCS study, injuries resulted in 56.8%, medical care was required for 23.7%, and hospitalization was necessary for 14.3%. Twenty-one percent of the victims lost one or more days from work as a result of the attack. Fifty-five percent reported the victimization to the police. In surveys such as the CUVS and the NCS that are defined to the victim as crime surveys, report rates to police for assaults by husbands are relatively high and comparable to other types of assault (Dutton, 1987b; CUVS = 37%, NCS = 55%). In surveys of family conflict resolution that measure spousal violence per se (e.g., Schulman, 1979; Straus & Gelles,

1985), rates of reporting serious assaults (defined by the *CTS* subscale) to the police are only 14.5% (17% and 10% weighted by respective sample sizes). One interpretation of this discrepancy is that many interspousal acts of violence are not considered criminal by the victim. To the extent the victim considers the action criminal, she is more likely to report to police and more likely to report the act to an interviewer interested in crime against the respondent. To the extent the victim does not consider the action criminal she is less likely to report the act in a crime survey while more likely to report it in a conflict-resolution survey (see Table 1.3).

TABLE 1.3   Likelihood of reporting wife assault to police as a function of seriousness of assault

	Sample Size	Percent Reporting Severe Violence	Percent Reporting to Police
	A. Conflict Tactics Surveys		
Schulman (1979): State of Kentucky	1,793 women	8.7%	17%
Straus et al. (1980): U.S. National Sample	1,183 women	12.6%	n.a.
Straus & Gelles (1985): U.S. National Sample	6,002 households		10%

Survey	Sample Size	Item	Percent Reporting to Police
	B. Crime Victim Surveys		
National Crime Survey (U.S.) (1980)	72,000 households	Spouse/ex-spouse assaults	54.8% (56.8%)[a]
Canadian Urban Victimization Survey (1983)	61,000 people	All assaults against women	44.0%
		Last in a series of assaults against a woman	48.0%
		All assaults by relatives (on victims of both genders)	38.0%
		All assaults against men	32.0%
		All robberies	45.0%
		All crimes	48.0%

[a]Gaquin (1977) reports 54.8%; the U.S. Department of Justice (1980) reports 56.8% for the same data.

SECTION SUMMARY Two types of surveys of family violence exist. The crime victim survey (CUVS, NCS) finds rates of reporting wife assault to the police that are comparable to the rates for other assaults. However, these surveys probably fail to detect violent acts used by one spouse against the other that are not defined as criminal by the victim. A second type of survey, which uses the *CTS* and asks respondents to report modes of conflict resolution in the family, avoids the problems of whether a respondent defines the action as criminal or not.

When *CTS* surveys are considered, two major results stand out. First, rates of reporting serious assault (by the *CTS* definition) to the police drop to 14.5% (from the 37%–55% report rate found by the crime victim surveys). This discrepancy is consistent with the suggestion that much family violence goes undetected by crime victim surveys. The crime victim survey seems to generate reports of incidents that are more likely to be defined as crime by the victim and more likely to be reported to the police.

A second result of the *CTS* surveys is that incidence rates for wife assault are 21% to 27.8% for all violent acts occurring at any time in the marriage and 8.7% to 12.6% for severe assault. In about two-thirds of couples where assault occurs once, it is repeated within a year. This finding, as we shall see in Chapters 5 and 6, has relevance for theories about recidivism in wife assaulters.

Surveys of Client Populations

By coding 174 hours of taped calls from citizens for police services in an urban setting, Levens and Dutton (1980) determined that 17.5% of all calls were for family disputes and 13.5% of all calls were specifically for husband-wife disputes that frequently involved wife assault. In Chapter 5, when we consider policy issues for controlling wife assault, we will have to consider this rather huge demand on police resources caused by family disputes. Figure 1.2 demonstrates this relationship.

A similar relationship exists for hospital use or for police services. Schulman's (1979) respondents reported requiring medical attention for 15% of the serious assaults against them. In urban areas, this usually means emergency room care (62% of all hospital treatment). The NCS survey respondents reported receiving medical attention in 23.7% of spouse/ex-spouse incidents (Gaquin, 1977), and the Canadian Urban Victimization Survey reported that 27% of women attacked by their spouses required medical treatment. Again most of this attention (53.2%) was hospital emergency care.

Viewing demand for hospital service as another social cost of wife assault, Stark, Flitcraft, and Frazier (1979) examined hospital records for an urban emergency room and concluded that 33.2% of all injuries presented by women were probably caused by assault by an intimate and 22.5% definitely were caused by such an assault. The Schulman (1979) survey found that injuries inflicted

FIGURE 1.2   Relationship of total estimated incidence of wife assault to demand for police intervention

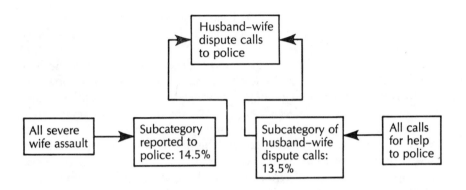

[a]Schulman, 1979; Straus et al., 1980
[b]Levens and Dutton, 1980

by a male partner resulted in 4.4 physician visits per year per 100 women. Two-thirds of these were emergency room visits. A survey of 1,210 women in Texas found a 1% per annum rate of injuries that required medical treatment (Teske & Parker, 1983). Straus (1986) pointed out that if one extrapolated the Kentucky and Texas results to the entire U.S. population, about 1.5 million women per year receive medical attention because of assault by a male partner. The picture is thus similar to that for use of police service; although only a fraction of all assaults get presented, the drain on resources is already high.

1.2   A BRIEF SOCIAL-LEGAL HISTORY

The development of social history methodology in the last 20 years has provided the means for studying the life of average citizens in various historical periods. We now have studies available of the social evolution of love (Hunt, 1959), sex (Taylor, 1954; Tannahill, 1980), sex and power (de Reincourt, 1974), manners

(Elias, 1978), folly (Tuchman, 1984), and even torture (Peters, 1985). A comprehensive social history of wife assault remains to be written, largely because the private nature of the event creates problems for historians in gaining access to adequate data.

What little historical work has been done has focused on attitudes of misogyny, especially in theological tracts such as the *Malleus Maleficarum* (Summers, 1928), *Gratian's Decretum* (Davidson, 1977), or the writings of St. Paul and St. Augustine (Daly, 1973, 1978), and on legal sanctions (or lack thereof) of wife assault. The theological tracts are of relevance because of the great influence they exerted in both guiding and exonerating behavior, especially during the Middle Ages. The *Decretum* (c. 1140), the first enduring systematization of church law, specified that women were "subject to their men" and needed castigation or punishment for correction. This punishment was made necessary by women's supposed inferiority and susceptibility to the influence of devils. Jacob Sprenger's *Malleus Maleficarum* carried misogyny to the extreme, using susceptibility to diabolic influence as the rationalization for murdering women during the Middle Ages in order to suppress witchcraft. It is interesting to note that one basis for suspecting a woman of witchcraft was male impotence.

Modern concepts of personal responsibility for violent behavior were foreign to the medieval mind, where violence was excused as part of a great cosmological scheme or justified as being in the best interests of the victim (to help her avoid the influence of devils). As we will see in Chapter 3, this tendency to externalize the causes of violent behavior is still common in males who assault women, although cosmic influences have been replaced by alcohol as a favorite excuse. Victim blaming is still common as well, through attributing the cause of the violence to the female victim. Female susceptibility to diabolic influence has been replaced as an exonerative cause of male violence by the concept of female masochism (Caplan, 1984; Dutton, 1983) or provocation (see Chapter 3).

Unfortunately, knowledge of medieval misogyny tells us little about the prevalence of wife assault during the Middle Ages. Davidson (1977) reports that in sixteenth-century France a group of carnival actors called *charivaris* who existed in each community staged pranks upon any members of the town whose actions deviated from the local norms. This dramaturgical social control focused on any husband who allowed his wife to beat him. The unfortunate male was dressed up, seated backwards on a donkey, draped with kitchen paraphernalia, and punched in the genitals. That no such derision descended upon battered women suggests to Davidson that wife beating was normative, since only counternormative behavior was punished by the *charivaris*.

Davidson also cites the eighteenth-century Napoleonic Civil Code that influenced French, Swiss, Italian, and German law as vesting absolute family power in the male and recognizing violence as a grounds for divorce only when the courts decided that it constituted attempted murder. Hence, the male had a legal right to use violence up to the point of attempted murder to protect his absolute power within the family.

This situation also apparently existed in England, prompting John Stuart Mill in 1869 to write his famous essay, "The Subjection of Women," which Davidson cites as the first significant document to raise public consciousness about the plight of battered wives. In this essay, Mill decried "bodily violence towards the unhappy wife," which he viewed as arising from men's "mean and savage natures" (p. 62). These natures were checked and resisted in public transactions but went unchecked at home because their wives could not repel or escape them and because they viewed their wives as chattels "to be used at their pleasure" (p. 63).

Mill's essay helped spark controversy about family violence and a report to the British Parliament in 1874. At that time British common law allowed a man to beat his wife with a rod no bigger than his thumb. This "rule of thumb" was believed to be humane because it replaced an older law that allowed beating "with any reasonable instrument."

By the end of the nineteenth century, wife assault even by the "rule of thumb" had become illegal under British common law and in many U.S. states (Goldman, 1978). However, in practice, the criminal justice system in England, the United States, and Canada routinely ignored family violence unless a murder occurred. This discrepancy between the law and criminal justice policy was pointed out in the 1970s by the women's movement as it identified wife assault as a social problem of considerable magnitude and incidence and as it brought attention to the lack of action by the criminal justice system in dealing with wife assaulters.

1.3 SINGLE-FACTOR EXPLANATIONS FOR WIFE ASSAULT

John Stuart Mill's attribution of wife assault to the "mean and savage natures" of some men exemplifies nineteenth-century explanations of human behavior: actions were attributed to an inferred construct residing within the person, referred to as nature. Such reasoning was clearly circular: the construct was used as cause for the behavior, but the only proof for the construct's existence was the behavior itself. Considerable credence was given to a belief that nature, be it savage or superior, was the product of breeding.

Explanations of wife assault disappeared for a century after Mill's essay. Wife assault was summarily dismissed and ignored by social detection systems. Others have written at length about society's inattention to this private crime (Straus, Gelles, & Steinmetz, 1980; Walker, 1979a; Martin, 1977), and in Section 1.3.3 we shall consider some bases for societal inattention to family violence.

For present purposes, however, it should be clear that if no social problem is detected, there is nothing to explain. Those cases that did come to the attention of authorities were exceptional in the extent of their violence since nothing short of extreme assault or attempted murder led to conviction (Field, 1978) or else were revealed in psychiatric treatment of individuals who presented with other psychological problems. These few exceptional case studies served as a basis for the overgeneralized conclusion that all men who assault their wives do so because of pathology or psychiatric disorder. Clinical syndrome explanations of wife assault attributed it to pathological dependency (Snell, Rosenwald, & Robey, 1964; Faulk, 1974), brain lesions (Elliot, 1977), or sadistic character (Pizzey, 1974). Such explanations helped reinforce the view of wife assault as rare and the men who committed it as unusual, atypical, and pathological.

1.3.1 In the Psyche of the Assaulter

The *Diagnostic and Statistical Manual of the Mental Disorders (DSM-III;* 1981) contains a variety of disorders that share symptomatologies with descriptions of wife assaulters given by their wives (Rounsaville, 1978; Rosenbaum & O'Leary, 1981), by clinicians working with the wife assaulters (Ganley & Harris, 1978), or by the men themselves (Gayford, 1975). These include conjugal paranoia, with delusions of sexual infidelity by one's spouse; intermittent explosive disorders, including temporal lobe epilepsy (Elliot, 1977), with intense acceleration of autonomic activity and postepisode amnesia; and borderline personality disorders with intense mood swings, interpersonal disturbances, anger, and suicidal gestures. Also, Rounsaville (1978) and Gayford (1975) reported substance abuse syndromes in approximately half of an assaultive population, although Rounsaville reported that only 29% had been drinking at the time of the assault. Furthermore, Rounsaville found that only 6 of 31 wife assaulters in his sample had a history of psychiatric contact and 15 had no prior contact.

These shared symptomatologies do not represent a psychiatric profile of all wife assaulters. Men who assault their wives may belong to subpopulations with psychiatric disturbances, as do nonassaultive males. The appearance of similarity between descriptions of assaulters and some *DSM-III* categories is not a substitute for a systematic analysis. The clinical explanation of wife assault was based on an overgeneralization from small clinical samples obtained under extremely selective circumstances.

Faulk (1974), for example, discussed the "psychiatric disturbance of men who assault their wives" based on a sample of 23 men "remanded in custody for charges of seriously assaulting their wives." The extremity of this sample is indicated by the fact that all men in it had either murdered their wives (8), tried to murder them (9), or wounded or seriously injured them (6). Faulk reported that 16 of these 23 men had a "psychiatric disorder," but 7 of these were suffering from anxiety or depression that might have been a consequence of their violence and ensuing incarceration.

Faulk's methodology exemplifies the problems associated with early clinical views of wife assaulters: the sample is small and nonrepresentative. The extremity of the violence is not considered prior to generalizing to less violent wife assaulters. The empirical basis for the psychiatric diagnoses is not fully described but seems to be based on prison records, depositions, and an interview. What these early studies lacked was a large sample of wife assaulters drawn not just from prison populations but more representative of the typical nonincarcerated wife assaulter. Furthermore, consideration of whether several subpopulations of wife assaulters existed was lacking. Faulk differentiated overcontrolled types of wife assaulters (whom he called passive-dependent) from undercontrolled (whom he called violent and bullying), but the differentiation was rudimentary and unsystematic. Comparison with appropriate control groups also was lacking. In Chapter 3 we will see the implications of this weakness: that conflict, anger, and the use of violence were confounded in surveys of experimental populations.

More recent psychiatric studies are methodologically sounder but still suffer from some serious interpretative problems. For example, Bland and Orn (1986) presented data from an urban random sample (n = 1,200) of an adult population that used the *Diagnostic and Statistical Interview Schedule* (Robins, Helzer, Croughan, Williams, & Spitzer, 1981), which asks 259 questions related to diagnostic criteria from the *Diagnostic and Statistical Manual of the Mental Disorders (III)* and the use of violence. Only 20% of contacted persons refused to participate (295/1,495). The authors reported only three diagnostic categories: antisocial personality disorder, major recurrent depression, and alcohol abuse/ dependence. For respondents with any one of the above diagnoses, there was a 54.5% chance of violent behavior (hitting or throwing things at their partner). For respondents with no diagnosis based on the *Diagnostic Interview Schedule*, the self-reported violence rate dropped to 15.5%. When alcoholism was combined with either or both the antisocial personality disorder or depression, the violence rate jumped to 80% to 93%. The study was largely descriptive and did not seek to causally disentangle family violence from the other diagnoses reported. Hence, the reader does not know whether depression causes violence to the spouse or whether both are produced by some unreported third factor.

Hamberger and Hastings (1986) report clinical assessments of 105 men attending a wife assault treatment program. Using the *Millon Clinical Multiaxial Inventory* to assess disorders (based on the *Diagnostic and Statistical Manual of the Mental Disorders* or *DSM-III*), Hamberger and Hastings factor-analyzed the protocols, identifying three orthogonal factors, which they labelled as schizoidal/borderline, narcissistic/antisocial, and passive-dependent/compulsive. Their assaultive sample fell equally (10–16 men each) into these three orthogonal categories, into four other categories that combined various aspects of the first three pure categories, and into one category that had no aspects of the clinical pathology indicated in categories 1 through 3.

Subsequent comparison of assaultive males with a nonassaultive population indicated greater difficulty in the assaultive population of modulating affective states and feeling comfortable in intimate relationships. As is relatively frequent in family violence research, the authors reported that subject-selection factors may have influenced their results. Also, the test used to establish the clinical assessments in this study, the *Millon Clinical Multiaxial Inventory,* may not accurately represent *DSM-III* classifications of disorders. The content validity of the Millon is debatable as far as the *DSM-III* is concerned (Widiger, Williams, Spitzer, & Frances, 1985). However, the implications of this study—that assaultive males tend to exhibit personality disorders—suggest that treatment programs may have limited success since personality disorders are notoriously difficult to change via short-term therapy.

1.3.2 In the Genes: Sociobiology and Wife Assault

Sociobiologists have extended Charles Darwin's (1871, 1872) notion that physical characteristics and behaviors of species develop over time through the process of natural selection. Characteristics and behaviors that enable a species to function in a specific environment are maintained and gradually evolve to enable the species to survive. In more recent years, the evolutionary point of view has been extended to account for the *social* behavior of animals (Wynne-Edwards, 1962) and humans (Wilson, 1975, 1978).

In extending evolutionary ideas to human social behavior, sociobiologists attempt to account for cooperation, competition, and aggression from the standpoint that each behavior has an evolutionary function; that is, it maximizes the likelihood that individuals who demonstrate the behavior will survive and that their offspring will survive (Bigelow, 1972) or that their contribution to the gene pool will be maximized.

In so doing, sociobiologists tend to focus on social behavior that is common to humankind across all cultures (rather than on cultural variations as anthropologists do). They regard these common types of social behavior as part of an evolutionary heritage. So, for example, groups and individuals who developed aggression in early hunting cultures would be more likely to compete successfully for territory and mates, thus maximizing the survival of themselves and their offspring. Sociobiological theory comes in for strong attack from most social scientists who claim that it underestimates the impact of sociocultural factors on contemporary social behavior and overestimates the biological or inherited aspect of such behavior (Gould, 1983). It is not necessary to get into the current controversy, however, in order to raise a question that is difficult for sociobiologists to answer: How does one explain domestic violence and in particular the killing of one's spouse? It seems a less-than-optimal way to increase one's contribution to the gene pool. In fact, it seems evolutionarily unsound; yet it has occurred with alarming frequency since the beginnings of recorded history (Davidson, 1977; de Reincourt, 1974).

Wilson (1975, 1978), a sociobiologist, concedes that the evolution of aggression has been jointly guided by three forces:

1. the genetic predisposition toward learning some form of aggression
2. the necessities imposed by the environment in which a society finds itself
3. the previous history of a group that biases it toward adopting one cultural innovation over another

Wilson views humans as disposed to (1) respond with "an unreasoning hatred to external threat" and to (2) escalate hostility sufficiently to overwhelm the source of threat by a wide margin of safety. If we apply this analysis to cases of sexual threat, the sociobiologists would predict an inherited predisposition of aggression toward invading *males,* but there is nothing in the sociobiological argument to account for jealousy based on sexual threat resulting in violence toward the intimate partner. Simeons (1962), for example, argues that men have a genetic disposition to react with rage to sexual threat. However, the stimuli that constitute sexual threat are often, as we will see, socially determined, and the response to such stimuli, while most certainly a form of physiological arousal, is itself often labelled (as rage, hurt, or anxiety) in ways that are also culturally shaped.

Finally, the behavior that follows from the emotion is again directed by what the culture deems more or less acceptable. Indeed, most recently sociobiological writers (e.g., Symons, 1980) on the evolution of human sexuality argue that molar behavior (with the exception of simple motor patterns) "is too variable and too far from the genes" (Symons, personal communication, 1981). Indeed, Symons states, "I imagine that many psychological systems are involved (in uxoricide)—emotional goals, cognitive abilities to appreciate the relations between various events (real and imagined) and goals, anger, and the like" (Symons, personal communication, 1981).

Hence, it is our argument that the strongest statement on wife assault that can be made on sociobiological grounds is that men have an inherited tendency to secrete adrenalin when they *believe* themselves to be sexually threatened and that they will experience this state as arousing. The label applied to this arousal, however, will be socially determined, and, the tendency to label this arousal as anger, the behavioral response of acting out anger aggressively, and the choice of a target for aggression are all shaped by societal values and learned dispositions. In order to understand these societal values more fully, we turn our attention now to North American macrocultural explanations of wife assault.

1.3.3 In the Culture: Patriarchy and Wife Assault

Sociological explanations for wife assault developed in the 1970s endeavored to correct the impression created by psychiatric explanations that wife assault was a rare event that was committed only by men with diagnosable psychiatric disturbances. Rather, sociologists viewed wife assault as a common event, generated by social rules that supported male dominance of women (Goode, 1971; Dobash & Dobash, 1978) and tacit approval by society (Straus, 1976, 1977a, 1977b, 1977c).

Straus (1976) and Gelles (1972) revealed what psychiatrists had ignored: that wife assault was mainly normal violence committed not by madmen but by men who believed that patriarchy was their right yet lacked the resources to fulfill that role. As Straus (1977b) claimed, "Our society actually has rules and values which make the marriage license also a hitting license." The sociological claim, therefore, was twofold: that society was patriarchal and that the use of violence to maintain male patriarchy was accepted. As Dobash and Dobash (1979) put it, "Men who assault their wives are actually living up to cultural prescriptions that are cherished in Western society—aggressiveness, male dominance and female subordination—and they are using physical force as a means to enforce that dominance" (p. 24).

As support for this claim, sociological writers cited evidence that included criminal justice system inaction and the protection husbands enjoy against civil actions by wives for damages resulting from assault. A survey by Stark and McEvoy (1970) found that 24% of men and 17% of women approved of a man slapping his wife "under appropriate circumstances." This latter finding, however, hardly seems to prove a cultural norm for the use of violence against wives. First of all, only a minority of men or women approved a man slapping his wife under *any* circumstances. Viewed from another perspective, the survey result tells us that the majority believe slapping is never appropriate. Second, the wording of the question was ambiguous. The phrase "appropriate circumstances" loads the question; we do not know what egregious transgressions may be conjured up by respondents as necessary before a slap is appropriate. Finally, the question tells us nothing about the degree of violence that is acceptable. While 24% of men may approve of slapping a wife, fewer may approve of punching or kicking a wife and still fewer may approve of beating or battering a wife.

When we add the Stark and McEvoy survey of acceptance of wife assault to the incidence surveys reviewed above (which indicate that a small minority of men assault their wives), the case for wife assault being normative is weakened. Also, as we will see in Chapter 3, many men who have been convicted of wife assault do not generally feel that what they did was acceptable. Instead, they feel guilty, minimize the violence, and try to exculpate themselves in the manner of one whose actions are unacceptable to oneself. The sociological view of violence as normal would lead us to expect the opposite: that no guilt would follow from normal behavior.

The reluctance of the criminal justice system to prosecute wife assault also fails to offer clear-cut evidence for tolerance of wife assault as sociological writers would have us believe. As we will see below, criminal justice inaction over domestic disturbances may not be substantially less than for other crimes. Furthermore, police reluctance to intervene in family trouble may stem from an admixture of emotional discomfort in witnessing strident conflict, beliefs about the inefficacy of charges, beliefs about women dropping charges, and informal professional socialization (Dutton, 1981a; Levens & Dutton, 1980). The claim that this indicates "legitimation of husband-wife violence" (Straus, 1976) is somewhat facile given, as shown in Chapter 5, that the criminal justice response to wife assault is not appreciably different from other forms of assault.

Shotland and Straw (1976) performed a bystander intervention study in which a man verbally abused and physically threatened a woman in order to investigate both third-party perceptions of this event and the likelihood of the third party intervening. Shotland and Straw had one male and one female actor engage in a verbal altercation in an elevator whose door opened across the hall from where experimental subjects awaited another study. In one experimental condition the woman yelled, "Get away from me, I don't know you!" and in another, "Get away from me, I don't know why I married you!" In all other respects the conditions were the same, with moderately high levels of verbal abuse and low levels of physical conflict. Subjects who witnessed the fight between strangers took intervening actions 69% of the time, while those who believed the couple was married did so only 19% of the time.

Subsequent examination of the beliefs and perceptions of third-party witnesses to a film of a man-woman fight revealed that when the couple was believed to be married (as opposed to being strangers), onlookers believed the woman to be in less danger and less likely to want their help. The man was perceived as more likely to stay and fight. In other words, an entire constellation of perceptions about the seriousness of the violence and the costs of personal intervention altered with the belief that the couple were intimates. Some of these perceptions may be erroneous (such as the belief that the violence is less), and some may be rationalizations of personal inaction. Nevertheless, the complex alteration of perception is more fundamental than mere tacit approval of wife assault.

What is required to clarify this issue is a systematic extension of the Shotland and Straw study that varies degree of violence and the social relationship between the third party and the couple in conflict. Complex issues affect intervention decisions and when professional objectives (such as arrest and conviction for police officers) are added, it becomes difficult to deduce approval for wife assault from intervention decisions per se (see Section 5.4 in Chapter 5).

The result of the sociological analysis of wife assault, however, has been the acknowledgment of the powerful, if complex, role of social factors in creating the context in which violence occurs. The shortcoming of the sociological approach has been its inability to explain why men exposed to similar normative contexts behave so differently. If social license determines violent behavior we would expect a majority of men to be violent, but only a minority are. Also, as the violence becomes more extreme, the size of this minority group of perpetrators shrinks.

Hence, a complete explanation for wife assault must distinguish men who repeatedly and severely assault their wives from men who do so sporadically and in a less serious way. It must explain why many wife assaulters commit wife assault only once (Schulman, 1979). While psychiatric theories err by setting their focus too narrowly and overlooking the context of wife assault, sociological theories set their focus too broadly and miss the variations in assaultive behavior in common contexts. A complete theory of wife assault must avoid both shortcomings: it must locate a man's violence in the normal learning environment to which that man has been exposed and it must be able to differentiate assaultive from nonassaultive males on the basis of differences in that learning environment.

Therefore, while sociological theories provide important analyses of the social context of wife assault, this context has to be combined with characteristics of the assaultive male in order to explain variation in behavior.

1.4 GENDER AND THE USE OF VIOLENCE

One other empirical finding that is difficult for the sociological viewpoint to explain is the finding from the U.S. national survey (Straus, Gelles, & Steinmetz, 1980; Straus, 1980) that the use of violence within marriage is approximately equal for males and females. If violence is a last resort used to defend a patriarchal status quo, we would expect to find males using violence much more than females. However, Straus (1980) reports that the annual incidence rate for use of violence by husbands was only slightly higher (12.1 per hundred husbands) than it was for wives (11.6 per hundred wives). Straus found that contrary to the expectation that each spouse would tend to cover up his or her own violence, rates were slightly higher when the computation was based on data provided by respondents on their own use of violence.

Straus also found that wives were slightly more likely than husbands to use severe violence (11.8 versus 11.4 per hundred) and that when acts of severe violence are considered (kicking, biting, hitting with an object, beating up, attacking with a weapon), the proportion of acts where the woman was the only one using violence increases. When less violent actions are considered (e.g., pushing, slapping, shoving), more mutual use of violence is reported. As Straus reports, "Contrary to our original expectations, the wives in this sample maintain their rough equality with respect to violence, irrespective of whether one measures it by incidence rate, mutuality of violence, degree of severity of the violent act, or prevalence of violence at each level of severity" (pp. 685–686).

Straus attempts to explain away this surprising result by differentiating self-defensive violence (where women used minor violence and their husbands used severe violence) from other violence (where the woman used severe violence and the husband used only minor violence). To support the defense of patriarchy view, one would have to assume that female violence was primarily self-defensive, and this is what Straus does. After admitting that in 36% of all self-reported cases of female violence the husband was not violent, he then assumes that wherever the husband was violent, mutual violence was initiated by the male 80% of the time. However, since his data have no reports of temporal sequence, there is no empirical basis for this assumption.

The Bland and Orn (1986) study referred to in Section 1.3.1 did include temporal sequence questions in assessing the incidence of family violence. Of those males in Bland and Orn's sample (n = 355) who reported hitting or throwing things at their wife (14.6%), 57.7% said they were the one to do so first. In a sample of 616 women, of the 22.6% who reported hitting or throwing things at their husband, 73.4% said they were the one to do so first. These data suggest that the women were somewhat more likely than the men to escalate arguments into the realm of physical acts.

These gender data raise three issues that are important to an understanding of family violence. The first issue is that the sociological explanation of family violence as caused by defense of patriarchy is not well supported. If we focus on the use of violence, it appears that, within marriages, men and women both use violence as a means of resolving conflict, although outside of marriage men are overwhelmingly more likely to use violence (Straus, 1980). An alternative view is that defense of patriarchy is only one of many causes of violence in intimate relationships and one which requires specific empirical testing.

A second point to be raised from these data is that any explanation of human action must apply to both male and female action. Some sociological views of wife assault have implied that patriarchy fosters violence because men are naturally violent (Davidson, 1978; Dobash & Dobash, 1979). It follows from this view that women's violence, to the extent it happens at all, occurs in response to male-initiated violence, but male violence occurs automatically (e.g., in response to unwarranted jealousy or unrealistic expectations about a woman's housekeeping responsibilities). My own view is that both men and women will use violence if they are rewarded for doing so and alternative actions are not available. If this is so, why is wife assault a more serious problem than husband assault?

The answer to this question brings us to our third point. Straus's data are for use of violence. Social explanations focus on actions. However, whether an action constitutes a social problem depends on its effects. The effects of male violence are far more serious than those of female violence. Berk, Berk, Loseke, and Rauma (1981) analyzed 262 domestic disturbance incidents reported to police, using a scale of effects that ranked the severity of injuries sustained by the victim. When assaultive incidents are classified by injurious effects rather than use of violence, women are the victims 94% of the time compared to 14% for men.

Berk et al. also report that data from the National Crime Survey, collected from a nationally representative sample of households, indicated that when victimization occurs between spouses, 95% of the time it is the woman who suffers. This discrepancy between mutual violence and unilateral victimization of women may have a distinctly simple and nonsocial explanation: greater male strength and different musculature creates greater capability to cause injury (Steinmetz, 1977). In any event, husband assault is not a major social problem because few males are injured by female violence. Wife assault, on the other hand, does produce serious injuries and physical risk.

1.5 INTERACTIONIST EXPLANATIONS: A NESTED ECOLOGICAL APPROACH

One of the points of consensus that developed among family violence researchers in the late 1970s was the need for more sophisticated, multifactor theories that took into account both the intrapsychic features of the violent offender and the interpersonal context in which the violence occurred. Gelles and Straus (1979) reviewed the contribution of 15 theories toward an understanding of wife assault and described the contributions and limitations of each. Sociology, psychiatry, psychology, and sociobiology have all made theoretical contributions, and as Gelles and Straus point out, their contributions tend to be complementary rather than competitive. Some theories, such as sociological theories, pertain more to the explanation of rates or incidence of violence in target populations. Psychological, psychiatric, and sociobiological theories focus more on an explanation of the violence of an individual or group of individuals with similar qualities. These theories further subdivide into those that seek to explain expressive violence (the use of force to cause pain or injury) and those that explain instrumental violence (use of force for control over another's behavior).

Since such a broad range of theories has been applied to family violence, attempts to disentangle theories are necessarily cumbersome and lead the reader into the area of metatheory and philosophy of science. Even single theoretical contributions such as Straus's (1973) general systems cybernetic model is so complex that in the 12 years since Straus published it, adequate empirical testing has not been possible (see Figure 1.3).

Rather than attempt to disentangle this welter of theoretical perspectives, we will instead describe our own criteria for a theory of wife assault and then go on to describe the development and testing of such a theory. Social-psychological theories concentrate on the individual as a unit of analysis. Hence our interest will be in building a theory to explain the behavior, feelings, and beliefs about the individual wife assaulter. This will involve a focus both on internal, or intrapsychic, events and those interpersonal, or social, relationships that influence assaultive behavior.

Instead of analyzing social relationships in the top-down fashion of sociology, which begins with broad macrosystem analysis, social psychology determines first which social relationships are of relevance to the individual whose behavior is to be explained. Theories are then built from the bottom up, for example, from the context of the lifespace of an individual (Lewin, 1951).

This approach allows social-psychological analysis simultaneously to be sensitive to the sociopolitical context that shapes behavior and to account for individual differences in behavior in a common sociopolitical context. Rather than argue that a norm exists that allows wife assault to occur (Straus, 1977a, 1977b; Dobash & Dobash, 1979), we are interested in:

1. How much violence toward wives is considered acceptable by various social groups and under what circumstances?
2. How does this vary from one social group to another?
3. Does an assaultive male's behavior fall within this range of acceptability?
4. If not, how does he justify his behavior to himself?
5. How do broader social values shape individual experience?

By originating inquiry at the psychological level, some fine tuning of sociological perspectives is possible. Straus, Gelles, and Steinmetz (1980) state that predictive checklists based on economic, demographic, and family power measures make too many false-positive identifications: they predict that many males will assault their wives who, in fact, will not (p. 219). Straus, Gelles, and Steinmetz (1980) point out the "obvious need to include data on the psychological characteristics."

In selecting these psychological characteristics, care must be taken to avoid the reductionism of the psychiatric explanations of wife assault. Characteristics should be chosen that have prima facie relevance for male-female interaction (such as power motivation) in intimate relationships (e.g., intimacy anxiety). In Chapter 2 we will describe how our therapeutic program with men convicted of wife assault provided a list of characteristics, which we then empirically tested.

The theoretical structure into which these social and psychological characteristics are fitted is called a *nested ecological theory* (Belsky, 1980; Dutton, 1981b, 1985). Nested ecological theories were developed primarily by developmental psychologists and ethologists (e.g., Tinbergen, 1951; Brofenbrenner, 1977; Garbarino, 1977; Burgess, 1978).

Belsky (1980) integrated Bronfenbrenner's (1979) analysis of the social context in which individual development takes place with Tinbergen's (1951) emphasis on individual development, which he called *ontogeny*. Bronfenbrenner divided this social context or ecological space into three levels: (1) the macrosystem; (2) the exosystem; and (3) the microsystem. The *macrosystem* refers to broad cultural values and belief systems that influence both ontogenetic development and the exosystem and microsystem. For example, patriarchy, as

FIGURE 1.3   The Straus general systems theory of family violence

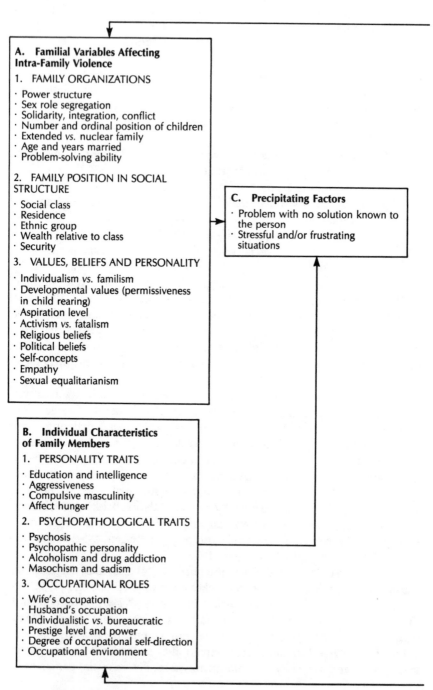

Source: Straus (1973)

FIGURE 1.3   (*continued*)

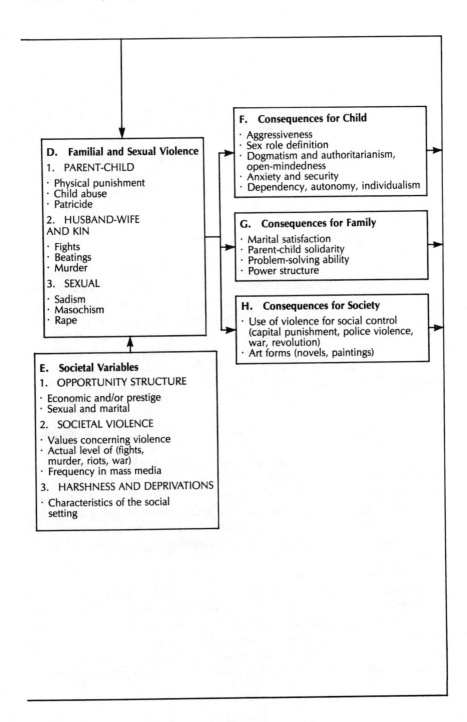

D.   Familial and Sexual Violence

1.   PARENT-CHILD

· Physical punishment
· Child abuse
· Patricide

2.   HUSBAND-WIFE AND KIN

· Fights
· Beatings
· Murder

3.   SEXUAL

· Sadism
· Masochism
· Rape

E.   Societal Variables

1.   OPPORTUNITY STRUCTURE

· Economic and/or prestige
· Sexual and marital

2.   SOCIETAL VIOLENCE

· Values concerning violence
· Actual level of (fights, murder, riots, war)
· Frequency in mass media

3.   HARSHNESS AND DEPRIVATIONS

· Characteristics of the social setting

F.   Consequences for Child

· Aggressiveness
· Sex role definition
· Dogmatism and authoritarianism, open-mindedness
· Anxiety and security
· Dependency, autonomy, individualism

G.   Consequences for Family

· Marital satisfaction
· Parent-child solidarity
· Problem-solving ability
· Power structure

H.   Consequences for Society

· Use of violence for social control (capital punishment, police violence, war, revolution)
· Art forms (novels, paintings)

a macrosystem value, might influence both the development of individual expectations about appropriate levels of authority in a male-female relationship
and the nature of social interaction at the family level.

The *exosystem* refers to "social structures both formal and informal that
impinge upon the immediate settings in which that person is found and thereby
influence, delimit or determine what goes on there" (Belsky, 1980, p. 321).
Hence, work groups, friendship or support groups, or other groups that connect the family to the larger culture represent the exosystem. Work stress or the
presence or absence of social support might increase or decrease the likelihood
of wife assault.

The *microsystem* refers to the family unit or the immediate context in which
wife assault occurs. The interaction pattern of the couple, the conflict issues that
were salient to them, and the antecedents and consequences of assault (how the
man felt, how the woman acted after it was over) would constitute the
microsystem level of analysis.

The *ontogenetic level* refers to individual development and defines what
a particular individual brings into this three-level social context as a result of
his or her unique developmental history. By examining the interaction of ontogenetic characteristics with features of the social context, we can begin to make
predictions about individual behavior patterns. Hence, two men may both have
been raised with the same cultural beliefs, have similar work and support networks, and equal amounts of conflict in the home environment, yet one man
may react with violence to this social context while the other does not. The basis
of this differential reaction is sought in the different learning experiences of the
two men: different exposure to violent role models, different response repertoires for handling conflict, and different emotional reactions to male-female
conflict.

Conversely, these individual characteristics are not viewed as existing in
a vacuum. Rather, they require a particular social context in which to manifest
themselves. Two hypothetically identical individuals (in terms of relevant
behaviors) would behave differently with different micro-, exo-, or macrosystems.
It is in this sense that the levels of explanation are said to be nested, one under
the other. Table 1.4 lists the types of variables associated with each level of
analysis, the scales used in our own research, and the types of questions these
scales attempt to answer about causal variables affecting the likelihood of wife
assault.

The profile of an assaultive male produced by a nested ecological theory
borrows factors from all four levels in predicting risk for assault. For example,
wife assault would be viewed as likely when a male with strong needs to dominate
women (ontogenetic) and exaggerated anxiety about intimate relationships (ontogenetic), who has had violent role models (ontogenetic) and has poorly
developed conflict-resolution skills (ontogenetic) is currently experiencing job
stress or unemployment (exosystem), is isolated from support groups (exosystem),

TABLE 1.4 A nested ecological model for wife assault

Level of Analysis	Variable	Scale	Question
The macrosystem	attitudes beliefs	Burt Attitude Scales	• Does man think women are enemies/adversaries? • Does man believe use of violence is acceptable? • Does man adhere to patriarchal double standard for male/female behavior?
The exosystem	isolation stress	Demographic Information Sheet	• Is man employed? • Is job stressful? • Does man use support group?
The microsystem	couple conflict communication pattern	Spanier Dyadic Adjustment Scale	• Is primary relationship rewarding, conflicted, etc.? • What is communication pattern?
The ontogenetic level	verbal skills	Assertiveness scales Test of emotional style	• Does man have communication skills? • Can he express affect?
	emotional response	Videotape analogue studies	• Does he have exaggerated anger response to male-female conflict?
	conscience empathy	Studies of own explanation for violence	• How does he excuse his violence to himself?
	learned habits	Childhood CTS	• Did he witness use of violence in family of origin?
		Crowne-Marlowe	• Is he telling the truth on the other scales?

is experiencing relationship stress in terms of communication difficulties (microsystem) and power struggles (microsystem), and exists in a culture where maleness is defined by the ability to respond to conflict aggressively (macrosystem).

This hypothetical profile combines both sociodemographic and family-interaction factors with psychological characteristics in the form of response repertoires, relevant motives, and anxieties. The combination produces a more finely tuned profile of a hypothetical assaultive male that remains sensitive to the social factors described by sociologists. One way of testing such a theory would be to investigate representative samples of assaultive males with samples who were not assaultive but who shared a variety of common characteristics (e.g., same demographics, similar degree of marital conflict). By so doing, the search for essential characteristics associated with assault can be more finely focused. The long-term objective is to ascertain which of the several ingredients suggested by a nested ecological approach plays the major role in determining wife assault. An ultimate objective would be like a chemical formula that could tell us what amounts or weights to give to each factor in contributing to the likelihood of wife assault. We now consider some factors at each level that might increase this likelihood.

1.5.1 The Macrosystem

Broad sets of cultural beliefs and values of relevance to wife assault constitute the macrosystem level of analysis, which has been the main focus of sociological investigation. Dobash and Dobash (1979), for example, focus on patriarchy and claim that "the seeds of wife beating lie in the subordination of females and in their subjection to male authority and control" (p. 33). The ideology of patriarchy holds that male supremacy is natural and that control of women and strong reactions to their insubordination are vital. Dobash and Dobash trace the history of this ideology and its buttressing via legal and religious dogma.

Historically, in Western societies the impact of this macrosystem belief on the family unit was to increase the power of the husband in nuclear families and the Crown while disenfranchising large feudal households. At the same time the belief that hierarchy was the natural order was encouraged. The patriarchal belief system presumably contributes to incidence of wife assault by simultaneously creating in males the expectation that their wishes will not be opposed by their wife and justifying the use of violence to obtain this natural right. Societies that regard women as chattel, and maintain a strong double standard according to this view, should demonstrate higher rates of wife assault (to the extent that male authority is occasionally resisted).

It is not known whether both the cognitive and behavioral aspects of the patriarchal ideology occur concomitantly. Bugenthal, Kahn, Andrews, and Head (1972) report that a majority of North American males approve of the use of violence to achieve political ends; however, Stark and McEvoy (1970) reported that only a minority (25% of North American males) approved of slapping a wife under "appropriate circumstances."

One relatively unexplored consequence of hierarchical systems is their influence on subjective emotional states. When someone who believes that he or she should be in a position of authority and is challenged as such, might this challenge produce an enhanced arousal/anger reaction? Would the same conflict generate less anger if that person did not define himself or herself as an authority with the concomitant expectations? We are suggesting (and will explore in greater detail below) that one psychological mechanism that may connect patriarchy to wife assault is the shaping of a male emotional response to male-female conflict. Specifically, we suggest that that response is more likely to be experienced by the male (as opposed to the female) as anger. Anger does not lead inextricably to violence but may increase the probability of violent behavior (Rule & Nesdale, 1976).

1.5.2 The Exosystem

Straus, Gelles, and Steinmetz (1980) reported that wife abuse rates increased with the number of stressful events a family experienced (as measured by a modified version of the Holmes and Rahe [1967] stress scale). However, as the authors concluded, "Counting stressful events and relating the tally to percentages of violent families does support the theory [that stress increases wife assault] but it does not convey the reasons for the relationship" (p. 184).

Exosystem factors that could contribute to wife assault include job stress, low income, part-time employment, unemployment, and the presence or absence of social support systems. The mechanisms that connect employment difficulties to wife assault include increased contact, greater likelihood of conflict over financial matters (Parke & Collmer, 1975), lowered self-esteem in the unemployed male (Gelles, 1976), and redirected aggression whereby frustration that accumulates from an unsatisfying work situation is taken out in the form of aggression toward the wife (Gelles, 1976). These exosystem factors considered alone would lead to the prediction that economic downturns would be followed by increases in wife assault, via some or all of the above mechanisms. An alternative view that we will consider in Chapter 7 is that exosystem factors interact with microsystem and ontogenetic factors so that increases in unemployment produce violence only in families with dysfunctional interaction patterns or in men with learned dispositions to react to stress with violence.

Dooley and Catalano (1984) point out the difficulty in testing the relationship between economic factors and pathological behaviors. Tests founded on aggregate measures of unemployment and pathological behaviors (such as wife assault) commit what they term the *ecological fallacy:* they attribute individual symptoms to individual economic circumstances based on aggregate data. Dooley and Catalano avoided this methodological problem by taking both economic and psychological measures on individuals as well as aggregate economic measures. Via this type of analysis they discovered that unemployment had a significant relationship to symptoms of psychological problems, but the relationship was much stronger when unemployment rate was considered in combination with a person's being in the work force (as opposed to being retired or a student) and with education level. Unemployment rates do not affect everyone equally but have their greatest impact on middle-status groups in the work force. (Low-status groups already have high rates of undesirable individual economic events.) Hence, these authors caution against simplistic application of exosystem main effects on behavior.

Unemployment and job stress represent exosystem instigators that increase the likelihood of wife assault. Informal support groups, on the other hand, represent a potential ameliorative variable within the exosystem. By providing emotional support, corrective feedback, and so forth, friendship groups could prevent individuals from acting out their worst excesses. Isolation has been found to be associated with child abuse (Belsky, 1980), which leads Belsky to point out "the crucial assistance that members of one's social network can contribute in times of stress." Such an analysis, however, assumes people to be motivated to make use of support systems when under duress. An alternative possibility is that people with available social support systems fail to utilize them out of either a belief that they should be able to handle their problems on their own or the failure to perceive that they have a problem. An exosystem view of wife assault would predict wife assaulters to be either more isolated or less capable of using available support groups under duress (or both).

1.5.3 The Microsystem

The microsystem refers to the interaction pattern that exists in the family itself or to structural elements of that family. Straus, Gelles, and Steinmetz (1980), for example, refer to structural elements like marital power as being related to incidence of abuse. Straus et al. used the Blood and Wolfe (1960) power index, which measures who has final authority in six common household decisions (e.g., buying a car, having children, money spent on food, and so on) and relates this measure of marital power to marital violence. They found that acts of violence toward wives were most common in husband-dominant households, second most common in wife-dominant households, and least common in democratic households. The explanation they provide for this relationship is that violence is used by the man to either legitimize his dominant position or as an attempt to gain dominance.

Psychological studies of the microsystem have tended to focus on the interaction process as a contributor to eventual assault. Some of this research has focused on verbal and nonverbal communication patterns in conflicted versus nonconflicted couples (Notarius & Johnson, 1982; Levenson & Gottman, 1983). Levenson and Gottman's intriguing work on interpersonal psychophysiology indicates that marital satisfaction is closely related to "physiological linkage" during discussion of problem areas in the marriage. Specifically, conflicted couples communicate negative affect, reciprocate the negative affect, and produce parallel patterning of physiological responses between the spouses. The authors see this process as the basis for the subjective state of being trapped or locked into a destructive, self-sustaining interaction pattern.

Margolin (1983) reviews marital interaction classification procedures and their use in predicting marital distress, but to date, the application of such techniques to the analysis of interaction in assaultive couples has not been greatly developed. Margolin (1984) has reported preliminary findings comparing physically abusive couples with verbally abusive, withdrawn, and nonconflicted couples. Margolin tentatively reports that physically abusive and withdrawn couples are quite similar in certain communication styles such as low assertiveness and conflict avoidance. Margolin's work, although in preliminary stages, suggests the potential already developed in the study of parent-child interaction (Patterson, 1981; Reid, Patterson, & Loeber, 1981; Wahler, 1980).

Patterson and his colleagues at the Oregon Social Learning Center have concentrated on reducing children's aggressive behaviors (tantrums, disobedience, acting out, and so forth) by altering parent-child interaction patterns. Specifically, Patterson focuses on interaction as a communication process in which expectations for behavior and rewards or punishments for fulfilling those expectations are communicated well or poorly. One conclusion from Patterson's work is that violent intrafamily behavior has its roots in the mismanagement of banal daily routine (Patterson, 1979).

A coercion trap develops when a child demands an act of compliance from a parent through performing behavior that is aversive to the parent (e.g., by whining or screaming). The parent provides punishment (by doing something that is aversive to the child) and the child (in response to the punishment) either stops making demands or acts defiantly by repeating the original aversive demand. When these three-part interchanges become a characteristic feature of the parent-child relationship, both parties are trapped into using coercive interchanges frequently in their daily interaction (Patterson, 1981).

Some parents respond to the child's aversive demands with their own set of behaviors (that are aversive to the child) intermittently accompanied by a positive reinforcer. This periodic positive/negative reinforcement and punishment keeps the coercion trap functioning. The child, in return, intermittently stops his or her aversive behavior in response to the parent's punishment, reward-ing the parent's actions. Thus the parent and child put each other on an inter-mittent reinforcement schedule, inadvertently maintaining each other's aver-sive behaviors.

The main point of Patterson's and Wahler's work for our purposes is that it represents the advances that have been made in interaction analysis and shows how aggressive behavior can be produced by dysfunctional interaction. Margolin's work applies such analysis to wife assault. Furthermore, Margolin's preliminary finding that the interactional characteristics of physically assaultive and withdrawn couples are similar presents the possibility that assaultive behavior is a joint func-tion of microsystem processes, ontogenetically learned traits, and response hierar-chies to conflict. While microsystem processes may produce conflict and anger, the individual's behavioral response to this anger (withdrawal, depression, or aggression) may be ontogenetically learned.

Giles-Sims (1983) has also developed an interactive approach to understand-ing wife assault. Her model accepts that predispositional factors exist but views repeated violence as being a system product (i.e., a product of the interaction of two individuals). Giles-Sims views family interaction process as evolving in stages. Stage One requires analysis of the following questions: How do patterns established in other social systems affect the family system? How does the com-mitment that establishes family boundaries evolve? What rules concerning power relationships and the use of violence are part of the family system in the initial stage?

Stage Two begins with the first incident of violence and focuses on ques-tions such as how the couple interaction at the time of the first violent incident affected the possibility of future incidents. For example, to what extent were the goals of the violent person satisfied? How did the victim respond? Giles-Sims found that, of 31 battered women she studied, 86% felt angry after the first incident but did not respond in an angry, retaliatory, or rejecting way, and 64% sought no intervention and did not leave the house. Giles-Sims then goes on to analyze how this victim response feeds back to the batterer, stabilizing an interactive pattern that includes rewards for violence (e.g., getting own way) and hence for generating intermittent violence.

1.5.4 The Ontogenetic Level

Ontogenetic-level factors focus on features of the individual's developmen-tal experience that shape his or her responses to microsystem or exosystem stressors. From an interactive perspective, both the cognitive appraisal of what is stressful and the emotional and behavioral reactions to the stressor are learned predispositions shaped by the unique experience of the individual. Hence, one obvious area of interest has been the wife assaulter's own developmental experience with violence in his family of origin. Straus, Gelles, and Steinmetz (1980) correlated *Conflict Tactics Scale* reports of violence by wife assaulters with reports of parental violence. They reported that "men who had seen parents physically attack each other were almost three times more likely to have hit their own wives during the year of the study" (p. 100).

Straus et al. are careful to point out, however, that many wife assaulters had not experienced violence in their family of origin. (Also, many men who witness father-mother assault are not violent themselves.) The experience of violence used as a conflict tactic in the family of origin was one modeling source for learning violence. Similarly, being a victim of parental violence increased the likelihood of wife assault: males who were physically punished as teenagers had a rate of severe violence toward their wives that was four times greater than those whose parents did not hit them. We will discuss this intergenerational transmission of violence in Chapter 7.

Finally, Straus et al. report the double-whammy effect: the men who both observed and experienced violence were five to nine times more likely to be violent (depending on the specific violence measure). What the Straus et al. survey did not reveal was exactly how this modeling mechanism operates: do sons in violent families learn to define potential conflict issues as more serious (i.e., do they perceive more causes for anger?)? Do they react to conflicts with more anger? Do they automatically use violence as a means of dealing with conflict? The answers to these questions await comparison studies using violent and nonviolent men with matched experiences of violence in their family of origin.

The Straus et al. survey reported that people fought most frequently over "money, housekeeping, social activities, sex and children" (p. 173). In treatment groups, assaultive males frequently reveal the emotional meaning of such conflict sources in the course of therapy. Money, housekeeping, and child-raising issues often involve beliefs and expectations about power and authority in the household. In part these beliefs may be shaped by macrosystem notions about family and patriarchy, but they also indicate a variety of expectations shaped in part by experience in the family of origin and in part by individual needs for power and control over family process.

Issues arising from social activities and sex often involve anxieties about too little or too much intimacy with one's spouse. Power and intimacy needs represent another constellation of perceptions and affective responses learned in the family of origin and hence represent another ontogenetic feature that could interact with stress and conflict at micro- or exosystem levels. A conflict event, such as a wife's desire for increased independence from her husband, could trigger vastly different reactions in men with different power and intimacy needs. In Chapter 2 we will examine the role of power and intimacy in shaping reactions to couple conflict.

SECTION SUMMARY   Nested ecological approaches to explaining wife assault do not decide, a priori, whether to focus exclusively on individual or cultural determinants of assaultive behavior. Rather, contributions from four levels of analysis are assessed and the specific interactions between levels are viewed as likely causal models. At our present stage of knowledge about wife assault, most research proceeds within one particular level of analysis. In the near future, however, we may see more sophisticated causal modelling techniques that allow us to test the importance of each level in determining the likelihood of assaultive actions.

1.6   EXPLANATIONS OF WIFE ASSAULT AND THEIR IMPLICATIONS

What is done about wife assault depends in part on how wife assault is explained; that is, how it is seen to be caused. Hence. Elliot (1977), who views explosive rage as stemming from an "episodic dyscontrol" syndrome, recommends pharmacological and psychiatric treatment. Shainess (1977), who sees wife battering as a personality problem, recommends counseling and self-esteem building for wives. Straus (1977a, 1977b, 1977c), who views wife assault as supported by culture norms condoning normal violence, suggests a radical restructuring of society to alter those norms.

Caplan and Nelson (1973) distinguish between person blame and system blame causal attributions for social problems. *Person blame* views the problem as caused by individual characteristics (ontogenetic factors), while *system blame* views the problem as caused by social system characteristics (macro- or exosystem factors). Person-blame explanations lead to inherently conservative solutions: change the individuals who cause the problem. An example of person blame–oriented policy would be the practice of tertiary intervention into wife assault whereby identified offenders (typically men convicted by the courts) are ordered into cognitive-behavior modification programs as a condition of their probation (see Chapter 6).

System-blame explanations are more consistent with radical solutions requiring a basic restructuring of societal institutions (such as the patriarchal family). Hence Straus (1977a, 1977b) calls for elimination of the husband as head of the family in law, religion, and administrative procedure. This policy is described as primary prevention and is aimed at lowering the incidence of wife assault in a general population by removing a societal structural cause.

A policy based upon an explanation that combines person blame and system blame is secondary prevention involving programs that seek to identify high-risk groups through improved diagnosis and treatment. Since treatment typically still involves the alteration of individuals as opposed to social structures, secondary prevention is philosophically closer to tertiary prevention.

If one were to establish an intervention strategy on purely pragmatic rather than political grounds, then prevention would be based on (1) an assessment of the major contributors to wife assault across all levels (individuals, family, societal) and (2) an appraisal of the ease with which any of those levels could be changed. A nested ecological approach lends itself particularly well to the first of these criteria in that it does not decide a priori whether the problem is inherently a person or system problem. If social-structural factors accounted for most of the statistical variance in measures of wife assault, then these factors would be the likely causes of wife assault. If considerable variance were unaccounted for after relevant societal factors had been assessed, then psychological-individual factors should be considered. If the inclusion of these factors accounted for a significant amount of the variation in incidence of wife assault, then tertiary intervention solutions should be considered.[1]

If neither societal nor individual factors adequately accounted for variance, alone or in interaction, then social science analysis is not yet prepared to suggest policy. From our reading of the current literature, we suggest that the jury is still out on what constitutes the major causes of wife assault. Nevertheless, we are at a stage where we have the analytic capability and methodology to answer such questions. What remains is the political will to invest in an adequate answer.

Since wife assault is a topic that arouses passions and political opinions, a dispassionate analysis of its causes is not easy. Early psychiatric explanations of wife assault occasionally blamed the victim for triggering the assault (Snell, Rosenwald, & Robey, 1964). As a reaction to this type of explanation, feminist analyses balked at any line of research that attributed some responsibility to the assaulted female (see Hilberman, 1980). Consequently, examination of dysfunctional interaction patterns was discouraged because such examination would attribute at least some responsibility to females.

Some females are responsible for contributing to some conflict patterns, but the use of violence to deal with the conflict is a response of, and hence a responsibility of, the assaultive male. Reid, Patterson, and Loeber (1981) describe some abused children as instigators in that they provide a high number of aversive behaviors that make parents irritable and that parents are inept at terminating. Reid et al. found significant correlations between the rate of aversive/oppositional acts and the likelihood of the child getting hit. Reid et al. conclude that "most children are at serious risk of instigating their own abuse at some time during their development" (p. 52). An instigation means any act or statement by a person that increases the likelihood of being hit. Judgments of blame can be independent of instigations: we might not blame a woman who refuses to run an errand for her husband at midnight after working all day, although such refusal can constitute an instigation. Our own judgments about what constitutes acceptable behavior or a level of compliance enter into such determinations.

We now present two brief case studies of men in our own treatment group called the Assaultive Husbands Project. These cases show how wife assault can have widely different etiologies by providing concrete examples of the difficulty of using single perspectives to explain all cases of wife assault.

Case #1: Robert

Robert was referred to our treatment group while his wife was still hospitalized for injuries sustained through his beating. He appeared tense and volatile, even making other men in the group nervous. He would rock back and forth in his chair and clench and unclench his fists repeatedly. He looked to be on the verge of tears. He reported no feelings and was surprised to find out that other men viewed him as tense and angry.

The incident that led to his being in the group occurred at his wife's office party: about 30 people were drinking and chatting when, according to Robert, his wife disappeared (i.e., he could not find her in a large, unfamiliar house). After 10 to 15 minutes he did see her and insisted that they leave the party. He recalled feeling nothing at this point. They drove home, she went to bed, and he began to watch television. His next memory was of seeing her lying in a pool of blood and realizing that he had severely beaten her. He called relatives and the police.

In treatment Robert revealed that he believed his wife was having an affair and that when she disappeared at the party she was having sex with a co-worker. (She was talking to two female co-workers on an outside balcony.) Two months into treatment Robert phoned me in a panic that he was "about to kill his wife." He had returned from an out-of-town business trip to find "a key with a man's name on it." (It was the name of the key manufacturer.) He again assumed his wife was having an affair and became enraged. It took him three days to completely calm down despite having his erroneous assumption about the key pointed out by a therapist.

Subsequent therapy revealed that Robert had been put up for adoption at age two. Whenever he failed to comply, his adoptive parents threatened "to send him back." He experienced strong arousal states at the prospect of abandonment. His delusional beliefs about his wife and his chronic anxiety mutually reinforced each other. A psychiatric label for Robert would be *conjugal paranoid*.

Case #2: Dan

Dan came into treatment on a court order, having been convicted of assault. He was articulate and intelligent, if a little disorganized. The incident that led to his being in the group occurred when Dan was phoning a movie theater to find out when a film started. His wife called to him from another room and he somewhat curtly told her to be quiet because he couldn't hear the telephone announcement. His wife became enraged and began screaming, smashing furniture, striking Dan, and verbally berating him. The color in her face turned to purple. Dan tried to leave but his wife threatened to follow him and publicly embarrass him and to kill herself. After five hours of abuse, Dan "lost it" and struck his wife. She called the police.

Dan's wife had been sexually and physically abused by her stepfather and would fly into rage states when she felt dismissed or neglected. She promised to seek treatment after these episodes were over but subsequently reneged. Dan was strongly attached to her but felt powerless to either change or leave her.

As the above case examples show, highly varied causal patterns can produce wife assault. Stereotypes of assaultive males as pathological bullies are as incomplete as the early psychiatric theories based on incarcerated samples of wife assaulters. Social scientists attempt to find common threads that link wife assaulters and differentiate them from other males. Therapists working with wife assaulters are impressed with the variety and idiosyncracy of each client's background and use of violence. As a therapist trained as a social scientist, I have attempted to reconcile these two opposing views. The result has been the adoption of a theoretical framework that allows for individual differences in the client population while seeking a common set of background causes. In the next chapter we will review this theory, and in Chapter 3 we will examine some initial attempts to test it empirically.

CHAPTER SUMMARY

In this chapter we have reviewed the incidence of wife assault and concluded that severe assaults occur in 8.7% to 12.6% of marriages and are repeated about two-thirds of the time. Repeat assaults may be the ones that are preventable through outside intervention. The demand created by wife assault on both police and hospital emergency services is considerable and warrants more effective intervention to reduce the substantial social costs incurred.

Social history reveals that wife assault was beginning to be recognized as a social problem in nineteenth-century England, leading to the beginning of legal reform. In practice, the criminal justice response throughout the first part of the twentieth century was inadequate. By 1970, women's groups began to lobby for more effective criminal justice action.

Explanations for wife assault began by attributing it to a single factor (pathology in the male, biologically inherited dispositions of males to aggress when sexually threatened, or patriarchal norms), although accumulating empirical evidence now suggests multiple-factor or interactionist causal models. A nested ecological approach is one such model that seeks to account for wife assault through the interaction of factors at the individual, microsystem, exosystem, and macrosystem levels. The most effective policy for diminishing the incidence of wife assault should be guided by an informed and systematic assessment of the relative influences on the wife assaulter's behavior of each of these four levels.

ENDNOTE

1. This conclusion, of course, is based on the assumption that factors from each level directly influence the likelihood of wife assault. As we will see in Chapter 7, however, the path from societal causes to individual reactions is complicated by indirect causal chains. Causal modelling techniques such as LISREL (Joreskog, 1979) make the statistical assessment of such indirect pathways possible and may be required for the eventual test of nested ecological models.

CHAPTER 2

The Social Psychology of the Wife Assaulter: The Theory

The core of sadism, common to all its manifestations, is the passion to have absolute and unrestricted control over a living being. It is transformation of impotence into omnipotence.
—E. Fromm, *The Anatomy of Human Destructiveness* (1973, pp. 322–323)

Against the backdrop of demographic descriptors provided by sociologists, psychological perspectives focus more narrowly on the individual who uses violence against his wife. In the language of the nested ecological theory described in the last chapter, the psychological focus is on the ontogenetic level, where individual habits of aggression are acquired, and on the interaction of these individual habits with the microsystem, or family unit. Clearly, not all men who assault their wives have the same etiology. In the next chapter we will examine some of the subcategories of assaultive males that exist. In this chapter, however, we will concentrate on the development of a general psychological theory of wife assault. The requirements for such a theory are as follows:

1. It must account for the use of violence in the majority of wife assaulters and show how, as a group, wife assaulters differ from nonassaultive males.
2. It must originate with the individual, attempting to develop theoretical constructs from his life space.
3. It must account for the development of wife assault as a habitual behavioral response and must indicate how the habit is sustained (and, by implication, how it could be changed).
4. It must make predictions that can be subjected to experimental testing.
5. It must be nonreductionistic; that is, it must explain behavior at the psychological, not the neurological level.

    6. It must have utility for treatment of wife assaulters.

    7. It must attend to the social context in which wife assault occurs.

Accordingly, to develop such a theory we began with the collection of some clinical hunches, or working hypotheses, about assaultive males that were developed in the course of providing treatment to groups of men convicted of wife assault (about which more will be said in Chapter 6). These clinical hunches were not subjected to empirical testing right away but rather were compared to clinical descriptions of other therapists who worked with nonincarcerated populations of wife assaulters (e.g., Ganley & Harris, 1978; Ganley, 1981) and to descriptions of batterers obtained from their wives (e.g., Gelles, 1975; Martin, 1977; Rounsaville, 1978).

Our objective at this point was merely to select explanatory variables that had some face validity based on our clinical observations and the observations of other therapists. These subjective clinical hunches were then subjected to empirical testing. Based on this approach, two potential explanatory variables were selected that met the criteria of occurring frequently in the therapeutic revelations of batterers and being described in the clinical literature on batterers. These variables were (1) power motivation and (2) intimacy anxiety. In the remainder of this chapter, we will develop our theoretical rationale for studying power and intimacy issues, and then show how these issues can be integrated into a social learning analysis of wife assault.

2.1 POWER AND INTIMACY IN MALE-FEMALE CONFLICT

Power issues were described by men in treatment groups through frequent mention of the need to control or dominate the female, by descriptions of female independence as loss of male control, and by frequent attempts to persuade or coerce the female into adopting the male's definition of relationship structure and function.

Intimacy issues included sudden increases in the wife's demands for greater affection, attention, and emotional support and, at the other end of the intimacy continuum, increased demands for greater independence, or freedom from control by the male. Gelles (1975) and Rounsaville (1978) reported that for 40% of repeatedly assaulted wives, the onset of assault coincided with a sudden transition in intimacy such as marriage or pregnancy. Daly, Wilson, and Weghorst (1982) describe sexual jealousy, which might be viewed as a reaction to perceived relationship loss, as an instigator of wife assault.

Changes in socioemotional distance between the man and his wife can serve as instigators of wife assault. The concept of socioemotional distance can serve as a unifying concept to link reports of wife assault that occurs in response to ostensibly opposite instigators such as increases and decreases in intimacy. An understanding of the interplay of power dynamics on issues of intimacy or socioemotional distance can provide an explanatory framework to deepen our understanding of men who are assaultive only in their primary relationship.

2.1.1 Power Issues

Although the consequences of the need for control and perception of control have been broadly researched (see, for example, Adler, 1966; Baum & Singer, 1980; Perlmuter & Monty, 1979; Bandura, 1977; Langer, 1983; Seligman, 1975), the need for control in primary relationships is not as thoroughly developed in the psychological literature.

McClelland's (1975) Type III power orientation describes men who satisfy their need for power (*n*-power) through having impact on or control over another person. McClelland views power orientations as analogous to Freudian stages of psychosexual development, and accordingly views the Type III as phallically fixated. Winter (1973) applied McClelland's Type III to males who compulsively seduce and abandon women. The Don Juan syndrome, as Winter described it, originates from twin motives to sexually conquer (or have an impact on) and flee from women. In such a transaction, a male purposely increases intimacy with a female up to the point of sexual seduction, and then decreases intimacy immediately after. Sexual and power motives are intertwined, and ambivalence about intimacy produces a repeated approach-avoidance pattern on a continuum of socioemotional distance between the male and the objectified female.

Dutton (1985) extended Winter's analysis to males in monogamous relationships, arguing that the same combination of strong power motivation and ambivalence operates to create strong needs to control socioemotional distance in order to move alternatively closer (through courtship, conquest, and impact) and further away (through emotional withdrawal, verbal criticism, or extramarital affairs). The specific behaviors involved in these control attempts may vary from one individual to the next as a function of idiosyncratic reward histories. Margolin (1984), for example, reported similarities in intermittently assaultive and intermittently withdrawn couples.

Stewart and Rubin (1976) obtained data consistent with this analysis, finding that college-age males who scored high on the *Thematic Apperception Test* measures of *n*-power (need for power) were more likely to dissolve premarital monogamous relationships than were males scoring low on *n*-power. This dissolution was created by high *n*-power males in two ways: first, through threatening the primary relationship by forming other romantic attachments (which fulfilled the need for new conquests) and second, through the generation of extreme control attempts in the primary relationship. These control attempts took the form of generating conflict through criticism of the female and constant attempts to modify her attitudes and behavior in order to have renewed, discernible impact on her. Perceived change in the female's behavior was tangible evidence of their impact.

High scores on *n*-power correlate significantly with frequency of arguments (McClelland, 1975) and with a variety of behavioral indicators of aggression, such as destroying furniture or glassware (Winter, 1973). In addition, high scorers write stories with themes reflecting adversarial sexual beliefs (Slavin, 1972) that portray women as exploitive and destructive. Whether these beliefs are a cause or a consequence of their adversarial behavioral tendencies toward women is not currently known.

As we report in Chapter 3, however, men in our own research who react with the greatest anger to scenes of husband-wife conflict tend to be men who report high degrees of verbal and physical abuse from their mothers (but not from their fathers). Interestingly, Winter (1973) proposes that men who develop the conquest-abandonment Don Juan syndrome do so in response to mixed communications or double-bind communications (Bateson, 1972) from mothers whose nurturance was mixed with hostility. This occurs, Winter speculates, in patriarchal societies where women were repressed and reacted with anger toward the only safe male target: their son. The ambivalence from the mother creates ambivalence toward women in the son. In a study we report in Chapter 3, self-reports of feelings of both anger and humiliation (in response to watching videotaped husband-wife conflicts) were significantly correlated to both verbal and physical abuse from the mother.

If a certain amount of transference occurs from the opposite-sex parent to one's spouse, then we might expect sons who were verbally or physically abused by their mothers to feel quite powerless in adult relationships. Male sex-role socialization, however, teaches men that powerlessness and vulnerability are unacceptable feelings and behaviors (Pleck, 1981). We then might expect exaggerated power concerns in such men, along with mistrust of females and anxiety about intimacy with a female (except when the male feels in complete control over the extent of the intimacy—i.e., able to increase or decrease it as he pleases). Any perceived threats to male control over the amount of intimacy should produce exaggerated arousal and anxiety in such males. In Chapter 3 we will report a test of this prediction that uses videotaped couple-conflict scenes to present subjects with socioemotional threats.

2.1.2 Intimacy Anxiety

Pollack and Gilligan (1982) reported images of violence in *TAT* stories written by men in response to situations of affiliation. They suggest that while fear of success scores demonstrate reliable gender differences (with women scoring higher), fear of intimacy is a predominantly male anxiety and that males perceive intimate relationships to be dangerous. The working hypothesis we have adopted is that intimacy anxiety has both trait (permanent) and state (short-term) properties. State properties involve increases in anxiety in response to sudden uncontrollable changes in the socioemotional distance between spouses. This distance we assume to be negotiated by both parties to a point that represents an optimal zone. An *optimal zone* for each person is that degree of emotional closeness or distance between themselves and their partner with which they feel comfortable at any given time. This comfort zone may be similar to optimal zones for interpersonal spacing (see Patterson, 1976) in that, as with interpersonal spacing zones, invasions (too much intimacy) or evasions (too little) may produce physiological arousal. Clinical reports (e.g., Ganley, 1981; Gondolf, 1985a) suggest that assaultive males tend to label such arousal as anger.

Invasions by the female (from the male's perspective), we term *engulfments;* evasions are called *abandonments.* Fear of engulfment can be produced in three main ways: first by the female moving emotionally toward the male through increased demands for closeness, attention, and affection. Second, by the female remaining static and the male developing an increased need for greater distance than is currently provided. Third, by shifts in formal role demands such as marriage or fatherhood. Ehrenreich (1983) has incisively described the sociological ramifications of the male breadwinner role and of male attempts to flee from its responsibilities and ensuing engulfment. Affective reactions to engulfment may vary but probably carry an admixture of anxiety and resentment, along with a sense of guilt. When coupled with a lack of verbal assertiveness to extricate oneself from engulfment, the probability of verbal or physical abuse may increase.

From the male's perspective, abandonment anxiety involves perceived uncontrollable increases in socioemotional distance. Abandonment anxiety could be produced by (1) sexual threat or any other instance of the female moving emotionally further away (or reinvesting her energy outside the primary relationship) or (2) by the male developing an increasing need for intimacy but not successfully expressing it so that a stationary female stays at what was previously an optimal distance but which is now too far. The consensus of clinical reports (Ganley & Harris, 1978; Walker, 1979b) is that for battering males acute anxiety accompanies perceived rapid changes in socioemotional distance (or intimacy) within relationships. Given the typical emotional isolation of such men and their exaggerated dependence on the female, accompanied by their often traditional sex-role attitudes (Dutton & Browning, 1987) that tend to make them view their wives as chattel or a possession, this disguised panic reaction may be viewed as similar to anxiety-based aggression in response to rapid depletion of any resource that is perceived as both necessary and scarce. For assaultive males, the psychological and behavioral result of perceived loss of the female produces panic and hysterical aggression. Formal redefinitions of the marital role can also produce shifts in intimacy. For example, motherhood redirects female attention toward the child (while simultaneously increasing male responsibility).

Finally, many clinical reports indicate that males exacerbate abandonment anxieties by behaving in such a way as to maximize the likelihood of abandonment by the female. Walker (1979a) describes the battering cycle, a process whereby assaultive males, having gone through an acute battering phase, experience guilt, remorse, and anxiety that their wife will leave. If she moves to a new lodging they put her under surveillance, call her repeatedly, try to convince her to return, and promise they will never be violent again. Men in therapeutic groups who are in an abandonment panic idealize the woman and obsess over her and their mistreatment of her. They reveal the exaggerated dependency they have on her—previously masked by their attempts to make her dependent on them or by their exaggerated control of her behavior through physical assaults and threats.

Sexual jealousy, especially to the extent that it involves delusions or distortions, may represent a form of chronic abandonment anxiety. Jealousy is mentioned frequently by battered women as an issue that incited violence (Rounsaville, 1978; Whitehurst, 1971; Roy, 1977; Daly, Wilson & Weghorst, 1982). Recent studies (Murstein, 1978; Clanton & Smith, 1977; White, 1980) have viewed jealousy as a mediating construct, produced by anticipated relationship loss. Jealousy produces a range of behavioral responses (including aggression and increased vigilance) and affective reactions (including rage and depression).

In many relationships, the degree of intimacy or socioemotional distance is a key structural variable that has dramatic impact on individuals in the relationship. Power and control over the degree of intimacy is especially important to the extent that (1) intimacy with one's spouse satisfies emotional needs unique to the primary relationship, (2) intimacy represents a major structural variable defining the form of the dyad, and (3) ontogenetically learned anxieties about intimacy transfer onto the spousal relationship. Perceived inability to homeostatically maintain the degree of intimacy within the optimal zone should produce arousal in assaultive males.

2.1.3 Arousal

While arousal may be clinically viewed as a component of state anxiety, a variety of mechanisms operate to induce males to experience the arousal as anger (Novaco, 1976; Dutton, Fehr, & McEwan, 1982). Male sex-role socialization is more compatible with expressions of anger than fear (Fasteau, 1974; Pleck, 1981; Gondolf, 1985b). Feelings of anger, potency, expressiveness, and determination accompany the expression of anger (but not fear) (Novaco, 1976). Dutton and Aron (1984) found that males viewing scenarios of interpersonal conflict demonstrated significant positive correlations between self-reports of arousal and anger. Females demonstrated significant positive correlations between arousal and anxiety. This finding is consistent with clinical reports that assaultive males tend to label many forms of emotional arousal as anger (Ganley, 1980; Gondolf, 1985a).

Males experiencing anger as a result of perceived loss of control over intimacy could behave in a variety of ways besides using violence, including verbal expression, self-abasement, or discussion with friends. Behavioral aggression may be more likely for males who (1) have poor repertoires of verbal-expressive skills and (2) who believe they should be in a position of coercive power vis-à-vis their wife. Hence, one way that macrosystem norms may influence violence toward women is through shaping the interpretation of arousal states in males produced by loss of control over intimacy with their wives. Our current research is testing the notion that arousal produced by witnessing intimate conflict may be a function of gender; males may be more likely to experience such arousal as anger, females as anxiety.

Some researchers have also suggested that aggressive or violent behavior may arise because of a need to seek stimulation in order to raise arousal levels. Berlyne (1967), Fiske and Maddi (1961), and Leuba (1955) have shown that a person will attempt to increase or decrease his or her level of stimulation depending on the prevailing level of input. Some findings consistent with this position can be taken from the research conducted with psychopaths. These are individuals who appear to be highly impulsive, who do not seem to learn from past experience, and who cannot delay gratification. In a number of studies, Hare (1965a, 1965b, 1968) has supported the notion that psychopaths have lesser autonomic reactivity than nonpsychopaths.

Since low-stimulation states appear to be unpleasant, violent behavior could occasionally arise from lack of stimulation (see also Fromm, 1973). That is, assuming that violent or aggressive people have a more rapid adaptation to stimulation than do psychopaths, they may have a need for stimulation variation to occur more rapidly and with greater intensity than other individuals. They therefore may create situations of conflict, novelty, or surprise in their personal relationships in order to raise arousal levels that they find positively reinforcing. Viewed in this light, aggressive behavior could be motivated by a need to increase rather than decrease stimulation.

On the other hand, some individuals engaging in violent acts of homicide and wife assault appear to be suffering from the effects of overarousal. Easterbrook (1959) has suggested that when arousal is low, selectivity is low, irrelevant cues are accepted uncritically, and performance is poor for all but the simplest tasks. As arousal increases, selectivity also increases, and performance improves because attention focuses on relevant cues while irrelevant cues are more likely to be rejected. However, as the individual becomes more aroused, the range of usable cues is correspondingly restricted so that even relevant cues are ignored. The consequence of raising arousal levels beyond the optimal point, then, is an increase in the number of input sources competing for the individual's dwindling attentional capacity.

These input sources range from situational cues, such as recognition of a victim's distress signals, to cognitive processes, such as a consideration of alternative behavioral strategies, to physiological signs, that is, the biological indicators of heightened arousal such as increased heart rate and galvanic skin response. More important, there is a tendency for individuals to resort to stereotypic behavior under conditions of high arousal, stress, or threat. It is possible that these stereotypic behaviors represent those that the person has seen a role model perform. In Chapter 7 we shall see how witnessing parental violence increases the likelihood of wife assault. Finally, Mandler (1975) has suggested that during heightened arousal there is an overall reduction in processing efficiency resulting from competition for limited cognitive resources. Given that these attentional deficits are created by high arousal, theory and treatment programs that emphasize behavioral choice may need augmentation with stress reduction techniques, since a person in a state of high arousal cannot examine the alternatives or consequences of their behavior. Surprisingly, very little of the voluminous literature on decision making has directly varied the decision maker's state of arousal (Abelson & Levi, 1985). The implications of this notion for anger-management therapy—with its emphasis on choice and personal responsibility for violence—needs future consideration.

Our research emphasis on the psychological role of power, intimacy, and arousal can be integrated into a well-established theory of aggression. Social learning theory focuses on ontogenetic and microsystem factors that sustain habits of aggression. We turn now to the application of this theory to wife assault.

2.2   A SOCIAL LEARNING THEORY OF WIFE ASSAULT

Bandura (1979) has developed a comprehensive theory of aggression that views aggressive responses as shaped through the individual's learning history and that has relevance for the specific form of aggression called wife assault, although the theory has been developed in other aggressive contexts. In this section, we will apply Bandura's social learning theory analysis to wife assault and then relate this analysis to the concepts of power motivation and intimacy anxiety described in the last section.

Bandura's analysis focuses on three major determinants of aggression: (1) the origins of aggression, (2) the instigators of aggression, and (3) the regulators of aggression (see Table 2.1).

2.2.1   The Origins of Aggression

Social learning theory views biological factors, observational learning, and reinforced performance as the main origins of aggressive behavior. *Biological*

TABLE 2.1 Social learning analysis of behavior

Origins of Aggression	Instigators of Aggression	Regulators of Aggression
Observational learning	Modelling influences	External reinforcement
	disinhibitory	tangible rewards
Reinforced performance	facilitative	social and status rewards
	arousing	expressions of injury
Structural determinants	stimulus-enhancing	alleviation of aversive
		treatment
	Aversive treatment	Punishment
	physical assaults	inhibitory
	verbal threats and	informative
	insults	Vicarious reinforcement
	adverse reductions in	observed reward
	reinforcement	observed punishment
	thwarting	Self-reinforcement
	Incentive inducements	self-reward
	Instructional control	self-punishment
	Bizarre symbolic control	neutralization of self-
		punishment
		moral justification
		palliative comparison
		euphemistic labelling
		displacement of
		responsibility
		diffusion of
		responsibility
		dehumanization of
		victims
		attribution of blame to
		victims
		misrepresentation of
		consequences

Source: Bandura, A. (1979). The social learning persepective: Mechanisms of aggression. In H. Toch (Ed.), *Psychology of crime and criminal justice*. New York: Holt, Rinehart, & Winston.

factors such as activity level, physical stature, and musculature "set limits on the type of aggressive responses that can be developed, influence the rate at which learning progresses," and "predispose individuals to perceive and learn critical features of their immediate environment" (Bandura, 1979, p. 201). People are endowed with inherited physical properties that enable them to behave aggressively, but the activation of these mechanisms depends on appropriate stimulation (i.e., instigators) and is subject to cognitive control (i.e., regulators or feedback from cognitive belief systems).

From a social learning point of view, males may be biologically predisposed to act aggressively, since they inherit greater musculature than females. This musculature increases the probability that physically aggressive responses will produce their intended effect, thereby generating reward for the performer of the response.

Observational learning constitutes a major determinant of the acquisition of behaviors, allowing the individual to develop a conception of how behavior is performed through attending to the modelled behavior, coding it into permanent symbolic modes, and integrating it through motor reproduction. Studies that indicate a higher likelihood of wife assault in a population of males who witnessed their mother being assaulted by their father provide data consistent with an observational acquisition of this behavior. Straus, Gelles, and Steinmetz (1980), for example, found that males who had observed parents attack each other were three times more likely to have assaulted their wives (35% of men who had seen this had hit their own wife in the year of the study, compared with 10.7% of men who had not witnessed this event). As Straus et al. conclude, "The scale of violence toward spouses seems to rise fairly steadily with the violence these people observed as children between their own parents" (p. 101).

Kalmuss (1984) found that such modelling was not sex-specific. Exposure to fathers hitting mothers increases the likelihood of both husband-wife and wife-husband aggression, and both sons and daughters who do so are more likely to be victims as well as perpetrators of violence against their spouse. Kalmuss suggests that exposure to father-mother violence communicates the general acceptability of marital aggression rather than particular rules about which sex parent is an appropriate perpetrator or victim. We shall discuss issues in the intergenerational transmission of violence in Chapter 7.

Social learning theory does not assume that any behavior observed will be practiced. For an acquired response pattern to be enacted by an individual, it must have functional value for them and be either rewarded or at least not punished. The enactment of an acquired behavior such as wife assault depends then on (1) appropriate inducements, (2) functional value, and (3) reward for or absence of punishment for performance (Bandura, 1979). An appropriate inducement for wife assault, from the perspective of the assaulter, might be a statement or action by his wife that challenges his authority. The functional value would be the utility and meaning that an individual ascribes to using violence to restore that authority. Reward might include termination of an aversive stimulus (his wife's insubordinate statements or actions). Punishments could include anything from police intervention, to his wife leaving him, to feelings of guilt for his violence. If these punishments are absent, re-enactment becomes more likely.

Bandura (1979) suggested three major sources for observational learning: the family of origin (see Straus et al., 1980), the subculture or microsystem in which the family resides (see Short, 1968; Wolfgang & Ferracuti, 1967), and televised violence (Leyens, Camino, Parke, & Berkowitz, 1975; Hendrick, 1977). The mechanisms involved in each source involve (1) explicit demonstration of an aggressive style of conflict resolution, (2) a decrease in the normal restraints over aggressive behavior, (3) desensitization and habituation to violence, and (4) a shaping of expectations.

Social learning theory also emphasizes symbolic modelling as an important source of response acquisition. Hence, any new behaviors introduced by salient examples (e.g., television portrayals of macho use of violence, use of stereotyped violent responses to conflict situations) would contribute to a generalized, adopted role that integrated such responses.

Finally, social learning theory describes how aggressive behaviors can be acquired through direct experience and shaped through trial and error. Although modelling sources for aggression are universally present, successful enactments of aggression can rapidly entrench an aggressive habit. Patterson, Littman, and Brickner (1967) reported how passive children could be shaped into aggressors through a process of victimization and successful counteraggression. Passive children who were repeatedly victimized but occasionally succeeded in halting attacks by counteraggression, not only increased their defensive fighting over time but began to initiate attacks of their own. By comparison, passive children who were seldom maltreated because they avoided others or whose counter-aggressions proved unsuccessful remained submissive.

Wife assaulters also learn to use physical aggression in an autodidactic fashion. The behaviors involved (e.g., punching, shoving) are not complex and, as Bandura points out, have been universally modelled. If a male uses these behaviors against his wife and is rewarded through (1) regaining control or dominance, (2) feeling expressive or agentic (i.e., acting out and taking charge in a fashion consonant with male sex-roles (Novaco, 1976), and (3) terminating an aversive state of arousal or upset, and if he is not punished for using violence, the likelihood increases of his using these actions again in a similar conflict situation.

Although the likelihood of wife assault increases if the assaulter has witnessed parental violence, the majority of wife assaulters have never witnessed parental violence. This suggests that learning may have occurred from another source—solely from their own experience or from some blend of the two. Kalmuss and Seltzer (1986) concluded from a transrelationship study of the use of violence that violence repertoires appeared to be learned in the first adult romantic relationship and tended to persist in new relationships.

2.2.2 Instigators of Wife Assault

Social learning theory holds that acquired behaviors will not be demonstrated unless an appropriate stimulus or instigator exists in the contemporary environment. Some of these instigators apply more frequently to acts of group aggression, such as *modelling instigators* where one person present in the current environment performs the aggressive acts serving to direct and disinhibit the aggressive actions of others, or *instructional instigators* where one receives a directive to act aggressively (from a formal authority, for example).

For wife assault in particular, three types of instigation mechanisms seem typically to apply. These are aversive instigators, incentive instigators, and delusional instigators. In social learning terms, the motivation to act aggressively comes either from an aversive stimulus—which, by definition, is something we would work to remove—or from an incentive inducement: an anticipated payoff for aggressive action.

Aversive stimulation (see Table 2.1 and Figure 2.1) produces a general state of emotional arousal that can activate or facilitate a variety of learned responses, including aggression, achievement, problem solving, withdrawal, dependency, psychosomatic illness, and blunting (i.e., self-anetheticization with drugs or alcohol). Which response occurs will depend on (1) the individual's acquired cognitive appraisal of the arousal source—specifically, whether he can control the response or not. The active responses to an aversive stimulus—achievement, problem solving, and aggression—follow from an appraisal of the source being controllable, according to this analysis. (2) The modes of response learned for coping with stress—the individual's unique reinforcement history for using aggression as opposed to other responses (or to observing them used)—and the rewards or punishments that accompanied that use in the individual's personal development. Both the mode of appraisal and the mode of action are acquired by the individual's unique reinforcement history. They are predispositions that individuals have acquired and utilize under appropriate conditions.

FIGURE 2.1 Relationship of aversive events to aggression

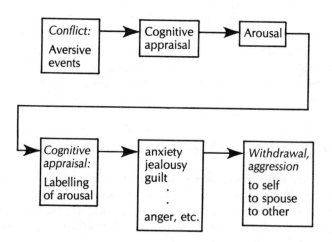

The arousal generated by aversive stimulation has both a physiological and an experiential component to it; that is, when exposed to an aversive stimulus, subjects (1) demonstrate arousal via conventional physiological indices (such as heart rate, galvanic skin response, or pulse transit time) and (2) feel aroused or tense.

The emotional consequence of such arousal depends, however, on a cognitive appraisal of the instigator and on the situation (Hunt, Cole, & Reis, 1958; Schachter & Singer, 1962; Mandler, 1975). Social learning theory has not placed great emphasis on the role of affect or emotion. Hence, anger is viewed as a by-product of aversive arousal that is not necessary for aggression, although anger does increase the likelihood of aggression (Rule & Nesdale, 1976).

Konecni (1975) postulated that anger and aggression had a bidirectional relationship in which each could influence the level of the other. The emphasis of social learning has been the appraisal of aversive events and consequent aggressive behavior. The relationship between these concepts is depicted in Figure 2.1. In this model, several relationships operate that have empirically demonstrated relevance for the onset of aggression:

1. When people are disposed to behave aggressively, nearly any source of emotional arousal can heighten aggression (Rule & Nesdale, 1976; Tannenbaum & Zillman, 1975).
2. Aggression can be self-generated by ruminating about anger-provoking incidents (Bandura, 1973).
3. Aggression can increase anger (Konecni, 1975).
4. Anger can increase aggression (Konecni, 1975).
5. Aggression is increased by perceiving actions of the other person as intentionally aggressive (Taylor & Epstein, 1967), as threatening to one's self-esteem (Rosenbaum & deCharms, 1960), or as causing one's own aversive arousal (Geen, Rakosky, & Pigg, 1972).
6. By varying the anticipated consequences, the same aggressive acts can either increase or decrease arousal (Hokanson, Willers, & Koropsak, 1968).

Other relationships are implied by the model in Figure 2.1. Aggression, for example, is controlled by perception of its immediate consequences, by prior anger, and by generalized arousal. However, any one of these factors is sufficient for aggression to occur. The other factors play a facilitating role. Therapists working with wife assaulters describe the assaultive males as engaging in cognitive processes that are consistent with this aggression model. Ganley (1981), for example, describes wife assaulters as personalizing disagreements with their wives so the conflict is viewed as intentional (i.e., as an intentional personal attack on them). Ganley also describes the tendency wife assaulters have of expressing a wide range of emotions as anger so that emotional states other than anger can lead to assault. Gondolf (1985a) describes the *male emotional funnel system* whereby a wide range of arousal-producing emotions are experienced as anger (see Figure 2.2). Both therapists view this affective narrowing as being caused by male sex-role socialization.

Social learning theory views anger arousal (see point 6 above) as facilitative rather than necessary for aggression. The arousal itself has a cognitive basis based on an appraisal of the situation. Its relationship to aggression also has a cognitive component based in part on the anticipated consequences of aggressive behavior. Novaco (1976) describes how the expression of anger has several built-in reward functions: it can be energizing, expressive, and lead to feelings of potency and determination. It can short-cut feelings of vulnerability and generate a sense

FIGURE 2.2   The male emotional funnel system. Repeated incidents of misidentified feelings push men toward violence.

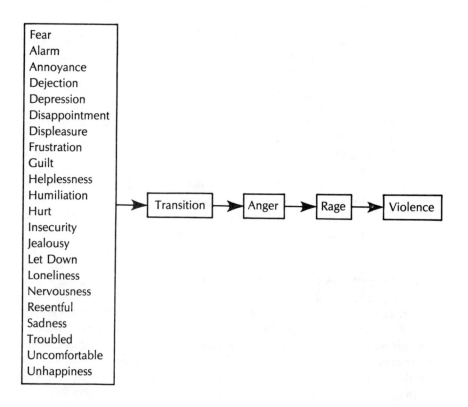

Source: From Gondolf (1985)

of personal control. Many of these functions are shaped by male sex-role expectations of agency (of taking action).

In primary relationships, these sex-role expectations may also define limits of acceptable male-female behavior by determining expectations of power, dominance, and the mode of conflict expression. Female behavior that exceeds those limits may be viewed as aversive. Hence, both perceived aversiveness and consequent expression of anger may be shaped by sex-role expectations.

Social learning theory has examined physical assaults, verbal threats and insults, and adverse reductions in the conditions of life as three types of stimuli that produce aversive arousal. Its major contribution has been to generate evidence to refute simplistic notions that aggression in response to pain is unlearned reflexive behavior. Bandura describes how avoidance and flight are prepotent responses to pain when environmental constraints to flight are removed. Correspondingly, Toch (1969) found that counterattacks were evoked more by humiliating affronts or threats to reputation and manly status than by physical pain.

Clinical reports of wife assaulters rarely cite physical attack by a woman as an instigator for assault, although a verbal threat that challenges authority and feelings of humiliation are frequent instigators. As with the population of assault-prone individuals studied by Toch (1969), high sensitivity to perceived devaluation and deficient verbal skills to resolve disputes (and to restore self-esteem) may characterize wife assaulters.

2.2.3   Intimacy Anxiety Recast

In Section 2.1.2 we proposed that intimacy anxiety was a by-product of male socialization that, in combination with other traits, could predispose males to wife assault. From this perspective, sudden uncontrollable changes in intimacy with one's wife could produce aversive arousal.

Hence, if a man perceived his wife to be increasing or decreasing socioemotional distance beyond an optimal zone and did not have the verbal skills to restore equilibrium, aversive arousal would ensue. Male sex-role socialization would increase the probability of that arousal being felt as anger (Pleck, 1981; Gondolf, 1985b). With men who develop verbal modes of expression for anger, that expression can serve to reduce anxiety and enhance feelings of power. However, with men in whom a verbal repertoire is not developed, or with men whose violent aggression has been rewarded in the past, violence is a more likely response to aversive arousal.

If the violence worked by reestablishing male dominance (at least temporarily), ending female verbal demands, and creating a feeling of male control, the consequences of the use of violence would be to make violence more likely in similar future situations.

Other consequences could include the women's leaving the relationship or threatening to leave as a result of the violence, feelings of guilt and remorse over the violence, and criminal justice intervention (arrest and a court appearance). Even if aggression only intermittently produces expected rewards, it is a difficult habit to extinguish (Turner, Fenn, & Cole, 1981). In Chapter 3 we report some empirical studies that examined the relationship between power, intimacy change, and anger in a population of males who had been convicted of wife assault.

2.2.4 Adverse Reductions in the Conditions of Life

Relative deprivation refers to the negative conclusion reached through comparison of one's present economic circumstances with one's past, one's expectations, or the circumstances of a relevant reference group (Turner et al., 1981). Relative deprivation is itself an aversive instigator that produces aggression in people who have a predisposition to aggression (Bandura, 1973). Social learning theory would predict that discontent leads to attempts to increase control in people with a history of personal success or efficacy. These people believe themselves capable of regaining control over aversive circumstances. People who lack feelings of self-efficacy respond to aversive stimuli with avoidance or withdrawal. They are more prone to use passive responses to aversive stimuli, including substance abuse or television addiction. Recall Margolin's (1984) study referred to in Chapter 1, which described certain similarities between physically abusive and withdrawn couples (in terms of communication problems). Hence, aggregate reductions in economic conditions (resulting in relative deprivation) would produce increases in violent behavior only in violence-prone individuals, not those with other learned habits in response to stress. As we shall see in Chapter 7, Dooley and Catalano (1984) found that economic downturns adversely affected only economically marginal groups. In these marginal groups, symptomatology occurred most frequently in those with passive habits (psychosomatic illness, depression, withdrawal). Only a subcategory of the marginal group indicated increases in intrafamily assault. Taken from the perspective of this latter subgroup, however, wife assault increased with the degree of stress (Straus et al., 1980) as measured by the *Holmes and Rahe Scale* (1967).

2.2.5 Delusional Instigators

Social learning theory acknowledges that the perception of an instigator is highly subjective. Bandura cites a study by Weisz and Taylor (1970) that shows that presidential assassins are typically delusionally instigated or have a bizarre belief system.

Some wife assaulters also have bizarre belief systems. One form of such a system is called *conjugal paranoia (DSM-III)* and is described as persecutory delusions and delusional jealousy that convince an individual, without due cause, that his mate is unfaithful. The case study of Robert in Chapter 1 is an example. However, determining what constitutes bizarre beliefs in longstanding interactions is more complex than merely dichotomizing males into deluded and nondeluded categories.

Beliefs about sex-role appropriate behavior, power, and legitimate use of violence exist on continua. In some cases, the bases of conflict arise in differing male and female views on relationship rules. A male may have a traditional view of gender relations that his wife does not share. In this context, his expectations of her and perceptions of her behavior may be a source of conflict. The instigators of aggression in that context may exist on a continuum between consensually defined instigators (such as threats or attacks) and delusional instigators. This becomes obvious when we treat intimacy change as an aversive stimulus. What constitutes veridical perception on this dimension? When is perception of threat real or delusional?

Furthermore, the social learning focus on the immediate instigator prior to violence overlooks the potential forcing function of the aggressor's behavior in producing the behaviors in his victim whom he subsequently punishes. Kelley and Stahelski (1970) showed how in interactive games some people act in a consistently competitive fashion. These conflict-generators attribute more competitiveness to their opponent and view their opponent as the cause of their own competitiveness, even though they themselves have produced the competitive reactions in that opponent.

Therapists working with batterers (e.g., Ganley, 1980) describe the batterer's tendency to project anger onto others. Clearly, batterers also produce extreme anger in their victims, which is frequently indirectly expressed (i.e., through emotional withdrawal or irritability) since direct expression carries a threat of physical retaliation. Unexpressed reactions to less extreme forms of abuse can accumulate over time, generating behaviors in the female victim that are then perceived as aversive instigators. It is perhaps important to stress that describing the victim as producing aversive instigators is in no way a form of blaming the victim. There may be extremely valid reasons from that victim's perspective as to why such behaviors were produced. The term *aversive* refers to the perspective of the assaultive male.

The social learning focus on the immediate instigator of an aggressive act and the categorizing of that instigator as delusional, aversive, or incentive, assumes a world of discrete stimuli and responses. However, in a long-term marital interaction, each person's response becomes their partner's stimulus in a continuous shaping and reshaping of each other's behavior. Under these circumstances the simple discrete categories of social learning sometimes fail. Determining whether one member of a couple is deluded or not may entail an elaborate analysis of the behavior of his or her partner and its meaning to him or her.

2.3 REGULATORS OF ASSAULTIVE BEHAVIOR

As we saw in Chapter 1, about two-thirds of males who commit wife assault once, repeat within a year. Straus (1977a) reported that within a victim survey sample reporting wife assault, the mean frequency of serious assault was eight times a year. These repeatedly assaultive males constitute the most serious risk for injury to their wives.

Bandura (1979) describes a variety of regulators or maintaining mechanisms that sustain aggression. These include intermittent reinforcement (Walters & Brown, 1963) that functions to make aggression especially persistent. In the case of wife assault, when aggression serves to regain control for the male in a male-female conflict, thereby reducing aversive arousal, reinforcement occurs.

Patterson's (1979) analysis of hyperaggressive children documented the role of intermittent negative reinforcement in promoting aggressive behavior. In such families, children are inadvertently trained to use coercive behavior as a means of commanding parental attention or terminating social demands. The children's antagonistic behavior rapidly accelerates parental counteraggression in an escalating power struggle. By escalating reciprocal aggression, each member provides aversive instigation for the other, and each is intermittently reinforced for behaving coercively by overpowering the other. Patterson found mutual coercion was a locked-in interaction pattern in families referred to his clinic for problem children (Reid & Patterson, 1976).

Berk, Berk, Loseke, and Rauma (1981) dismissed the mutual combat myth based on injuries sustained by females from the violence of males. However, mutual combat simply suggests that both males and females use violent conflict tactics, perhaps in the reciprocally aversive fashion described by Patterson. Straus's (1980) data support the notion that use of conflict tactics does not differ greatly by gender. However, even if the conflict tactics used were essentially verbal, and the male escalated to physical tactics because he perceived himself to be losing the verbal battle, if the physical tactics put a stop to the dispute (in the male's favor), reinforcement would occur for the male using these physical tactics.

Social learning theory argues that when this outcome (favorable to the male) occurs intermittently, strong reinforcers for using violence will exist. However, even if this outcome does not occur, the feelings of agency associated with anger expression would still have reinforcement value. Hence, from a social learning perspective, wife assault would tend to be a repeated action because of the variety of sources of reward associated with it. Only expectations of punishment would serve to stop the habit once initiated.

2.3.1 The Expression of Pain by the Victim

Two points of view exist on whether expressions of injury by a victim increase or decrease the likelihood of future assault. One perspective argues that because the purpose of aggression is the infliction of pain, aggression is reinforced by signs of the victim suffering (Sears, Maccoby, & Levin, 1957; Feshback, 1970).

Another point of view argues that signs of suffering function as inhibitors of aggression. This latter perspective bases its argument on the fact that most social groups establish strong prohibitions against cruel and destructive acts (except under special circumstances) because of the dangers of intragroup violence. As a result of such socialization, most people adopt self-evaluation standards that adjudge ruthless aggression as morally reprehensible. Consequently, aggression that produces evident suffering in others elicits both fear of punishment and self-censure that inhibits further injurious attacks. Empirical support for this position derives from studies on the effects of pain expression on assaultive behavior (Geen, 1970).

Aggressors behave less punitively when their victims express anguished cries than when they do not see or hear their victims suffer (Baron, 1971a, 1971b; Sanders & Baron, 1977). Pain cues from a victim reduce aggression, whether assailants are angered or not (Geen, 1970; Rule & Leger, 1976). When an aggressor sees his victim suffering, aggresion is reduced even more than when he hears the victim suffering (Milgram, 1974).

Hence, laboratory studies of aggression seem to indicate that expression of pain should inhibit further aggression. To what extent could such studies be generalized to wife-assault situations? The degree of arousal and anger generated in the lab does not match that generated in genuine husband-wife conflict. And as Bandura (1979) points out, when one party injures another whom they perceive to be an oppressor, pain cues from the injured party may signal the alleviation of aversive treatment. However, in cases of wife assault, expressions of pain by the female victim may not inhibit aggression when the male's arousal is so high that his focus of attention is shifted away from his victim (Zimbardo, 1969; Dutton, Fehr, & McEwen, 1982). In Section 2.5 of this chapter we will examine a situation where the expression of pain has no inhibitory effect on the assaulter: deindividuated aggression.

2.3.2 Punishing Consequences

A fundamental tenet of social learning theory is that behavior is regulated by its consequences. So far we have examined the gains or rewards that might attend the use of violence against one's wife. We have also reviewed one other consequence: expressions of pain in the victim, whose ability to regulate behavior is ambiguous. At this point we will examine two sources of punishment, one external or social, the other internal or personal, which should function to limit aggressive actions.

External Punishment

Much has been written about the inability or unwillingness of the criminal justice system to punish men for wife assault (U.S. Commission on Civil Rights, 1978; Field, 1978). In Chapter 5 we will examine these claims to see whether stronger criminal justice action would deter wife assault (Dutton, 1986a). For present purposes, our focus is on the effectiveness of external punishment in controlling aggressive behavior.

Bandura (1979) reviews the empirical literature on this issue and concludes that for external punishment to be effective, a variety of factors must be considered. These include:

- the benefits derived from aggression
- the availability of alternative means for obtaining these benefits
- the likelihood of punishment
- the nature, severity, timing, and duration of punishment

Bandura concludes that when alternative means are available and the risk of punishment is high, aggression decreases rapidly. However, when aggression is rewarded or when alternative means of obtaining rewards are not available, punishment must be forceful and consistent to suppress aggression. Even when this is so, control is only temporary. Functional aggression (i.e., aggression that obtains rewards) recurs when threats are removed and is readily performed when the probability of punishment is low.

These results have implications for the regulation of wife assault where external punishment for assault, in theory, could be applied by the wife-victim, by a friendship or kinship group, or by the criminal justice system. In practice, however, the wife-victim may not have sufficient power or resources to punish the aggressor, and informal kin groups may or may not have knowledge of the assault and may be unwilling to interfere. Criminal justice punishment is rare for wife assault (Dutton, 1987a). In any event, Bandura's conclusions suggest that for future assault to diminish, alternative means of obtaining a goal (that the oppressor normally obtains via assault) must be developed. Alternative means are typically one objective of treatment groups for wife assaulters that seek (1) to alter unrealistic male expectations about their wives, (2) to improve assertive communications as a means of nonviolent conflict resolution, and (3) to improve the male's empathy for his victim and build in processes of self-punishment for aggression.

Conscience and Reprehensible Behavior: Self-Punishment

The existence of self-regulatory mechanisms such as self-punishment implies that people respond not only to external consequences of their behavior but to internal reactions as well. Through intuition and modelling, people adopt certain standards of behavior and respond to their own actions in self-punishing (or self-rewarding) ways. These standards of behavior are the by-product of social norms and mores, subgroup influences, and personal experiences.

With regard to wife assault, tremendous variation in self-regulation exists. Walker (1979a) describes a cycle of violence where assaultive males go through a phase of guilt and contrition about their violence, indicated by exaggerated positive responding to their wives. Dobash and Dobash (1984), however, dispute Walker's theory, claiming that for the majority of Scottish men, wife assault is followed by total denial of the event, after which they proceed as if nothing had happened. Therapy with wife assaulters reflects this variation: some men believe their conviction was unjust and their violence justified; others are filled with self-recrimination.

In Chapter 3 we report an empirical study of wife assaulters' own explanations for their violence. This study confirms that a variety of explanations or rationalizations exist in an assaultive population. While variations about the propriety of assaultive behavior exist among wife assaulters, Bandura's theory makes the point that wife assault could stem from two generally different etiologies: It could occur because some men simply view it as acceptable behavior or because some men obtain reward through its use both by dominating their partner and by feeling personal pride about their use of violence. Sociological theories suggesting wife assault has normative support would favor the latter etiology (e.g., Dobash & Dobash, 1979).

Alternatively, wife assault could occur because some men, who have socialized constraints against the use of violence toward their wife, violate their own self-constraints because of high arousal, anxiety about relinquishing control to their wife, and the perceived seriousness of the conflict issue. As Bandura (1979) puts it, moral (i.e., normally socialized) people perform culpable acts through processes that disengage evaluative self-reactions from such conduct rather than through defects in the development or the structure of their superegos.

2.4 THE NEUTRALIZATION OF SELF-PUNISHMENT

When people violate their own self-standards, a variety of cognitive processes may result to keep negative self-evaluation (and consequent guilt) from becoming overwhelming. Self-deterring consequences are activated most strongly when the connection between conduct and the detrimental effects it produces are clear (Bandura, 1979). To dissociate consequences from behavior, one can (1) cognitively restructure the behavior through euphemistic labelling, palliative comparison, or moral justification; (2) cognitively restructure the relationship between behavior and its effects on the victim by displacing responsibility; (3) cognitively restructure the behavior through euphemistic labelling, palliative comnoring the consequences for the victim; or (4) cognitively restructure their perception of the victim through blaming her for the violence (see Figure 2.3).

In the case of wife assault, some form of all these cognitive restructurings

FIGURE 2.3 Mechanisms through which behavior is disengaged from self-evaluative consequences at different points in the behavior process

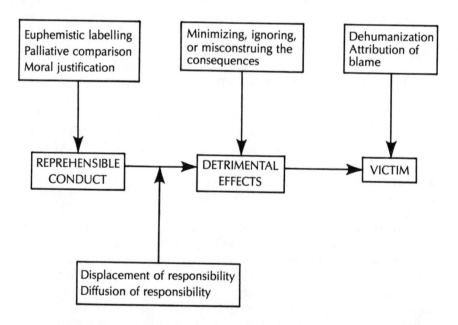

Source: Bandura, A. (1979). The social learning perspective: Mechanisms of aggression. In H. Toch (Ed.), *Psychology of crime and criminal justice.*New York: Holt, Rinehart, & Winston.

appears to occur for assaultive males (as we will see in Chapter 3). Treatment manuals (Ganley, 1981; Sonkin & Durphy, 1982) provide explicit directions for therapists to confront clients' use of each of the forms of neutralization of self-punishment described above. Men in treatment for wife assault frequently cognitively restructure their behavior so that it is described as being less violent than it actually was.

Browning and Dutton (1986) obtained Straus *CTS* ratings by husbands and wives in 30 couples where the man had been convicted of wife assault. Men reported less than half the frequency or severity of violence as their wives reported them committing. Men's recall and reporting of their own violence were frequently at odds with reports of police and hospital emergency room reports of women's injuries. *Euphemistic labelling* occurs when a serious assault is described in nonserious terms (i.e., "The night we had our little problem. . . ." "You know, when I pushed her."). *Palliative comparison* in treatment groups is also frequent. Some convicted wife assaulters will volunteer the observation that all men beat their wives and only they themselves had the misfortune to get caught. *Moral justification* takes the form that the nagging, infidelity, or other unacceptable behavior of their wives needed to be brought into line. Recall the medieval emphasis on the "need" women had to be punished that we described in Chapter 1.

For wife assaulters, the connection between their own actions and the injurious consequences to their victim is obscured by displacing responsibility. Some therapists feel that assaultive men sometimes get drunk in order to get violent. Alcohol is involved in 30% to 56% of domestic dispute calls attended by police but in only 10% of cases did the complainant allege that their spouse was drunk (Bard & Zacker, 1974). The role of alcohol in wife assault is not completely clear; although it is a disinhibitor and thus can be viewed as having a pharmacological main effect that contributes to violence, it is also known to be a disinhibitor and, hence, can be chosen by men who want to act out or be violent. Marlatt and Rohsenow (1981) have shown that expectations about the disinhibiting effect of alcohol usage are as powerful as the pharmacological effect of the drug itself.

The seriousness of injuries and psychological trauma to the victim are frequently overlooked by assaulters as well, so that the consequences of the assault are restructured by the assaulter. His action is rendered less reprehensible by denying to himself that it caused pain and distress for his victim. Finally, the victim is frequently blamed as being the cause of the man's violence through her own actions. Ganley and Harris (1978), Walker (1979a,b), and Dutton and Painter (1980) all report the excessive minimizing of personal responsibility for the wife assault, which goes on during the first month of therapy with assaultive males. Often this is accompanied by fixating on some aspect of the wife's behavior, real or imagined, that is described by the batterer as having caused his violence.

As we shall see in Chapter 6, part of the traditional therapeutic approach in anger management with battering males (Novaco, 1975; Ganley & Harris, 1978) is to demonstrate to them that even if their wives do the things that they claim make them violent, it is *their* interpretation of their wives' behavior, *their* choice of an anger label for the resulting arousal, and *their* decision to express anger by directing violence at the women. In short, the therapy seeks to establish and strengthen a sense of personal responsibility that has been diminished by rationalization and lack of awareness. A major objective of treatment is to confront and alter these forms of neutralization of self-punishment.

2.5 SEVERE WIFE ASSAULT AND DEINDIVIDUATED VIOLENCE

Particularly severe forms of violence sometimes appear to violate the reward-and-punishment rules that typically control our behavior in the fashion described above. Normal constraints such as pleas from the victim sometimes do not operate to reduce aggression, and the aggressor launches into a self-reinforced series of progressively more destructive actions that are extremely difficult to terminate. These episodes, termed *deindividuated violence* by social psychologist Phillip Zimbardo (1969), appear to occur in the most extreme cases of wife assault (often termed *battering*).

These most severe cases of wife assault generally involve, on the part of the batterer, an inability to recall the actual assaultive incident, even after shame and embarrassment about reporting it have subsided. Reconstruction of the assaultive incident from interviews with the wife and from police and medical testimony depict the male as being in a highly aroused state of rage, unresponsive to begging or pleading from the victim, and, in some cases, beating her until he was too exhausted to continue. The men usually remember the events leading up to the actual battering and the aftermath (some were shocked and sickened by what they had done), but not the intervening battering. Several therapists working with assaultive husbands have reported this phenomenon (Ganley, 1980; Walker, 1979a; Martin, 1977).

Walker (1978) described the batterer's uncontrollable destructiveness and lack of responsiveness to cues from the victim. Ganley (1980) has confirmed the tendency of women victims to have comprehensive recall of the battering incident (since their lives depended on being able to defend themselves in whatever way from the blows) and of the male batterers to blank out on the actual battering incident.

Portions of Severe Wife Assault and Deindividuated Violence are reprinted by permission from *Victimology: An International Journal* 7(1982), 1–4(13) © 1983 Victimology Inc.

The descriptions of acute battering incidents provided by Walker and Ganley's interviews with victims and by our own (Dutton & Painter, 1980, 1981) present a description that appears to fit Zimbardo's (1969) analysis of deindividuated aggression. Certain key features of such violence stand out in both descriptions: (1) escalating violence that increases to a point of frenzy and (2) cannot be terminated, once begun, by the victim but (3) ends only when the aggressor is exhausted. Furthermore, several of the antecedent conditions that Zimbardo postulates as increasing the likelihood of deindividuated violence are present in severe wife battering: anonymity from public purview, diminished personal responsibility, generalized arousal, and altered states of consciousness.

The memory lapse on the part of the batterer might be explicable by another feature of deindividuated aggression: the shift in control over the batterer's behavior from external, environmental stimuli to internal, proprioceptive stimuli. With the exception of being able to locate and direct violence toward the victim, an individual in a deindividuated state is attuned to and registering only stimuli from within. What has not been stored in memory cannot be retrieved; hence, the persistent inability to remember external details of the battering incident.

Zimbardo (1969) depicts both sexual and aggressive behavior as being stringently controlled by social norms that have evolved to regulate behavior that could affect the size and longevity of social groups. For individuals living in such groups, both external normative control and internal control constitute the essentials of what we commonly refer to as socialization. Hence, we learn to inhibit inappropriate sexual and aggressive behavior for fear of negative consequences from a group that satisfies our social needs. The impulses to be sexual or aggressive, however, do not disappear, and their expression can be facilitated by any psychological state or social circumstances that temporarily minimize these controls.

Zimbardo's position is that proscribed emotional, sexual, and aggressive behavioral expressions are inherently pleasurable (Zimbardo, 1969). Such expressions are "self-reinforcing; therefore, once initiated, they should be self-maintaining and perpetuating until a marked change occurs in the state of the organism (e.g., exhaustion, emotional breakdown) or in environmental conditions (e.g., a weapon breaks)" (Zimbardo, 1969, p. 252). Zimbardo's innovative combination of psychoanalytic assumptions, social learning behavioral analysis, and social psychology produced a perspective for linking antecedent conditions with subsequent impulsive behavior, although as we shall see below, the evidence for the assumption that the expression of violence is inherently pleasurable is questionable.

As a social psychologist, Zimbardo has been primarily concerned with those social conditions that might decrease social controls over proscribed behavior. One of these social conditions is group size. People in crowds, or who are disguised, masked, or indistinguishable from others, are more likely to perform impulsive expressions of proscribed behaviors than they would if they were identifiable as individuals. Citing riots and mob violence as examples, Zimbardo speculates that crowds provide anonymity, action models, and a reduced sense of personal responsibility for ensuing behavior. Subsequent research on deindividuation has tended to focus on such group variables and their effect on aggression (Diener, 1976; Jorgenson & Dukes, 1976; Maslach, 1974; Watson, 1973).

At first glance, wife battering appears to depart from the group-induced violence that Zimbardo describes, yet the intrapsychic input variables that increase the likelihood of deindividuated violence are all present in wife-battering situations. The effect of anonymity is to reduce social control simply because an anonymous individual cannot be identified for reprisal or sanction. Immersion in a group is not, of course, the only way to produce anonymity. Anything that severs our connection to the everyday trappings of our social role (such as travelling in a foreign country), feelings of alienation from one's self and others, or any other circumstances that make one feel unidentifiable could produce anonymity.

While wife battering usually occurs in the home where, in one sense, the batterer should feel most connected to symbols of his identity, in this place the batterer also is most freed from public scrutiny and surveillance. In many jurisdictions, policy, attitudes, and beliefs make police less than eager to respond to family dispute calls (see Chapter 5) (Levens & Dutton, 1977; Dutton, 1977; Loving & Farmer, 1980). Furthermore, public attitudes about the privacy of the family (see, for example, Steiner, 1981) and the victim's own shame that often precludes her reporting the assault (Dutton & Painter, 1980, 1981), all may contribute to a wife assaulter's feeling of anonymity with respect to this particular offense. Furthermore, Belsky (1980) reports that isolation of a family (i.e., absence of informal support networks) is associated with the incidence of assault. Isolation also contributes to anonymity since, by definition, it connotes an absence of others who might make norms salient, judge, and individuate the batterer. Hence, one could argue that anonymity as a central input variable for deindividuated violence is present in cases of wife battering.

The action model supplied by the group or crowd can often be supplanted for wife batterers by role modelling in their family of origin. As stated previously, studies profiling batterers report increased likelihood of wife assault for men who have witnessed father-mother violence (Straus, Gelles, & Steinmetz, 1980; Kalmuss, 1984).

As we argued in Section 2.2.1, only minimal opportunity for learning proscribed behaviors is required for their expression. If the expression of sexual or aggressive behavior is self-rewarding, such behavior will be quickly amplified and shaped upon repetition. Indeed, evidence suggests that violence tends to escalate from initial discrete incidents until it becomes serious enough to warrant outside intervention (Wilt & Breedlove, 1977; Dutton & Painter, 1980;

Jaffe, 1982). This occurs because of self-rewarding mechanisms such as feelings of power, agency, and catharsis (Novaco, 1975, 1976) that augment proprioceptive feedback as the reward mechanism for the expression of accelerated aggression.

2.5.1 Personal Responsibility

The reduced sense of personal responsibility for the consequences of proscribed violence, although aided by immersion in a group, also can occur intrapsychically either through externalizing the violence to the use of alcohol or by blaming the victim. Zimbardo suggests that any drug that alters consciousness will tend to increase the likelihood of deindividuated behavior by diminishing cognitive control. Alcohol, therefore, may serve to diminish personal responsibility in acts of wife assault, as the aggressor often blames his violence on the alcohol despite incidents of being violent while sober (Dutton & Painter, 1980; Rounsaville, 1978). The criminal justice system often inadvertently reinforces this excuse by placing undue emphasis on alcohol usage per se (see Bard & Zacker, 1974; Levens & Dutton, 1980). Diminished responsibility is also brought about by blaming the victim of the assault, as we have described in the last section.

Interestingly, Diener (1976) posits that lessened self-awareness may be the crucial psychological construct that produces deindividuated behavior. While group or crowd situations may contribute to lessened self-awareness, they are certainly not necessary to produce it. The cognitive mechanisms described in 2.3.2 that neutralize self-punishment can also operate to diminish self-awareness.

2.5.2 Arousal and Deindividuated Violence

A final major antecedent variable posited by Zimbardo is arousal that "increases the likelihood that gross 'agitated' behavior will be released, and that cues in the situation which might inhibit responding will not be noticed" (Zimbardo, 1969, p. 257). Again, Zimbardo cites social bases for the generation of extreme arousal, while our own research investigates arousal generated within intimate relationships as a function of perceived uncontrollable intimacy change (described in 2.1 above). Hence, we would argue that the expression of extreme anger in intimate relationships is supported by a variety of mechanisms in addition to those posited by Zimbardo. Furthermore, as we discussed in 2.1, high arousal states tend to narrowly focus attention and to "simplify" behavioral repertoires.

2.5.3 Alternative Sources of Reinforcement
for Deindividuated Violence

Zimbardo sees the deindividuated expression of violence as originating when some crucial conjunction of anonymity, arousal, and diminished responsibility occur and, presumably, some instigating stimulus is perceived by the aggressor. From that point on, once normative control is lost, the aggressor focuses on proprioceptive (physical) feedback from their own body, which Zimbardo assumes to be pleasurable, hence "a self-reinforcing amplification process is generated. Once begun, each subsequent response should have progressively shorter latencies, coupled with greater vigour" (Zimbardo, 1969, p. 259). Blows, stabs, trigger pulls, or other acts of violence accelerate, coming faster and faster and with greater vigor up to the point of exhaustion. Of course, if pleasurable proprioceptive feedback is the key to this output pattern, we should expect to see it occur more with actions that provide more proprioceptive feedback (e.g., hitting a pillow from an overhead position provides greater proprioceptive feedback than pulling a trigger).

If, on the other hand, the environmental result is more important than Zimbardo speculates, then actions that produce disproportionate reactions should produce the self-accelerating pattern (e.g., pulling a trigger to shoot out plate glass windows would be more rewarding than smashing a pillow [see, for example, Allen & Greenberger, 1978]). Zimbardo's own empirical test of portions of his theory provided little opportunity for proprioceptive feedback, as subjects merely pushed a shock button. However, later demonstrations of deindividuated vandalism led him to conclude that the ideal conditions occur where the physical act is energized and expressive, thus producing considerable noncognitive feedback. It is pleasurable to behave at a purely sensual, physical, unthinking level—regardless of whether the act is making love or war (Zimbardo, 1969).

This may indeed be the case. However, it is our contention that considerable reinforcers exist for the expression of aggression in addition to proprioceptive feedback. Batterers in therapeutic groups report feelings of power, even sexual arousal, following battering incidents, bringing to mind Eric Fromm's statement, which opens this chapter, that sadism (physical control of another) is an attempt to convert feelings of impotence into a temporary feeling of omnipotence (Fromm, 1973).

Novaco (1976) has outlined the variety of reinforcers built into anger expression: feelings of energy, expressiveness, and potentiation, which are all consonant with the romanticizing of violence and with traditional male sex-role values. In addition, anger serves the defensive function of short-circuiting anxious feelings of vulnerability. Since these other potential sources of reward exist for the expression of anger through histrionic aggression, an alternative explanation exists for the suggestion that proprioceptive feedback determines accelerating aggression.

As is often the case when new phenomena are fit to theory, the theoretical conception provides new insights into the etiology of the phenomenon and is itself transformed by the new data pattern. Zimbardo's notion of deindividuated aggression makes a valuable contribution toward the understanding of extreme wife assault, but the notion of deindividuation itself seems to require refinement in explaining wife assault, particularly in view of the reinforcers operating in the expression of such assault. Our own research has investigated the role of arousal produced by rapid, uncontrollable changes in intimacy as an instigator of aggression. In the next chapter we report these studies.

CHAPTER SUMMARY

In this chapter we have attempted to apply social learning theory to the explanation of wife assault. From the nested ecological perspective developed in Chapter 1, the emphasis of social learning theory is primarily on ontogenetic development and secondarily on the interaction of ontogenetic factors with microcosm factors. Considerable basic research on aggression that has tested predictions from a social learning model has been reported. This research provides a rich perspective on the etiology of wife assault. However, at this time little research on aggression has specifically tested these predictions in the context of intimate violence. While social learning analyses have been used in developing treatment programs for wife assaulters (Ganley, 1981), they have not as yet generated substantial empirical studies.

In the next chapter we report in detail some beginnings in this direction: intimacy and power are systematically studied as constituting elements of aversive stimuli, and the consequences for angry responses in assaultive males are compared to a nonassaultive control group. Also, the cognitive machinations that constitute the neutralization of self-punishment are examined in order to ascertain how repeat wife assaulters sustain a habit of violence.

The Social Psychology
of the Wife Assaulter:
The Research Studies

Sit down before fact like a little child, and be prepared to give up every preconceived notion.
—Thomas Henry Huxley, quoted in Aldous Huxley, *The Human Situation*
(1980, p. 15)

In Chapters 1 and 2 we examined several theoretical explanations for wife assault. In Section 1.6 we established a framework for a nested ecological theory of wife assault that concentrated on the interaction of individually acquired dispositions with social-contextual features of the family, the subculture, and the broader culture. Using this framework, we established a hypothetical profile of an assaultive male that incorporated individually acquired factors such as (1) the desire to have control over or dominate women (see Section 2.1.1), (2) exaggerated anxiety about control over the amount of intimacy in a relationship (see Section 2.1.2), (3) violent role models for conflict resolution (see Section 2.2.1), and (4) poor verbal conflict-resolution skills. To this profile were added contextual factors from the microsystem (coercive interactions), the exosystem (unemployment, job stress, and social isolation), and the macrosystem (beliefs in patriarchal rights, double standards, etc.).

In Chapter 2 we developed a social learning analysis of the individual assaulter and examined the acquisition and maintenance mechanisms of the habit of wife assault. We suggested that for men who assault their wives, but are not generally assaultive, some special categories of aversive stimuli or instigators to assault may exist. These categories include (1) perceived actions by the wife that she wishes to change the degree of intimacy with the male and (2) perceptions by the male that he is powerless to stop her.

In this chapter we will describe some experiments conducted with wife assaulters and control subjects in order to test hypotheses generated by these theoretical notions. Our objective in doing this research has been to determine which factors, taken in combination, explain why males assault their wives. Recall that in Section 1.3.1 we were critical of psychiatric explanations for wife assault. The problem with these explanations was that they sought to connect wife assault with a clinical syndrome, such as an antisocial personality disorder, depression, or substance abuse, without demonstrating how the disorder per se could lead to an increased likelihood of wife assault. There is no logical reason why depression, for example, should produce wife assault, nor does alcoholism lead inevitably to assaultive behavior.

The logic of explanation, as we outlined in Section 2.1, must show how wife assaulters differ from married males with similar stresses, conflicts, and demographic profiles who do not assault their wives. Furthermore, this explanation must clearly specify how the combination of these differentiating factors produces the assaultive behavior.

We have begun to sketch out one possible multifactored explanation that fits these guidelines: we have speculated that wife assaulters may have exaggerated needs for dominance vis-à-vis their wives, poor verbal skills to enable them to establish such dominance, poor access to their emotions, exaggerated anxiety about relationship issues, such as degree of intimacy, and a learning history that reinforced the use of violence as a means of establishing control. The combination of a high need for power and poor verbal skills might produce chronic states of frustration in their relationship with their wives. For these men, any normal conflict issues such as time spent together or apart might produce exaggerated arousal-anxiety reactions. Male socialization tends to lead to the transformation of frustration or anxiety into anger. A learning history that reinforced the expression of anger through violence would increase the likelihood of aggression directed toward women.

We have begun to test this hypothetical model of wife assault by testing its components. Our research strategy has been to compare men with histories of wife assault with demographically matched controls. We have tested each link in our theoretical chain by using paper-and-pencil tests, reactions to videotaped male-female conflicts, projective tests, and so forth, so that we have assessments of the need for power, verbal assertiveness skills, intimacy anxiety, and exposure to violent role models for assaultive males. We will report the methods used and results obtained in the rest of this chapter in greater detail than in other chapters. For readers with less interest in methodological detail, summaries of results and implications for our theoretical model are provided at the end of each section of this chapter.

3.1 WHAT DIFFERENTIATES WIFE ASSAULTERS FROM OTHER MALES?

Our interest was in comparing a group of men who had histories of repeated wife assault with appropriate control groups on the dimensions described above.

We hypothesized, for example, that wife assaulters (W.A.) might have higher scores on tests of the need for power and dominance, might react with greater anger to scenes depicting male-female conflict over intimacy issues, and may have had greater exposure to violent role models than would our control subjects.[1]

We selected three groups of control subjects: (1) men who were demographically similar to our assaultive population but who were *happily married* (H.M.), (2) men who were demographically similar to our assaultive population and were *maritally conflicted* but not violent with their wives (M.C.), and (3) men who had assaulted their wives but who were *generally assaultive* as well (G.A.).

In contrast to this generally assaultive group, our *wife assaultive* group (W.A.) did not engage in violence outside their primary relationship. Inclusions of each of these groups allowed us to make specific comparisons that were informative: the happily married group presented some baseline information on frequency of conflict and types of conflict resolution and the maritally conflicted group allowed us to separate frequency of conflict from other factors as a cause of assault. The maritally conflicted group reported as much conflict with their wives as the wife assaulters but did not use physical aggression to resolve it. Finally, the generally assaultive group used physical aggression both inside and outside their primary relationship. Hence, we hypothesized that they might not react to the same specific aversive instigators as men whose violence was wife-specific.

The wife assaulters group and generally assaultive group were men who had been referred to the Assaultive Husbands Project, a treatment program run in conjunction with the Vancouver Family Court. These two assaultive groups participated voluntarily in order to obtain some feedback on their conflict-resolution techniques. The maritally conflicted group was comprised of men attending counselling groups for marital conflict; the happily married group were solicited through ads in local newspapers. These latter two groups were paid to participate in the research. All subjects first attended an assessment session where, among other questionnaires to be described below, they were administered the Straus *Conflict Tactics Scale* (see Section 1.1). In addition, so that we need not rely exclusively on the men's self-reports on the *CTS*, an added requirement for participation was that the men be currently in a relationship and that their partner fill out the *CTS* as well.

Men's and women's scores were averaged to establish criterion scores.[2] Criteria for selection were as follows: wife assaulters (at least three incidents of serious assault against their wife in the prior year, corroborated by their wife and no assault outside the relationship); generally assaultive (three incidents of serious wife assault [corroborated by their wife] in prior year and three or more incidents of serious assault outside the relationship); maritally conflicted (80th percentile or above for previous year's scores on the Verbal Aggression Subscale of the *CTS* and no physical violence (corroborated by wife); happily married

(65th percentile or below on Verbal Aggression Subscale and no physical violence [corroborated by their wife]). Table 3.1 demonstrates their scores.

Men in both assaultive groups were predominantly in blue-collar professions or unemployed, and their average age was 32. In order to achieve socioeconomic and demographic matching with these groups, men were selected for participation in the maritally conflicted and happily married groups who most matched this demographic profile. Men who did not fit this profile or whose scores on any subscale of the *CTS* fell outside the criterion range were rejected from the study. Table 3.2 demonstrates some demographic properties of these groups. The tests described below were not administered to every member of these four groups. Rather, subsets of tests were administered to subsets of subjects. Hence, the sample size may change from test to test.

3.1.1 General Procedure

Participants were required to attend two individual testing sessions, each lasting approximately two hours. The first session involved a prolonged rationale for the study with an emphasis on the necessity for honesty and completion of all items. Assaultive males were told that an accurate assessment of their anger and conflict-resolution problems necessitated their answering all items honestly. Since these men had volunteered for this research and were also in treatment

TABLE 3.1 *CTS* scores for experimental groups during prior year

	Wife Assaulters	Generally Assaultive	Maritally Conflicted	Happily Married
n =	45	18	45	45
Husband's ratings (of own behavior)				
Reasoning	7.6[a]	7.8	9.60	7.0
Verbal aggression	18.9	16.6	15.70	3.8
Physical aggression:				
with wife	10.9	2.3	0.67	0.2
outside marriage	0.8	8.9		
Wife's ratings (of husband's behavior)				
Reasoning	7.4	7.2	7.70	7.5
Verbal	21.2	12.2	13.80	5.7
Physical	17.2	16.8	0.90	0.3

[a]Reasoning Subscale is (0–18), Verbal Aggression Subscale is (0–36), Physical Aggression Subscale is (0–48). The 95th and 99th percentile scores for the general population are as follows: Verbal Aggression 19 and 30 and Physical Aggression 4, 14 (Straus, 1979).

TABLE 3.2   Demographic characteristics of experimental groups

	Wife Assaulters	Generally Assaultive	Maritally Conflicted	Happily Married
n =	45	18	45	45
Age	32.2	32.8	32.9	31.9
Education				
Some high school	40%	50%	35%	35%
High school grad	40%	35%	40%	40%
Some college	15%	15%	20%	20%
College grad	5%	0%	5%	5%
Occupation				
blue collar	85%	88%	82%	83%
white collar/prof.	15%	12%	18%	17%
Unemployment	45%	45%	25%	30%
Years married	6.8	6.9	8.6	9.1
Number of children	1.5	1.7	1.5	1.4
Number of drinks/wk	12.8	13.2	5.4	5.8

for anger problems, there is some reason to believe they would be motivated to answer honestly. The men completed a battery of questionnaires bearing on experimental hypotheses. After these were completed, *CTS* scoring was completed to establish whether each man met selection criteria. If he did, a second session was arranged that involved testing on the videotape analogue of the research. All men were provided with feedback based on their responses to session one. This feedback appeared to be a prime motivation for participation.

3.1.2   Questionnaire Assessment

We wished to assess features of each subject's (1) work and friendship network (exosystem), (2) beliefs and attitudes about women, acceptance of violence, and so forth, (3) assertiveness and communication skills, and (4) power motivation. The rationale and test used for each of these is described below:

1. *Demographic Information Sheet*
This sheet assessed the following exosystem factors: (1) employment situation—whether the man was employed or unemployed and how stressful

his life (and job) was using the Holmes and Rahe (1967) stress scale. Also assessed were (2) the frequency and quality of his contacts with friends or support group; for this, we used a modified version of the *Fischer Scale* (1982).

2. Power Motivation: The Thematic Apperception Test of n-Power

In Section 2.1.1 we described the work of McClelland (1975) and Winter (1973) on the power motive. Men with a Type III power motivation were described by Winter as having an exaggerated need to persuade and generate compliance. Such men appeared to generate conflict in primary relationships (Stewart & Rubin, 1976). If this tendency to generate conflict was combined with poor conflict-resolution skills and an exaggerated anger reaction to certain forms of perceived conflict, potential for assaultive behavior could increase. Hence, we wanted to test our assaultive populations against other populations on a measure of the need for power (*n*-power).

Winter (1973) developed a scoring system for *n*-power that has been widely used to test power motivation in male populations (e.g., McClelland, 1975; Stewart & Rubin, 1976; Winter, 1973). Winter's test measures a power motive described as having impact on the behavior or emotions of another person and was empirically derived from experiments designed to arouse the power motive in subjects. The scoring system allows power imagery to be scored from a *Thematic Apperception Test* story that includes references to (1) strong assertive actions, (2) actions that induce strong emotions in others, and (3) concern about the reputation of the actor.

Participants wrote stories in response to five pictures selected initially by Winter on the basis of their being able to elicit power imagery.[3] Participants look at the pictures one at a time and write short stories that answer the following questions: What is happening? Who are the people? What has led up to this situation? What is being thought? What is wanted? By whom? What will happen? What will be done? Trained raters scored these stories.[4] Our hypothesis was that assaultive males would demonstrate comparatively high scores of power imagery, suggesting a high need for power.

3. Measures of Assertiveness and Communication Style

Two measures of assertiveness were obtained for all subjects: The *Rathus Assertiveness Schedule* (Rathus, 1973), which is a 30-item inventory covering a wide range of assertive behavior, and the *Spouse-Specific Assertiveness Scale* (Rosenbaum & O'Leary, 1981), a 29-item scale that measures assertiveness and aggression within the primary relationship. The purpose of the above scale is to assess whether communication deficits, which may combine with other factors to increase the likelihood of physical violence as a means of conflict resolution, are characteristic of wife assaulters.

4. The Marlowe-Crowne Social Desirability Scale
(Crowne & Marlowe, 1960)

This is a 33-item scale designed to assess the need to respond in a culturally acceptable manner. While all subjects were told that feedback on their conflict-resolution problems required honest responses on all questionnaires, the *SDS* allowed us to assess for differential image management by group.

5. The Burt Attitude Scales (Burt, 1980)

These scales assess sex-role stereotyping (9 items: example: "A woman may have a career but her marriage and family should come first); adversarial sexual beliefs (10 items; example: "A woman will only respect a man who will lay down the law to her"); and acceptance of interpersonal violence toward women (5 items; example: "a man is never justified in hitting his wife"). Burt (1980) has argued that these attitudes serve to target and release violent assault and has demonstrated strong relationships in males between these scale scores and holding the myth that females enjoy being raped. The inclusion of these beliefs in the present study has a two-fold objective: (1) to establish whether wife assaulters have a generalized mistrust of women (i.e., adversarial sexual beliefs) and (2) whether assaultive males place a positive value on the use of violence. As described above, social learning theory would indicate widely differing etiologies for men who believe the use of violence against their wife is acceptable and those who do not so believe but act violently anyway.

6. Straus Conflict Tactics Scales: Childhood
Exposure to Violence

In addition to the husband-wife *CTS*, a *CTS* that assessed childhood exposure to violence was used. Straus, Gelles, and Steinmetz (1980) had reported higher rates of physical abuse as children in males who subsequently used violence.

3.1.3 Results of Questionnaire Assessment _____

As a general strategy of data analysis given the large number of variables examined in this study (and consequent concern for holding down the false-positive error rate), we first analyzed items where no differences were anticipated. The remaining variables were then grouped and subjected to multivariate analysis of variance (Marascuilo & Levin, 1983). If significant differences were found, the MANOVAs were followed up by univariate analyses of variance[5] in order to assess specific differences. Newman-Keuls multiple comparisons were performed on pairs of means as a follow-up to significant ANOVAs.

We used the Dyadic Adjustment Scale (1976) to assess degree of marital dissatisfaction. We had hoped for similar scores on this scale for the W.A., G.A., and M.C. groups in order to rule out degree of conflict and marital quality as confounds. This is what we found: there were no significant differences between these groups but all differed from the H.M. group ($p < .01$) using Newman-Keuls pairwise comparisons. Similarly, we had hoped that no one group would demonstrate exaggerated scores in the *Marlowe-Crowne Social Desirability Scale*. A one-way ANOVA on the *Marlowe-Crowne* did not reveal any significant between-group differences on this scale. The H.M. group had the highest scores (i.e., the most socially desirable) but they were not significantly higher than the other groups.

The remaining questionnaire items were ones on which we expected between-group differences. Accordingly, they were combined and analyzed via one way multivariate analysis of variance as follows: (1) attitudes toward women, (2) *n*-power, (3) assertiveness, and (4) exposure to childhood violence.

Do Wife Assaulters Have More Negative or Adversarial Attitudes toward Women than the Other Groups?

Our analyses revealed no differences between the wife assault group and other groups on scores on the *Burt Attitude Scales*. Wife assaulters as a group were not more stereotyping of females, more mistrustful of females, or more accepting of the use of violence toward females. Neidig, Friedman, and Collins (1986) also failed to find differences between wife assaulters and control groups on attitudes toward women using the Spence and Helmreich (1978) *Attitudes toward Women Scale*.

One obvious possibility for these failures is that too many demand characteristics (Orne, 1969) exist in research that measures attitudes. *Demand characteristics* are those cues available to subjects from the experimental settings and instructions that tell them what an appropriate or correct response might be to the experimenter's questions. Men who are selected for research on the basis of their having been violent try to answer attitudinal questionnaires in an exonerative fashion, which may diminish any possible differences between groups of subjects. Since the correct answer (in terms of exoneration) is usually obvious on attitude measures, real differences between groups of men tend to be obscured.

An alternative explanation for these failures to find between-group differences is that assaultive males may simply not hold particularly negative or adversarial attitudes toward women in general (i.e., any more so than control-group males) but simply act with a learned pattern of violence that is not consonant with general attitudes.

Do Wife Assaulters Have a Stronger Motive to Control or Dominate Women?

The measure of need for power used in this research indicated significant differences between our wife assault group and the happily married group when the stimulus materials used were male-female scenes.[6] However, wife assaulters did not differ from the maritally conflicted control group. (Generally assaultive males were not tested using this particular measure.) This suggests a stronger need to have impact on or dominate in a male-female context. *Thematic Apperception Test* stories are not so obviously related to violence against women as are direct attitudinal measures. Consequently, they are more difficult for subjects to answer in a socially desirable fashion.

Dutton and Strachan (1987a) have argued that, for this reason, *Thematic Apperception Tests* may be more revealing of broader motives related to dominance and control of women than are attitudinal questionnaires. Dutton and Strachan cite work by Pollack and Gilligan (1982) who scored men's and women's *TAT* stories for violent imagery in response to scenes cued for affiliation, achievement, and power motivation. Sex differences were found not only in frequency of violent imagery but in terms of which stimuli cued the imagery. Men wrote stories with a greater incidence of violent imagery overall, but the sex differences were most pronounced in response to scenes of men and women together (which the authors refer to as affiliation scenes). Women demonstrated the greatest frequency of violence themes in response to pictures of people in work situations (which Pollack and Gilligan refer to as achievement scenes).

Pollack and Gilligan interpreted violence themes as indicating perceptions of danger and concluded that men perceived more danger in intimate relationships, while women perceived danger in work-related social isolation. Pollack and Gilligan suggest that this sex difference in the perception of relationship danger is one basis for male-female conflict in intimate relationships. They speculate that males may develop exaggerated needs to control what they perceive as dangerous situations, namely, their relationships with women.

The need for power demonstrated by wife assaulters manifests itself only in male-female scenes. Browning (1983) found no significant between-group differences when a variety of gender relationships were depicted in the stimulus materials. There are, of course, many ways that a male could be high in power motivation vis-à-vis women and not be assaultive: he could merely have impact or establish control or dominance through verbal means. However, if a male with a strong motive to dominate was low in verbal skills, a certain amount of chronic frustration might develop, increasing the likelihood of violence.

Are Wife Assaulters Less Assertive than Other Men?

One measure of verbal competence is assertiveness. We measured both general and spouse-specific assertiveness in our subject groups and found qualified support for the expectation of low assertiveness in wife assaulters. Wife assaulters obtained the lowest scores of all four groups on general assertiveness, although these scores did not differ significantly from the rest.

However, on spouse-specific assertiveness, their scores were significantly lower (Browning, 1983; Dutton & Strachan, 1987a), replicating a finding obtained by Rosenbaum and O'Leary (1981). The profile that develops from our data so far is of wife assaulters as being high in a need for control and influence over their wives but low in one resource—spouse-specific assertiveness—required to manifest this influence. This latter deficit differentiates the wife assaulters from the maritally conflicted but nonviolent control group.

Where Is the Violence Learned?

The combination of the need for power over one's wife with poor verbal assertiveness skills might combine to produce a chronic frustration level in wife assaulters. If these men have learned to express frustration as anger and violence, then the power motive and verbal deficits, in combination with reinforced learning for violence, will interact to produce wife assault.

One source of learning for expressing frustration and marital conflict as violence is in the family of origin. A variety of published results indicate that observation of father-mother violence increases the likelihood of wife assault (Straus, Gelles, & Steinmetz, 1980; Kalmuss, 1984). Results of our research confirmed these earlier findings: wife assaulters had higher scores than all other groups for both observation of parent-parent violence and for being a recipient of violence from their parents. As we described in Section 2.2.1, however, another way in which violence is learned is when assaultive males successfully use violence to satisfy their personal needs for power and dominance and escape punishment. These reinforced learning experiences increase the probability of repetition of the violent acts.

SUMMARY: DIFFERENCES ON QUESTIONNAIRE AND PROJECTIVE TESTS The questionnaire assessment of our four groups revealed that wife assaulters did not differ from control-group males in attitudes toward women. This is not to say that wife assaulters in our sample did not have negative attitudes toward women, but they did not hold these attitudes to a greater degree than the other groups of men. Negative attitudes toward women do not seem to cause wife assault.

In terms of personal characteristics, wife assaulters did differ in that they were somewhat less verbally assertive and had a somewhat greater desire for power and control in a male-female context. This combination of traits suggests a potential chronic level of frustration. The wife assaulter does not have the verbal skills to satisfy his need for control. Also, as a means of responding to conflict, the wife assaulter is more likely to have learned to use violence through observation of violence used in his family of origin. This latter finding, of course, is not new but corroborates the findings of Straus, Gelles, and Steinmetz (1980). Of theoretical interest is the reporting by the wife assaulter population of greater verbal abuse by their mothers. To what extent does this abuse leave a legacy of heightened sensitivity to perceived criticism by a female with whom a man is in a significant relationship?

3.2 THE INSTIGATORS OF WIFE ASSAULT: THE VIDEOTAPE STUDIES

The questionnaire assessment reported above gave a general profile of the background factors that described our subjects. Against this backdrop, the videotape studies were designed to test specific arousal and anger responses of our experimental groups to vivid depictions of male-female marital conflict. We were especially interested in intimacy and dominance issues as described in Chapter 2 above. The general strategy was to present the subject with a series of videotaped scenes depicting verbal conflict between a man and a woman, encourage him to identify with the man, and obtain measures of physiological arousal and reported affect.[7]

This analogue format was derived somewhat from our observations in therapy groups that wife assaulters' anger was frequently experienced during guided fantasies of conflict situations with their wives. The use of videotapes allowed us to present a consistent (as opposed to imagined), yet vivid, stimulus to subjects. Conflict scenarios were varied on the dimensions of power or dominance and intimacy. The power/dominance dimension was meant to represent two levels of verbal control of a conflict situation, either by the man or the woman. The videotape scenario was meant to represent a conflict event (i.e., something that happened or might happen in a male-female relationship) and, to that extent, represent an aversive stimulus occurring in the microcosm or husband-wife interaction.

Clearly, however, the *perception* of that event by our subject population is important and may be affected by such predispositional factors as *n*-power. For example, a man high in *n*-power may perceive a moderate level of female control as female dominance. Similarly, a man with extreme anxiety about being rejected or abandoned may perceive moderate moves toward independence by his wife as abandonment. The delusional state is called *conjugal paranoia;* the case of Robert in Chapter 1 describes this tendency. Hence, careful checks on the manipulation of both variables were instituted.

General Procedure

1. Design
The videotape component employed a factorial design with four levels of subjects (W.A., G.A., M.C., H.M.), two levels of power (male-dominant, female-dominant), and three levels of attempted intimacy change (abandonment, engulfment, neutral). Power and intimacy change were manipulated by varying the videotaped scene. Therefore, there were six different videotaped scenes, one for each power x intimacy combination. The power variable was varied between subjects, while the intimacy variable was a within-subjects variable.[8] Specif-

ically, the participants in each group were randomly assigned to viewing either male-dominant scenes or female-dominant scenes. Each participant then viewed three videotapes, each depicting a different intimacy condition.

2. Videotaped Scenes

The scenes were between 5.5 and 7.5 minutes in duration. They all involved the same man and woman arguing heatedly over an issue. The subjects were told that the man and woman were a couple who had been involved in an in-depth study of marriage at the university and who had allowed a camera crew access to their home over a period of several months. In fact, the couple were professional actors.

Relative power was manipulated by having either the man or the woman in the scene dominate the argument verbally. Family interaction researchers (see Mishler & Waxler, 1968; Jacob, 1975) have specified a number of discrete behaviors that seem to constitute verbal dominance. These were employed here to manipulate relative power. Specifically, the powerful person was instructed to have a greater total talking time, interrupt his or her partner (successfully) more often, and to get their way in the end. In the male-dominant scenes, the man displayed this verbal prowess while the woman appeared cowed and submissive. In the female-dominant scenes, their roles were reversed.

Attempted movement toward intimacy was manipulated by varying the issue discussed during the conflict. There were three issues: one for abandonment (woman attempting to move away from the man), engulfment (woman attempting to move closer to the man), and the neutral (no attempted movement) condition. It was decided to have the woman instigate this movement in the tapes (rather than the man) because the dynamic of interest here was the man's attempt to control the woman's behavior, not the other way around.

The specifics of the enactment of the abandonment and engulfment issues were selected on the basis of clinical experience as well as descriptions in the literature of actions by battered women that appear to anger their husbands. The abandonment issue involved the woman stating that she wished to become more independent, spend more time with her friends (i.e., go away for a weekend with them), and join a women's group. The engulfment issue involved an argument in which the woman complained that the man did not spend enough time communicating his thoughts and feelings to her. Finally, the neutral scene involved an issue that is common to most couples, but did not involve a change in intimacy. The couple argued over whether they would spend their vacation camping (the man) or in the city (the woman). All the tapes were constructed so that the severity of conflict increased over the first part of the tape, peaking around the middle, trailing off toward the end, and finally resulting in acquiescence by the nondominant person. The conflict was purely verbal; there was no physical contact between the man and woman in the scenes. A detailed report of the checks on these manipulations is available in Browning (1983). In general, all experimental manipulations were successful.

c. Dependent Measures

Self-report measures of perceived affect were obtained immediately after each videotape scene. While a number of standardized measures of affective state are available (e.g., Zuckerman, Lubin, Vogel, & Valerius, 1964; Izard, Dougherty, Bloxom, & Kotsch, 1974), these instruments were considered too lengthy or too broad-based for the present purposes. Therefore, two scales used by Russell and Mehrabian (1974) to measure anger and anxiety were used. Each scale consisted of three adjectives that tap feelings of anger (angry, hostile, aggressive) and anxiety (tense, nervous, anxious). The scales had the advantage of being short while providing some breadth in the coverage of the two emotional states.Ratings on the anxiety scale were analyzed to see whether the men differed on this alternate subjective emotional state. A list of fourteen other adjectives describing affective states were selected from an extensive list compiled by Russell and Mehrabian (1974) and included in the form given to the men following each scene. These items were included primarily as a background on which to place the anger and anxiety items.

The adjective list was presented to the men using a nine-point semantic differential format, with the adjective at one pole and its negation at the other. About half the items were inverted so as to reduce the influence of a response set. Each man completed the checklist twice after each scene. The first administration requested a rating of his feelings while watching the scene and the second administration requested an estimate of his feelings had he actually been in the situation in real life. Scores on the first administration likely reflect some combination of the relevance of the scene's stimulus characteristics for the man plus ability to get into the scene and experience emotion. The second administration represents a more cognitive report of his typical emotional response in a situation of that kind. Both are of interest in the present research.

In addition to their ratings of affect, the men also rated each scene on a nine-point scale for realism and severity of conflict and on a seven-point scale for dominance and attempted intimacy movement. The latter two ratings provided manipulation checks for the power and intimacy factors.

In our initial research (Browning, 1983) we assessed *physiological measures,* or physiological arousal reactions, as well as self-reports of affect. Specifically, measures of skin conductance level and responding, pulse transit time, and respiration were all taken using a Beckman Type R Dynagraph and a respiration strain gauge transducer to which subjects were connected prior to observing the videotapes. A four-way MANOVA with repeated measures on two factors (time and intimacy) was used to analyze the data. No significant results were obtained from the physiological data and these tests were discontinued.

Videotape Analogue Data

The approach to analyzing the dependent measures in this portion of the research closely followed that outlined above with the questionnaire data. Repeated measures of MANOVAs were performed on logically combined groups of variables, followed by Bonferroni-adjusted univariate ANOVAs and Newman-Keuls post-hoc comparisons (given statistical significance in the preceding analyses).[9]

Self-Reports of Anger

Self-report measures of anger ("while watching the scene" and "had you actually been in the situation in real life") in response to the tapes were analyzed using a MANOVA. Means and standard deviations for these measures and prerating scores are presented in Table 3.3. The range of possible scores is 0

TABLE 3.3 Means and standard deviations for anger ratings

Group	Dominance	Prerating	Intimacy Condition		
			Abandonment	Engulfment	Neutral
Wife assaulters	Male-	6.05(4.61)	18.64(6.10)	9.80(5.90)	12.60(6.70)
	Female	5.36(3.05)	16.90(5.90)	10.60(6.10)	12.10(6.20)
Generally assaultive	Male-	6.00(4.61)	13.00(6.10)	10.33(5.90)	13.44(6.70)
	Female	5.22(3.05)	15.22(5.90)	11.00(6.10)	12.67(6.20)
Maritally conflicted	Male-	8.22(4.61)	15.78(6.10)	13.11(5.90)	14.78(6.70)
	Female	5.11(3.05)	14.78(5.90)	12.67(6.10)	11.78(6.20)
Happily married	Male-	5.78(4.61)	12.22(6.10)	11.11(5.90)	10.67(6.70)
	Female	3.78(3.05)	8.33(5.90)	6.11(6.10)	6.67(6.20)

Anger—Had You Been in the Situation

Group	Dominance	Prerating	Intimacy Condition		
			Abandonment	Engulfment	Neutral
Wife assaulters	Male-		23.20(6.10)	18.50(5.90)	17.80(6.70)
	Female		25.10(5.90)	16.90(6.10)	16.90(6.20)
Generally assaultive	Male-		19.60(5.12)	16.22(7.50)	19.80(5.30)
	Female		19.80(5.03)	16.44(7.55)	18.33(4.85)
Maritally conflicted	Male-		17.11(7.24)	18.44(4.75)	19.56(3.97)
	Female		14.44(8.25)	14.33(6.93)	16.11(6.45)
Happily married	Male-		12.33(7.25)	17.22(5.31)	18.67(6.31)
	Female		10.89(8.36)	10.22(7.23)	12.89(7.59)

to 27. Two way ANOVAs were performed on the two prerating scores. Analyses of preratings revealed that there were no group differences or differences by dominance condition (or interaction effects) on prerated anger.

A MANOVA of anger ratings in response to the scenes yielded a significant overall difference among groups[10] that remained significant when the anger ratings were corrected for initial levels of anger by using preratings (taken prior to showing the scenes) as a covariate. Observation of the means suggests a linear relationship, with the W.A. group rating the most anger and the H.M. group the least. Furthermore, specific comparisons indicated that the W.A. group reported significantly more anger to the abandonment scene than did the other three groups ($p < .01$). No main effect was found for male versus female dominance; the F score approached but did not attain the conventional (.05) level of significance. A similar analysis of anxiety ratings indicated no significant between-group differences.

Men were also asked to indicate their most likely response had they been the man in the conflict scene (see Novaco, 1976). These behavioral likelihood scales yielded consistent between-group differences, with the W.A. group reporting the least amount of constructive reasoning,[11] the most verbal aggression,[12] and the most physical aggression.[13] Post-hoc comparisons revealed the W.A. group to be significantly different from each of the other three groups on these measures. This was especially true for the abandonment scenes. Finally, the men were asked the relevance of the issues portrayed to their own relationships. The percentages generated by this question are contained in Table 3.4. An overall chi square performed on these data was significant ($\chi^2 = 38.3$, $df = 6$, and $p < .001$). It would appear from observation of the cell frequencies that the abandonment issue was the most relevant for the W.A. group and the least relevant for the other groups.

To generate directions for future research, some "data snooping" techniques were performed. Specifically, an internal analysis that correlated all anger ratings, collapsed across both subjects and videotapes, was performed. Composite self-report anger ratings correlated most highly with composite anxiety ratings ($+ .86$, $p < .001$) and humiliation ($+ .60$, $p < .001$). The emergence of humiliation as a key descriptor of affective reactions poses potential heuristic value. Self-

TABLE 3.4 Relevance of intimacy issue portrayed to own relationship

	Condition		
Group	Abandonment	Engulfment	Neutral
Wife assaulters	78%	58%	42%
Generally assaultive	54%	66%	40%
Maritally conflicted	39%	72%	56%
Happily married	29%	56%	0%

Note: $\chi^2 = 38.3$, $df = 6$, $p < .001$.

reports of humiliation while watching the conflict scenarios correlated + .4 (p = .001) with reports of being verbally abused by the mother. Correlations of humiliation with reports of verbal and physical abuse by the father, however, were not significant. This finding suggests support for Winter's notion of maternal mixed messages contributing to strong ambivalence about intimacy for wife assaulters and is, in our opinion, deserving of further study.

SUMMARY: THE PROFILE OF THE WIFE ASSAULTER   What are the most salient results of these studies using videotaped male-female conflicts? First, men who are wife assaulters (W.A.) differ from all other groups, including generally assaultive men (G.A.), in two crucial respects: (1) they perceive more abandonment from female-initiated independence and (2) they report more anger in response to this scenario than do other groups. Furthermore, they tend to see the issue as more relevant to their own relationship and to report that if something like it were to occur in their own relationship, they would use physical aggression to resolve it. Internal analyses indicated that, for all men in this study, anger scores were associated with feelings of humiliation and with the prior occurrence of abuse (both physical and verbal) by their mother.

'Wife assaulters also demonstrated, in response to male-female stimuli, high scores on the need for power and had poor verbal communication skills. What emerges is a composite profile of a man with an exaggerated response to abandonment situations, perceiving abandonment when other men do not, having a stronger need to control the amount of socioemotional distance between him and his wife, and lacking the verbal skills to do so. This combination produces feelings of lack of control and general arousal that are labelled as anger. The anger is expressed as violence, either because the wife assaulter has learned this mode of behavior through observing his parents, or has himself been reinforced for using violence. The consequent anger carries with it other, less acceptable feelings such as anxiety (+ .73) and humiliation (+ .42).

3.3 THE WIFE ASSAULTER'S CONSCIENCE: THE RATIONALIZATION OF WIFE ASSAULT

So far we have examined the exaggerated tendency of wife assaulters to become aroused and angry in response to certain aversive stimuli. Although anger is obviously not the same as aggression, anger has been found to increase the likelihood of aggression (Konecni, 1975). We have argued in Chapters 1 and 2 that this is especially true when the angered person has no alternative resource (e.g., verbal skills) for expressing anger and removing the aversive stimulus. As we established in Section 2.3.2, once a habit of aggression is established as a primary means of controlling an aversive stimulus, a normally socialized aggressor has to develop ways of perceiving his aggression as justified and its consequences as not serious. Otherwise, his behavior will clearly violate standards of self-conduct.

In this section we examine the excuses that wife assaulters use to justify their behavior, render it less reprehensible, and thereby maintain their habit of aggression. Recall that in Section 1.1 we estimated (based on the Schulman [1979] and Straus, Gelles, & Steinmetz [1980] surveys) that repeated or habitual wife assault occurred for about 63% of men who had assaulted their wives once. These repeat wife assaulters must find ways to rationalize their habit if they are to sustain it (see Section 2.3.2).

When normally socialized men commit behavior that violates their own self-standards, a variety of cognitive mechanisms become operative to neutralize self-punishment for reprehensible behavior. Clinical reports suggest that some of the cognitive restructuring tendencies described by Bandura are used frequently by wife assaulters. Both Ganley (1981) and Sonkin, Martin, and Walker (1985) describe this population as minimizing both their violent behavior and its consequences and victim blaming. In fact, a primary means of altering habitual assault is through therapeutic confrontation of these forms of neutralization of self-punishment in order to have the assaulter assume personal responsibility for his violence (Sonkin, Martin, & Walker, 1985).

Despite the clinical emphasis on the cognitive restructuring tendencies of wife assaulters, little in the way of empirical research has been reported on this question. Sheilds and Hanneke (1983) compared the attributions of wife assaulters with the attributions of their wives for the assault. They found that the husbands tended to externalize the cause of their assault by attributing it to their wife's behavior (45%) or to alcohol (23%), while the wives attributed the assault to a locus internal to the husband (e.g., his anger, personality, or intoxication). The finding that criminal actions tend to be externalized by the perpetrator was consistent with previous studies (Saulnier & Perlman, 1981; Felson & Ribner, 1981).

Felson and Ribner (1981) analyzed perpetrators' accounts of criminal violence, distinguishing between excuses (accepting that the act was wrong but denying personal responsibility) and justifications (accepting personal responsibility but denying that the act was wrong). For more criminal acts, justifications were more frequent than excuses (50% vs. 18.7%). However, when the victim was female, excuses became more prevalent.

Henderson and Hewstone (1984) replicated this finding with a maximum-security prison population having current offenses for murder, attempted murder, manslaughter, wounding, grievous bodily harm, or assault. Free responses were coded into (1) locus of attribution categories (victim, self, situation) and (2) excuses versus justifications. Again, justifications were more frequent than excuses (70% vs. 30%). When the victim was an intimate and no third party was present, 50% of the actions were attributed to the victim.

Unfortunately, Henderson and Hewstone did not specify the gender of the victim nor the victim's specific relationship to the perpetrator. Their method of assessing both attributions and excuses/justifications, however, provides a technique for generating a more complex analysis of a perpetrator's explanation for his own violent actions (see Fincham & Jaspars, 1980). These explanations could provide an insight into the means by which potentially negative self-evaluations are neutralized by wife assaulters. The relationship between excuses/justifications and the locus of attribution will be analyzed, and the results of this analysis for determining common forms of neutralization of self-punishment will be discussed in 3.3.2 and 3.3.3. Neither Felson and Ribner (1981) or Henderson and Hewstone (1984) focused on wife assault per se, although the latter study did include violent crimes committed on intimates in private situations.

We are interested in whether consistent patterns of neutralization of self-punishment occur. For example, when the effects of the assault are minimized, is the victim also blamed? When personal responsibility for the assault is accepted (justification), do other compensatory cognitions become more prevalent?

Finally, since research with wife assaulters suffers from sample-selection factors affecting results, we will compare the observed effects for two samples of wife assaulters: those self-referred for treatment and those sentenced by the courts for treatment.

3.3.1 General Procedure

Two groups of men who had assaulted their wives took part in this study. Self-referred men were men who had contacted the Assaultive Husbands Project directly, or via a community mental health clinic or social worker, seeking treatment for an acknowledged problem with violence toward their wives. Typically, their motivation for seeking treatment was to prevent their wives from leaving them. Court-referred men had been convicted of wife assault and were referred to the Assaultive Husbands Project as a condition of their probation. The two groups were matched demographically, in terms of average length of marriage, time since first wife assault, and number and severity of wife assaults.

To assess frequency and severity of wife assault, subjects and their wives filled out the Straus (1979) *Conflict Tactics Scale* (Form N). The men in our two groups generated the following self-report scores of physical aggression: self-referred = 14.8; court-referred = 14.2. Their wives generated the following scores for their husbands' use of physical aggression: self-referred = 22.1; court-referred = 21.8. Hence, both groups of men are in the top 1% of the population for frequency of use of physical aggression against their wives, both by their own ratings and by their wives' ratings. *CTS* scores by both the men and their wives in the self-referred and court-referred groups did not differ significantly with the referral source, nor did length of time married or duration of assaultive behavior.

All subjects were interviewed about their history of assaultive behavior, use of violence outside their marriage, and history of arrests, and were asked to describe the most recent assaultive action in detail. If not mentioned spontaneously, the following aspects were probed for:

1. *Victim:* Her age, relationship to the offender (married, common-law), years together.
2. *Situation:* Time of day when incident occurred, location, whether others were present, whether police were called.
3. *Precipitating events:* Type of interchange with victim, circumstances leading up to first blow, victim's behavior, alcohol use, prior history of violence between offender and victim.
4. *Details of incident:* Whether a weapon was used, what part of victim's body was attacked, injuries to victim, injuries to offender.
5. *Attitude:* Offender asked to relate his feelings at the time, whether he perceived he had control over his own aggression, whether victim deserved the attack, his own motivation.
6. *Explanation:* The offender was asked why the violence occurred.

Interviews were recorded verbatim where possible, lasted 45 to 70 minutes, and were carried out by four therapists with experience in treating wife assault. Following the coding procedure developed by Henderson and Hewstone (1984), the following coding scheme was used for responses to Item 6.

1. *Locus of attribution:*

a. *Victim:* Explanation for violence is attributed to the behavior or characteristics of the victim. This category includes reference to victim provocation or to perceived acts of aggression by the victim, victim denigration of the perpetrator's significant others, or verbal abuse by the victim.

b. *Self:* Explanation for violence involves own characteristics or behavior (temper, arousal, chronic alcohol problem, upholding reputation, or pride).

c. *Situation:* Explanation in terms of nonpersonal situational factors (e.g., acute stress or drunkenness where the interviewee has not described a chronic alcohol problem).

2. *Excuses versus justification:*

a. *Excuses:* A denial of personal responsibility for the act. This category includes drink, drugs, accidents, uncontrollable arousal, other situational factors.

b. *Justifications:* An acceptance of personal responsibility but also an attempt to justify the act in terms of valid reasons or norms. This category includes egregious (from the perpetrator's perspective) victim provocation, acting according to subgroup norms, self-defense, and so forth.

3.   *Minimizing:*

a.   *Of act:* Comparison was made of the offenders' description of the specifics of his assault with a composite description from the victim, social worker, probation officer, police, and court records. *High severity-minimizers* were defined as men who described their most severe act against their wife in the past year as two levels less severe than that described by their wife on the *CTS*. For example, if a wife reported beating as her husband's most severe act, and the husband reported kicking, biting, or hitting with a fist, the man was classified as high in severity-minimizing. For a description of within-couple discrepancies in reports of husband's violence, see Browning and Dutton (1986).

High incidence-minimizers were defined as men who reported less than half the total incidents of violence as their wives reported them to have committed on the Severe Physical Aggression subscale of the Straus *CTS*. If the man reported 6 acts, for example, and his wife reported 13, he was classified as high in incidence-minimizing. The 50% criterion was based on the finding by Browning and Dutton (1986) that a sample of (mainly self-referred) wife assaulters reported about 50% of the incidence of their violence toward their wives that their wives reported they had committed. It is not known whether the wife's report reflects incidence accurately. For a discussion of the veridicality of wives' reports, see Browning and Dutton (1986).

b.   *Of effects:* Comparison was made of the offenders' descriptions of the victims' injuries with victims' reports, hospital, and police reports. Berk, Berk, Loseke, and Rauma (1981) developed an eight-point scale for severity of effects of wife assault. High minimizers of effects were defined as men who described their wives' injuries as one level or more (on the Berk et al. scale) less severe than police and hospital reports.

3.3.2 Results

Table 3.5 illustrates the tendency to excuse or justify the assault as a function of the locus of attribution for cause of assault. Although it was theoretically possible for men to neither excuse nor justify their actions, all men in this study did so. As in the Henderson and Hewstone (1984) study, justifications were far more prevalent than excuses (n = 59, 16, respectively). These data are for both court-referred and self-referred men. Men who excuse their assault are most likely to attribute the assault to situational circumstances, whereas men who justify their assault tend to attribute it to the victim.[14]

As Table 3.6 illustrates, referral type differentially affects the locus of attribution for assault.[15] Self-referred men are more likely than court-referred

TABLE 3.5 Locus of attribution by excuse justification

| | Excuse (not responsible) | | | | Justification (responsible) | | | | Total | |
| | S.R.[a] | | C.R. | | S.R. | | C.R. | | S.R. | C.R. |
Locus	n	%	n	%	n	%	n	%	%	%
Victim	(0)	0	(1)	2	(4)	16	(20)	40	16	42
Self	(1)	4	(5)	10	(12)	48	(2)	4	52	16
Situation	(1)	4	(8)	76	(7)	28	(14)	28	32	44
Total % n	(2)	8	(14)	28	(23)	92	(36)	72	100	100

Note: Figures are percentages for each variable.
[a]S.R. = self-referred (n = 25); C.R. = court-referred (n = 50).

TABLE 3.6 Locus of attribution by referral type

| | Referral Type | | | |
| | Self-Referred | | Court-Referred | |
Locus	n	%	n	%
Victim	4	16	21	42
Self	13	52	7	14
Situation	8	32	22	44
	25	100	50	100

men to attribute the assault to themselves,[16] and court-referred men are more likely to attribute the assault to situational circumstances (44%) or to the victim (42%).

Locus of blame had no differential effect on the type of minimization pattern used by the men[17] (see Table 3.7). Men who minimized severity tended to also minimize frequency and effects independently of how they viewed the cause of the assault. The tendency of self-attributors to minimize less approached but did not reach significance when compared to other men. One-third of the men (25/75) used no minimization pattern. This proportion was not affected by referral type. Thirty percent of the men (22/75) used all three types of minimization.

In Table 3.8 we reclassify the men according to high (all three types of minimization), moderate (use of any one form of minimization), or no minimization. Self-referred men were overrepresented in this group of high minimizers.[18] The high-minimizer groups were comprised of 9 out of 50 (18%) court-referred men and 13 out of 25 (52%) self-referred men.

Locus of cause for assault had a strong effect on minimization when reclassified this way.[19] Men who attributed cause for assault to the victim were more likely to fall into the high-minimizing category (using all three kinds of

TABLE 3.7 Minimization pattern by locus of blame

Locus	Minimize		
	Severity	Frequency	Effects
Victim (n = 25)	16	19	13
Self (n = 20)	8	9	5
Situation (n = 30)	22	9	18
n = 75	46	37	36

TABLE 3.8   High, moderate, and low minimizers by locus of cause for assault

	High (22)	Moderate (28)	No (25)
Victim (n = 25)	12	6	7
Self (n = 20)	7	0	13
Situation (n = 30)	3	22	3

minimization), whereas men who attributed cause to themselves were more likely to fall into the no-minimization category.[20] Men who attributed cause to the situation fell overwhelmingly into the moderate-minimization category (27/28).

3.3.3 Patterns of Neutralization of Self-Punishment

One-third of the men in the current study attributed their assault to actions or provocations from the victim. Our court-referred sample of wife assaulters gave justifications 79% of the time and excuses 21%. Hence, the general pattern of attribution of cause for assault and excuses versus justifications for assault found by Henderson and Hewstone (1984) appears to have been replicated for a population of wife assaulters. Indeed, this current group responds very similarly on these categories to the group in the Henderson and Hewstone study who committed violent crime on intimates in private.

From the perspective of treating assaultive males, it is useful to know that different trends in attribution for assault occur with self- and court-referred men. In one sense the court-referred men present an additional treatment problem: that of getting the man to realize his causal role in violence since only 14% attribute the locus of cause for violence to themselves. The self-referred men appear to have already made this realization. They appear to compensate for acknowledging personal responsibility, however, by minimizing the incidence, severity, and effects of their actions. Fifty-two percent of self-referred men were high minimizers, compared to only 18% of court-referred men.

Also, though locus of attribution does not affect the type of minimization (e.g., severity, incidence, or effects), it does affect the total minimization pattern. Twelve of 25 (48%) victim attributors were also high minimizers, compared to only 7 of 20 (35%) of self-attributors. Interestingly, all 7 self-attributors who were high minimizers were self-referred. No court-referred self-attributors were high minimizers, suggesting a conviction-induced motive to "come clean" for a subsample of court-referred men. In fact, all 7 court-referred self-attributors fell into the no-minimization category. Self-referred self-attributors split into high (7) and no minimization (6) patterns almost equally. These two categories of self-attributors are deserving of further study to determine what factors contribute to their extreme differences in the use of minimization.

Wife assaulters do appear to cluster into various patterns in order to neutralize self-punishment. Those men who tend to view their wife-victim as the cause of the violence are also likely to minimize their violence. They do not differ in minimizing severity, frequency, or effects but tend rather to minimize all three.

Men who attribute the violence to an enduring characteristic of themselves fall into two categories with respect to minimizing. Category one is comprised of high minimizers (similar to victim-blamers in this respect); category two is men who do not minimize at all. Of all court-referred (7/9) and self-referred (6/13) men in this latter category, none minimized any aspect of their assault. This subsample (13/75) did not appear to neutralize self-punishment by the means described in clinical descriptions of wife assaulters (Sonkin, Martin, & Walker, 1985). They may have tried to excuse the violence as due to uncontrollable arousal or to justify it by reference to subgroup norms or to victim provocation. Their explanations for their violence, however, focused on attributes of themselves, and they did not minimize its incidence, severity, or effects.

Men who attribute their violence to the situation fell somewhere between these first two groups, exhibiting a moderate amount of minimization, tending to excuse or deny personal responsibility for the assault, and differing significantly from the victim-attributers in this respect. Self-attributors who do not minimize may sometimes justify their violence as acceptable via particular cultural norms.

CHAPTER SUMMARY

What do we know about the psychology of the wife assaulter as a result of this research? We know that he tends to have pronounced needs for interpersonal control vis-à-vis his wife but poor verbal skills to generate this control. We know that he reacts with exaggerated arousal and anger to scenes of male-female conflict. His anger is greatest when the female has verbal power and appears to be abandoning the male. Feelings of humiliation correlate highly with his feelings of anger.

Is there a common source for the need for control, the exaggerated anger and humiliation? We found that a background of verbal abuse by the mother correlated significantly with anger and humiliation responses to the conflict scenes. Psychoanalysts might argue that the man's feelings of powerlessness and humiliation experienced with his verbally abusive mother are transferring into his marriage and that the exaggerated anger response is the result. Recall from Chapter 2 Winter's analysis of male reactions to mixed maternal communications: the male is both vulnerable to maternal nurturance but humiliated by maternal anger-rejection. Winter suggested that these mixed communications were the result of patriarchal systems that frustrated women and led to ambivalent reactions to their male sons.

We have noticed considerable suspicion among assaultive males about female motives. Although not all assaultive males would qualify as conjugally paranoid, exaggerated perceptions of malevolent intent behind female actions are common. Our current research is beginning to indicate that a subgroup of assaultive males, whom we identified as *victim blamers* in the study on rationalization, have chronic attributional tendencies to regard female actions as intended to cause them pain, embarrassment, or humiliation. We describe this attributional style as one of perceiving malevolent intent in the actions of females vis-à-vis males. At present, we do not know the origin of this perceptual tendency.

We do know something about the rationalizations of wife assaulters. We know that they subdivide roughly into thirds (actually 25, 20, 30) in terms of whether they blame their wife, themselves, or the situation for their violence. We also know that victim blamers are also most likely to minimize their violence (its severity, incidence, and effects) and that self-blamers subdivide into two groups: one also minimizes their violence, the other seems relatively honest about both the extent of the violence and their causal role in it.

It is becoming clearer that all wife assaulters do not have similar etiologies. Instead they differ both in terms of what aversive stimuli trigger their violence and how they rationalize the violence to themselves. Our future research focus will be to more clearly elucidate these subcategories of wife assaulters—in order to ascertain whether different treatment emphases are indicated for each and, eventually, the prognostication for stopping the violence that exists for each subcategory. An informed social policy for wife assault will require better information about the psychology of the offender than currently exists.

It is toward these policy issues that we now begin to direct our attention. Although we may expect the victim of such crimes to take responsibility for reporting and testifying, some unique circumstances make these responses particularly difficult for assaulted wives. We turn now to an examination of the social-psychological circumstances of the victims of wife assault.

ENDNOTES

1. Data for 54 of the men reported here were collected by Jim Browning and constituted his doctoral dissertation. An earlier report on these 54 men is reported in Dutton and Browning (1984). Data and analysis of the additional assaultive males was conducted by the author, Brenda Gerhard, Andrew Gotowiecz, Hamida Hajee, Sally Harrison, Stephen Hart, and Catherine Strachan.

2. Browning and Dutton (1987) found that wives of assaultive husbands report about twice as much husband-wife violence as their husbands report (for Serious Violence Subscale items on the Straus *CTS*). Except where weapons are implicated, husband-wife correlations on specific items are in the + .32 to + .57 range, indicating considerable disparity in recall of violence.

3. Originally the pictures used represented a variety of gender relationships (male-male, male-female, female-female). The results of this original test indicated that between-group differences on the need for power seemed to occur only when the pictures depicted male-female relationships (Browning, 1983). A second experiment was run (Dutton & Strachan, 1987a) using five male-female pictures where both the setting and relationship were ambiguous. It is the results from this latter experiment that we report below.

4. The raters demonstrated agreement with expert scoring (rho = .87, category agreement on power imagery = .93) on 60 test stories (Winter, 1973).

5. The Bonferroni method of correcting alpha for experiment-wise error was used (see Harris, 1975).

6. For a more detailed report of these findings, see Dutton and Strachan (1987a).

7. For a complete description of this experiment, see Browning (1983) or Dutton and Browning (1987).

8. The power variable was chosen as a between-subjects variable because it would appear less realistic if the actors were to switch from dominant to submissive for a given viewer than to be merely arguing over different issues for a given viewer. In addition, since there are only two power conditions (either male or female dominant) this approach allows for a more efficient use of participants.

9. Since these analyses all involved at least one repeated measures factor, a sphericity test was performed for each repeated measures factor of the univariate ANOVAs to test the assumption of symmetry (i.e., that the orthogonal polynomials for any within factor were independent and had equal variance (see Anderson, 1958; Dixon, Brown, Engleman, Farne, Hill, Jennrich, & Joporek, 1981). If the sphericity test was significant, adjustments were made to the within-factor degrees of freedom via a procedure outlined by Greenhouse and Geisser (1959).

10. $F(3, 68) = 6.02$, $p < .01$.
11. $F(3, 68) = 10.01$, $p < .001$.
12. $F(3, 68) = 9.03$, $p < .01$.
13. $F(3, 68) = 11.6$, $p < .001$.
14. $\chi^2 = 5.9$, $df = 1$, $p < .02$.
15. $\chi^2 = 12.93$, $df = 2$, $p < .01$.
16. $\chi^2 = 12.3$, $df = 1$, $p < .001$.
17. $\chi^2 = 4.07$, $df = 4$, n.s.
18. $\chi^2 = 9.36$, $df = 1$, $p < .01$.
19. $\chi^2 = 48.6$, $df = 4$, $p < .001$.
20. $\chi^2 = 7.6$, $df = 1$, $p < .01$.

CHAPTER 4

Effects on the Victim

We may prefer to deflate ourselves in order to keep the relationship, even though we glimpse the impossibility of it and the slavishness to which it reduces us.
— Ernest Becker, *The Denial of Death* (1973, p. 167)

Over the last decade a considerable literature has developed on the psychological effects of victimhood, describing reactions to being a victim of rape (Schram, 1978), hostage takings (Strentz, 1979; Flynn, 1986), assault (Sales, Baum, & Shore, 1984), sexual assault (Scheppele & Bart, 1983), incest (Silver, Boon, & Stones, 1983), and technological disaster (Baum, Fleming, & Singer, 1983). Out of this victimization literature some insights have developed into the cognitive means that victims use to regain feelings of self-control (Janoff-Bulman & Lang-Gunn, 1985; Wortman, 1976), and models have been developed that try to account for successful victim recovery (Sales, Baum, & Shore, 1984). In this section, we will examine this general literature on victim reactions with a view to how it might apply to assaulted women.

4.1 VICTIM REACTIONS TO TRAUMATIC EVENTS

Studies on victim reactions have focused on the aftermath effects, both emotional and cognitive, and on post-trauma decisions such as reporting the attack to police, proceeding with charges, and staying with or leaving the abuser. Fattah (1981) reviewed these studies and concluded that as far as postvictimization reactions were concerned, generalizations were difficult to make. Victim reactions appeared to depend on a variety of factors, such as the nature of the experience and the circumstances surrounding it, the characteristics of the victims themselves, and the degree of violence experienced. Variability in both short- and long-term reactions were reported by victims of violence.

4.1.1 The Stockholm Syndrome

As early studies in victim reactions began to develop, two highly publicized hostage-taking events occurred that focused public awareness on the occasionally paradoxical reactions of hostage-victims. The first was the kidnapping of Patty Hearst, granddaughter of newspaper magnate William Randolph Hearst, by the Symbionese Liberation Army in California in 1974. Hearst was imprisoned in a closet and subjected to intermittent bouts of violence and to sexual and psychological abuse. Subsequently, she denounced her parents, joined the gang, and assisted them in bank robberies. When finally captured she took the Fifth Amendment to the Constitution (a total of 42 times) to avoid self-incrimination. A debate ensued over whether Patty Hearst was acting voluntarily or had been brainwashed by the SLA.

At about the same time in the mid-1970s, reports began to surface about something called the Stockholm Syndrome, a constellation of unexpected positive feelings developed by captives for their captors. The syndrome was named after an event in Stockholm, Sweden, where four bank employees were held hostage in the bank's vault for 131 hours by two escaped prisoners. The hostages in this event feared the police more than their captors, and when finally freed expressed gratitude toward their captors for sparing their lives (Strentz, 1979).

Early explanations for this phenomenon were psychoanalytic. Strentz (1979) cited Anna Freud's concept of identification with the aggressor where, in a life-and-death situation with a powerful authority figure, the ego identifies with the aggressor-authority to avoid punishment and anxiety. Bruno Bettelheim (1943) described a particularly vivid instance of identification with the aggressor: some Jewish prisoners in Nazi prison camps emulated their captors to the extent of sewing scraps together to imitate SS uniforms and taking over punitive rule-enforcement functions with new prisoners.

Flynn (1986) reviewed the literature on victim reactions to being held hostage and noted that the Stockholm Syndrome was most likely to develop when no serious physical abuse had occurred. But even victims who are injured when initially captured eventually identify with the offender and his cause during later phases of their captivity. What prevents the Stockholm Syndrome from developing, it seems, is when prisoners have a strong ideology that sustains them through captivity. One of the more fascinating literatures is the collection of reports on coping under extreme duress of captivity and harassment (Timmerman, 1981; Fallaci, 1981). The individuals who seem capable of sustaining such resistance, however, are a very small minority.

4.1.2 Stages of Victimization

More typical responses to severe victimization are a sense of helplessness, powerlessness, and *idiocide* (Flynn, 1986), which describes the total loss of the social self. Symonds (1980) describes the acute response to victimization as having four stages. The symptoms of the first stage are shock, disbelief, denial, and delusion. Only when the victim perceives the reality of the situation does the second stage begin. This is a terror-induced pseudo-calm that Symonds calls frozen fright, where feelings of isolation and powerlessness are so intense that a victim separates her consciousness from her body. This dissociation is occasionally reported by assaulted women (Walker, 1979b).

This acute phase gives way to a delayed coping response of rumination and busy work that frequently includes a review and reflection of one's past life with vows to change for the better if given another chance (Strentz, 1979).

The final stage is described as traumatic psychological infantilism, where individuals lose their ability to function as adults and regress to behaviors first learned in early childhood: compliance, submission, and ingratiation. If this final stage continues, attitude shifts that we have described above as identification with the aggressor occur. Symonds calls this attitude shift *pathological transference.*

Since the initial descriptions of the Stockholm Syndrome in the victim literature (Symonds, 1975, 1980), we have become more aware of its effects on victims of hostage takings and sudden, unpredictable traumas. A second line of reports suggests, however, that the compliant submissive stage can be reached in more prolonged, less traumatic situations.

Conway and Siegleman (1978), Sage (1976), and others have described the infantilism produced in cults to the extent that to counter the effect parents occasionally must kidnap and deprogram their children who have joined a cult. The literature on cult members describes a form of idiocide and infantilism that is reached gradually through isolation from normal social contacts and reward for behavior consistent with the new role. Schein (1971) described these factors as essential ingredients of what has come to be termed *brainwashing.*

As we shall see below, assaulted women also demonstrate some of the affective and cognitive reactions of these other victims. They frequently are unexpectedly positive about their abuser and may blame themselves for the abuse (Walker, 1979). They sometimes seem passive and inert about taking steps to leave the situation, even though visible impediments to their leaving do not exist. They are not under 24-hour surveillance by an armed guard, for example. Hence, some outside observers, for reasons we shall describe below, tend to view their staying in an abusive relationship as indicative of a masochistic predisposition.

4.2 DIFFERENTIAL VICTIM REACTIONS

As research on victim reactions grew more sophisticated, studies began to emerge that attempted to account for differential victim reactions. Sales, Baum, and

Shore (1984), for example, interviewed 127 rape victims to obtain retrospective reports of prerape symptoms, immediate postassault symptoms, and follow-up symptoms. They found a complex picture of postassault recovery that included immediate postassault increases in symptoms (anxiety and depression) that were followed by an apparent return to normalcy, with symptoms diminishing over a six-month period. However, a reactivation of symptoms occurred after six months and did not return to preassault levels over a three-year period. The Sales et al. study is important for two reasons: first, it demonstrated that a different pattern of results was obtained with long-term follow-up. Second, it began to examine factors thast explained the differential victim reactions found.

4.2.1 Predictive Factors

Sales et al. divided their predictive factors into three categories: (1) preassault factors—demographic and psychosocial aspects of the victim herself, including prerape psychological problems, chronic life stressors, and quality of relationships; (2) assault factors—degree of violence and relationship to perpetrator; and (3) postassault factors—criminal justice involvement and reactions of the victim's informal support system.

Demographic variables were not strongly predictive of postassault reactions; however, some relationship did exist between personality characteristics and postassault reactions. In both their own data and the studies of others, Sales et al. found postassault functioning to be affected by prior biosocial problems (psychosis, drug use, alcoholism, etc.). Coping ability was also reduced by prior life stressors such as economic stress and absence of social support. Degree of violence strongly predicted symptom severity; threats of death had a particularly strong impact on symptoms. Acquaintanceship with the aggressor had no effect on reported symptoms, nor did the reactions of the victim's informal support network after the assault.

One particularly interesting result was that victims who proceeded with charges initially showed fewer postassault symptoms (immediate and at six months) than victims who did not. However, further progress toward trial exacerbated the symptoms. Victims whose cases were tried showed heightened symptoms compared to those not pursuing their case. Sales et al. interpret this as suggesting that the legal process may inflict additional stress on victims or keep a victim from returning to normal functioning.

The Sales et al. study represents an example of the more sophisticated, multivariate studies of victim reaction beginning to emerge in the victim literature. It suggests a conceptual model for analyzing reactions of battered women that subdivides predictive factors into preassault circumstances, postassault circumstances, and the severity of the assault itself. Furthermore, it raises an issue that we will return to when we consider criminal justice policy for wife assault: if proceeding to trial can exacerbate the victim's suffering, what interest is served by doing so?

4.3 PERCEPTIONS OF ASSAULTED WOMEN: THE FUNDAMENTAL ATTRIBUTION ERROR AND THE "JUST WORLD" BELIEF

In Section 1.2, we examined victim surveys and concluded that serious, repeated wife assault occurred in about 6.8% of all marriages. The women who are repeatedly assaulted by their husbands in these marriages perplex and exasperate outside observers. The obvious question that arises for police, social workers, or transition house personnel who observe the aftermath of the assault and the woman's subsequent return to the marriage is simply, why doesn't she leave?

Casual discussion with police or other professionals typically generates an account of a woman who needed police intervention to save her life, who agreed to charge her husband, and who was given shelter in a transition home. After a few weeks, despite the support of transition house staff, and in the absence of face-to-face contact with her husband, she decides abruptly to return to the marriage and drop the charges. The state is left without its key witness if it proceeds to trial, the police mutter knowingly about "these women always dropping the charges," and inexperienced transition home workers wonder what they did wrong.

Rosenbaum and O'Leary (1981) report that, whereas nearly 70% of their sample of 52 battered women had experienced abuse from their spouses by the end of the first year of marriage (and of these, 15% experienced abuse even prior to the marriage), the women continued to live with their husbands for an average of over 12 years before they presented themselves at a clinic for problems related to marital violence. Rounsaville (1978), discussing the strength of the emotional bonds in his sample of 31 battered women, notes:

> The most striking phenomenon that arose in the interviews and in treatment with battered women was the tenacity of both partners to the relationship in the face of severe abuse sustained by many of the women. Even those who had divorced or separated from the partner stayed in contact with the partner beyond ordinary activities such as visitation of children. In all cases, this continued to lead to abuse such that only 3 of the women had been free from abuse for more than three weeks at the time of the interview, despite 10 of the women having been separated or divorced from their partners (Rounsaville, 1978, pp. 20–21).

4.3.1 Is Masochism a Factor?

Although economic factors (children, no job, etc.) operate for many women who return, they do not seem to be a major consideration for many others. Outside observers who witness repeated returns to the marriage begin to draw conclusions about the kind of women who return. Typically, these women are viewed as returning because they enjoy the violence or because the initial report of violence was hysterical and exaggerated. The action of returning is attributed to a predisposition in the victim such as masochism or pathological dependence. (For critical reviews of the professional literature drawing this conclusion, see Dutton [1983], Caplan [1984], and Shainess [1977].)

Unfortunately, the very agencies and resources to which the battered woman might turn for assistance often reflect such beliefs. Medical professionals often attempt to deal with the battered woman by treating her symptoms (e.g., her depression or anxiety), rather than recognizing that the origin of her emotional response was to an injurious or life-threatening situation (Davidson, 1978; MacLeod, 1980). Researchers (e.g., Truninger, 1971, cited in Gelles, 1978; Dutton, 1981a; Hogarth, 1980) have found that the courts are often mired in mythology about the victims of family violence and are thus unprepared to deal effectively with a woman's attempts to protect herself through the legal system. Social service agencies are likely to provide counseling that stresses the responsibility of the woman to adjust to the situation in which she finds herself rather than assist her in leaving that situation (MacLeod, 1980). In short, those who encounter a woman who has been beaten and who returns to her partner do not always respond sympathetically; to the contrary, they frequently blame her for her plight.

4.3.2 Masochism Defined

A variety of definitions of the term *masochism* exist in psychology. At the broadest level, Fromm (1973) uses the term to describe a giving up of personal control to another in order to satisfy existential needs for connection and freedom from existential anxiety. Deutsch (1944) uses the term to apply specifically to women in terms of willingness to accept pain paired with pleasure as part of life. She suggests that this "normal" masochism differs from *neurotic masochism*, where pain becomes a condition of pleasure. Unfortunately, derivative reports from Deutsch's work do not always make the distinction.

In addressing the concept of masochism as it may apply to a battered woman who remains with her tormentor, we refer to the narrow definition of masochism as used by Freud, where "gratification is connected with suffering or physical or mental pain at the hands of the sexual object" (Freud, 1938, p. 569). This definition would presume that battered women remain in abusive relationships because they derive gratification from being abused.

4.3.3 Fundamental Attribution Error

When a battered woman endures intermittent abuse or returns to an abusive relationship, outside observers are likely to attribute the woman's behavior to a predisposition or trait indigenous to the woman. While this attribution has been described by some as blaming the victim (Ryan, 1971) or as the need to "believe in a just world" (Lerner, 1977), it can also be explained by current research in social cognition (Nisbett & Ross, 1980), attribution (Jones & Nisbett, 1971), and human judgment (Kahneman & Tversky, 1973).

A woman returning to an abusive relationship represents a salient example of what, to common sense, is unusual or counternormative behavior. That is, outside observers, be they male or female, believe that they and others would act differently than the assaulted woman. Furthermore, from their perspective, there does not appear to be tangible impediments to her leaving: she is not physically confined, imprisoned, or under constant surveillance. When we observe behavior that appears unusual and not externally determined, we tend to attribute that behavior to a trait indigenous to the person who performs the behavior (Jones & Nisbett, 1971; Nisbett & Ross, 1980). We overlook the impact of subtle situational forces on the person's behavior. In social cognition research, this tendency is termed the *fundamental attribution error*. Hence, in the case of assaulted women, the outside observer may explain her behavior as caused by a trait of masochism.

4.3.4 The "Just World" Hypothesis

This tendency to attribute the victim's behavior to a predisposition is further strengthened when professionals believe, rightfully or wrongfully, that the criminal justice system cannot protect the assaulted women. Lerner (1975) discovered a cognitive bias in subjects that he described as a need to believe in a just world. People have this need, according to Lerner, because they need to believe that the universe is orderly and that their good actions will be rewarded. It both justifies one's behavior in the past and promises rewards for good behavior in the future. Good behavior simply means doing the type of thing that society has taught one to do.

When someone is victimized or suffers a tragedy, people look for a way to restore justice to that person, to right the wrong. When justice cannot be restored, that person's fate threatens our belief in a just world. In order to protect these beliefs, we find a way to view the victim as deserving of her fate. In the case of the assaulted woman, viewing her as provoking or enjoying the violence or as being psychologically flawed are all ways of restoring a belief in a just world. She is getting, in effect, what she deserves. One could argue that world-weary police officers should be the last people to believe in a just world, but Lerner's notion of justice goes beyond a narrow criminal justice system concept of justice. However, even with criminal justice professionals, Lerner would argue, a tendency exists to blame the victim in order to avoid the conclusion that the universe is chaotic and that consequences do not necessarily follow from actions.

The "just world" hypothesis would predict that to the extent the criminal justice system or other social agencies fail to provide early and effective assistance for an assaulted woman (and, therefore, fail to assist her to break away from a repeatedly assaultive relationship), the professionals who work in those systems may adopt the view that the woman herself was partially to blame for the violence by remaining in the relationship. This belief serves three functions: (1) It protects the professional from recognition that their particular system is not functioning efficiently. (2) It maintains the belief that the world is just, that is, that people get what they deserve. (3) It precludes the necessity of working for system change. It is ironic that these attitudes, when held by professionals within the medical, social, and justice systems, help to create the very social and legal climate that contributes to the battered woman's inability to get out of the battering relationship, thus creating a self-fulfilling prophecy.

4.4   PSYCHOLOGICAL HOSTAGES

The attribution of masochistic behavior to assaulted women depends on the outside observer's overlooking any situational factors that impede a woman's leaving her assaultive husband. Clearly, however, a variety of situational inducements to remain might exist, ranging from broad macrosystem pressures (such as economic deprivation or socialized beliefs that a woman must be loyal to her husband) to the use of threats of violence and intermittent surveillance by her husband. Furthermore, short-term reinforcers could occur after the assault that might operate to keep the woman from leaving.

4.4.1   The Macrosystem

The macrosystem (or cultural) explanations for the difficulty associated with leaving a violent relationship have focused on the socialization of women to feel responsible for marriage outcome, to rescue the male from his problems, and to demonstrate loyalty to the marriage in the face of adversity (Maccoby & Jacklin, 1974; Greenglass, 1984). Martin (1977) discusses how female socialization to be responsible for marital success leads to a sense of shame if the marriage fails and to attempts to save face, such as covering up bruises received in an assault. Martin and others describe the existential meaning of marriage to women, whereby self-worth becomes equated with marital success.

Similarly, a culturally developed nurturer role leads a woman to rationalize the outbursts of her husband as signs that he needs her. As Martin points out, this rationalization forms a tight circle of logic: the worse the man behaves, the more he appears to be sick and therefore to need the woman. Interestingly, while some feminist writers (e.g., Caplan, 1984) have decried the explanation of the loyalty of battered wives as due to masochism, the explanations of other feminist writers (e.g., Martin, 1977) sound like a form of socialized masochism in the broader sense of the term. Becker (1973) and Fromm (1973), for example, describe socialized masochism as a character form whereby someone else's existence takes precedence over the self. As Becker puts it, "We may prefer to deflate ourselves in order to keep the relationship, even though we glimpse the impossibility of it and the slavishness to which it reduces us" (1973, p. 167).

We shall return to this consideration below. For present purposes, this macrosystem explanation of the behavior of battered women suffers from the same problem as cultural explanations of assaultive husbands: it fails to account for individual differences. If the socialization of women to be loyal to abusive husbands was so compelling, the surprise, chagrin, and lack of comprehension of female outside observers raised with the same socialization would be hard to explain. Macrosystem factors again may direct or set parameters on the responses of battered women, but an interaction with factors from other levels seems required to understand fully the unusual loyalty of battered women.

4.4.2 The Exosystem: Access to Social and Economic Resources

It has been suggested that assaulted women fail to escape the battering relationship because of the many social and economic obstacles in their way (e.g., MacLeod, 1980; Strube & Barbour, 1983, 1984). These include economic dependence on the husband due to inequitable pay (women traditionally earn about 60% of men's salaries) or unequal employment opportunities for men and women, inadequate resources such as alternative accommodation, transition houses, family and friends nearby, and lack of adequate protection from the husband by the criminal justice system (poor police response, unenforced peace bonds, etc.).

Gelles (1976) interviewed a sample of women who had sought police intervention or social service assistance or who had begun divorce proceedings because of their husbands' physical violence. He found that those women who were entrapped (by a lack of formal education or job skills, unemployment, or young children) were less likely to seek a divorce or outside assistance after being beaten. While such system inequities do exist as barriers to a woman's leaving a battering relationship, and should be corrected, they still do not provide a sufficient explanation for the fact that women often stay in violent relationships.

Rounsaville (1978) found that the availability of outside resources (fewer children to care for, better jobs, better social adjustment, higher social class) did not discriminate those who left their partners from those who did not. Leaving the relationship seemed to be more a function of dynamics internal to the relationship (e.g., severity of abuse, fear of being killed by the husband, having called police, and/or having discovered that the husband was also abusing the children). As Rounsaville pointed out, "When these circumstances prevailed, it did not seem to matter whether there were adequate resources or not. Given sufficient motivation, women even with few resources found a way to leave" (p. 17).

Gelles (1976) also found that severity and frequency of abuse were the best predictors of a woman's decision to seek help or leave the relationship. In Section 4.7 below we will review recent empirical studies on the economic and psychological determinants of leaving or staying. In these studies, economic variables, taken by themselves, rarely account for more than 15% of the variance in leave or stay decisions.

4.4.3 The Microsystem: Dynamics of the Relationship

Several writers have suggested that the relationship of the battering couple is characterized by unmet dependency needs on the part of either or both partners (Kardiner & Fuller, 1970; Lion, 1977; Rounsaville, 1978; Shainess, 1977). The constant round of doomed attempts to satisfy one another's unrealistic needs fuels the arguments that lead to violence and keeps the couple locked in battle. For example, a high percentage of battered women report that their partners are jealous and possessive in the extreme, often to the point of obsession (Rounsaville, 1978; Walker, 1979a). Arguments about the woman's outside activities or imagined affairs are a frequent cause of violent episodes. The man attempts to restrict his partner's independent existence, which is a constant threat to his security. The woman, in hopes of avoiding arguments and reducing the accompanying violence, begins to organize her life completely around her partner and his demands.

The woman's compliance legitimizes his demands while systematically eliminating opportunities for her to build up a supportive network that could eventually assist her in leaving the relationship. Her compliance also builds up a store of repressed anger and frustration on her part. Compliance also deepens the woman's dependence upon her partner, as she devotes herself completely to fulfilling his needs. In time, the woman's self-esteem may become wrapped up with her attempts to placate her partner and to fulfill her wifely duties by keeping the relationship together. As Walker (1979a) notes, "Since most battered women adhere to traditional values about the permanency of love and marriage, they are easy prey for the guilt attendant on breaking up a home, even if it is not a very happy one" (p. 67). Thus, the battered woman becomes trapped in the relationship by both her own and her partner's expectations of her behavior and responsibilities.

4.4.4 Ontogenetic Factors

Family History, Parental Role Models,
and Role Expectation

As we described in Chapter 2, parents who behave violently toward or in the presence of their children are providing role models of behavior that the children readily learn. As with assaultive males, the women who are victims of wife battering are also likely to have witnessed domestic violence. A study by the National Organization of Women (NOW) in Ann Arbor, Michigan, found that one-third of battered women had seen violence between their parents (Fleming, 1979). There is also evidence that being the victim of abuse as a child is related to becoming involved in a violent relationship as an adult. In a large-scale study of family violence, Straus found that the more frequently a woman had been struck by her parents, the more likely she was to be in a domestically violent relationship (Straus, 1977a).[1] Gelles (1972) found that those who had been hit frequently as a child were likely to fight physically with their spouse. Hilberman and Munson (1977–78) found that the 60 battered women in their study had often been both witnesses to and victims of violence in their families of origin.

Children who witness violence not only learn specific, aggressive behaviors but are also likely to acquire the belief that violence is a legitimate way to solve personal problems. They are therefore likely to expect that they will be involved in violence as a part of their adult relationships. Furthermore, children who witness violence between adults may develop attitudes and sex-role orientations that predispose them to become involved in violent relationships as adults. Men who saw their mothers being beaten may develop an attitude that women are second-class citizens and deserve to be ill-treated. In the normal development process of adopting the female sex-role, girls come to identify with their mothers as the victims of aggression (Fleming, 1979). They may begin to see themselves as powerless and deserving of scorn, and may come to see the world as a place where they have no control over what happens to them.

Being predisposed to enter an adult relationship where they will be treated in the same way in which they saw their mothers treated, these women may believe that violence is simply an expected part of married life and accept it as they saw their mothers accepting it. Consequently, they are not inclined to believe that they deserve better, or that they would be able to survive in the world alone. They are therefore unlikely to leave their relationships and, if they do, usually return to their husbands to resume the kind of marriage that was modelled for them by their own parents.

Personality Characteristics

As described above, one of the traditional and most persistent explanations for why battered women remain in an abusive relationship centers around the notion that they are masochistic and thus consciously or unconsciously invite and encourage abuse (e.g., Snell, Rosenwald, & Robey, 1964). If it were the case that battered women invited or encouraged abuse, one would expect to find that these women would have a history of battering relationships in adulthood or other forms of self-destructiveness apart from the present battering relationship. The assessment of indirect self-destructive behavior as prima facie evidence for masochism (Farberow, 1980) unfortunately has not been connected to the problem of battered women. Since much of the battering occurs later on in a relationship and involves, as we will argue below, situational forces that diminish the control and volition of the battered woman, we would argue that battering does not constitute a form of indirect self-destructive behavior.

Furthermore, one investigation found that the majority of battered women do not fit a pattern of being abused in other adult relationships. In a sample of 31 battered women interviewed in hospital emergency rooms and a mental health facility, Rounsaville (1978) found that only 4 (13%) had been physically abused in previous relationships. Although Rounsaville notes that some of the women in his sample reported that they sometimes deliberately escalated arguments that they thought might lead to violence, he rejects the notion that battered women are masochistic and therefore stay in the battering relationship in order to suffer. An occasionally deliberate escalation of conflict by a woman was an attempt on her part to hasten the inevitable and "get it over with."

Psychological State

A second type of explanation often advanced for the fact that battered women stay in the relationship is that they are in a state of *learned helplessness*. Seligman's theory of learned helplessness (1974) states that when an individual learns through experience that he or she has no control over an unpleasant environment—that is, that certain outcomes are independent of his or her own behavior—the individual loses the motivation to change that environment or situation. Walker (1979a) has applied the concept of learned helplessness to the battered woman's position. She proposes that women come to expect battering as a way of life because they have learned that they cannot influence its occurrence. The experiences recounted by battered women certainly support this notion, with personal recountings of being awakened and dragged out of bed in the middle of the night and beaten by their enraged partners.

A corollary of the learned helplessness theory is that the feelings of helplessness learned in the primary situation generalize to other situations. Thus, the abused woman may come to believe that none of her behavior in any sphere will be effective, and her resulting sense of futility regarding alternative courses of action will preclude the possibility of her leaving the assaultive relationship. Furthermore, Frieze (1979) has suggested that when the assaulted woman internalizes the blame for the abuse (e.g., blaming herself for being a poor wife), her self-esteem is lowered more, which leads to even greater feelings of depression and helplessness. The situation may come to constitute a particularly vicious cycle if the woman blames herself for her failure to stop the abuse or control the behavior of the batterer. The very occurrence of abuse is then further evidence of how helpless and incompetent she is, contributing to lower self-esteem and the further unlikelihood that she will free herself from the relationship.

A controlled self-report study of battered women in the United States and New Zealand revealed significant differences in the areas of self-esteem, assertiveness, reality perception (e.g., what is normal behavior, who is responsible for the attacks, etc.) and sense of identity (Smart, Dewey, & Goodman, 1987). But contrary to the theory of learned helplessness, there were no significant differences between controls and abused women in the area of competence. This finding does not, however, necessarily refute the concept of learned helplessness. While on one level the battered women may have believed that they were competent individuals in certain aspects of their lives, the combination of low-self-esteem, lack of assertiveness, inability to realistically perceive their situation and alienation from self (e.g., "Sometimes I feel that things are happening to someone else, not to me," p. 9) may render any intellectual sense of competence irrelevant in dealing with the dynamics of a relationship that they perceive to be beyond their control.

Preabuse psychosocial functioning can be inferred from women's medical histories. Stark, Flitcraft, and Frazier (1979) examined medical records of 481 women who sought treatment at an urban hospital emergency room. Preassault medical records for assaulted women were remarkably similar to medical records of nonassaulted women. The two groups did not differ significantly on number of suicide attempts, drug abuse, frequency of use of psychiatric emergency services, community mental health center, or state mental hospital, although assaulted women had a higher incidence of alcohol abuse. Postassault comparisons revealed significant differences on all measures, suggesting that deficits in psychosocial functioning are more a result, than a cause, of assault.

Rounsaville indeed found a high level of depression in a sample group of assaulted women that he studied postassault (80% reported symptoms of depression). However, this may be the inevitable consequence of feeling trapped by violence, rather than an indication that assaulted women are in a state of learned helplessness. These women were not found to have generalized their feelings of helplessness and ineffectiveness to other areas of their lives.

Rounsaville and his colleagues found that the assaulted women in their study reported themselves to be competent in their work outside the home, in their relationships with their family of origin, and in their relationships with their children (Rounsaville, Lifton, & Bieber, 1979). Reports of impaired functioning were specific to the spouse relationship and to leisure-time activities. These data suggest that if a syndrome of learned helplessness exists at all, it may be a contributing factor to these women's inability to leave the battering relationship. It is not, however, an exhaustive explanation of the situation in which assaulted women find themselves.

4.5 TRAUMATIC BONDING AS A THEORETICAL FRAMEWORK

Each of the above explanations receives qualified empirical support. Yet taken individually or together, they do not adequately account for the sudden about-face that often characterizes the return of an assaulted woman to a relationship that has a high prognosis of future violence. Most of the above explanations, in fact, attempt to say more about a woman's initial choice of a relationship or else present a picture of an amotivational woman who has lost interest in attempting to change her situation.

While ambivalence may manifest itself behaviorally in an assaulted woman, most professionals would support the view that such a woman experiences very strong emotional states posttraumatically, and that these states serve to push her out or pull her back into the battering relationship. My colleague Susan Painter and I have developed a theory based on the social psychological research on power and social traps and the developmental research on the formation of emotional bonds. This theory links the tenacity and loyalty of assaulted women to special features of the abusive relationship, rather than to inferred aspects of her own personality or to the socioeconomic milieu in which she finds herself.

The formation of strong emotional attachments under conditions of intermittent maltreatment is not specific to assaulted women but has been reported in a variety of studies, both experimental and observational, with both human and animal subjects. For example, as described in Section 4.1, people taken hostage may subsequently show positive regard for their captors (Bettelheim, 1943; Strentz, 1979), abused children have been found to have strong attachments to their abusing parents (e.g., Kempe & Kempe, 1978), and cult members are sometimes amazingly loyal to malevolent cult leaders. The relationship between assaulted women and their partners, then, may not be an isolated phenomenon. Rather, it might be seen as one example of what we have termed *traumatic bonding*—the development of strong emotional ties between two persons where one person intermittently harrasses, beats, threatens, abuses, or intimidates the other.

There are two common features of social structure in such apparently diverse relationships as battered spouse-battering spouse, hostage-captor, abused child-abusing parent, cult follower-leader, and prisoner-guard. The first feature is the existence of a power imbalance wherein the maltreated person perceives himself or herself to be subjugated to or dominated by the other. Second is the intermittent nature of the abuse.

4.5.1   Power Imbalance

Attachment to a person or group larger or stronger than the self increases feelings of personal power (Becker, 1973; Fromm, 1941; Lion, 1977; McClelland, 1975). Social psychologists have found that unequal power relationships can become increasingly unbalanced over time, to the point where the power dynamic itself produces pathology in individuals (Ng, 1982). For example, Zimbardo, Haney, and Banks (1972) reported anxiety and depression in volunteer subjects playing the role of prisoners who were relegated to powerlessness in a simulated prison situation. Lewin, Lippitt, and White (1947) reported increased redirected aggression in powerless members of autocratic groups. As mentioned before, Bettelheim (1943) reported compulsive copying by Jewish prisoners of the behavior and expressed attitudes of their Nazi prison guards.

Recasting Anna Freud's (1942) concept of identification with the aggressor from its psychoanalytic, life-and-death mode, this concept would predict that in situations of extreme power imbalance, where a person of high power is occasionally punitive, a person of low power would adopt the aggressor's assumed perspective of herself, internalize aggression, or redirect it toward others similar to herself.

As the power imbalance magnifies, the person of low power would feel more negative in her self-appraisal, more incapable of fending for herself, and thus more in need of the high-power person, whether or not high dependency existed in the low-power person prior to the present imbalanced relationship. This cycle of dependency and lowered self-esteem repeats itself over and over and comes eventually to create a strong affective bond to the high-power person. Concomitantly, the person in the high-power position will develop an overgeneralized sense of his own power (just as the low-power person develops an inflated sense of her own powerlessness), which masks the extent to which he is dependent on the low-power person to maintain his self-image. This sense of power, however, is predicated on his ability to maintain absolute control in the dyadic relationship. If the symbiotic roles that maintain this sense of power are disturbed, the masked dependency of the high-power person on the low-power person is suddenly made obvious.

One example of this sudden reversal of the power dynamic is the desperate control attempts on the part of the abandoned battering husband to bring his wife back to him through surveillance or intimidation. In romantic relationships as well as in cults, power imbalances magnify so that each person's sense of power or powerlessness feeds on itself. What may have been initially benign, even attractive, becomes ultimately destructive to positive self-regard. In the process, both persons (or groups) become welded together to maintain the psychological subsystem that fulfills the needs created in part by the power dynamic itself.

4.5.2 Periodicity of Abuse

The second feature of traumatic bonding situations is the intermittency of abuse. That is, the dominant party intermittently and periodically maltreats the submissive party by threats, verbal, and/or physical abuse. The time between bouts of abuse is likely to be characterized by more normal and acceptable social behavior. Thus, the victim is subject to alternating periods of aversive or negative arousal and the relief and release associated with the removal of aversive arousal. The situation of alternating aversive and pleasant conditions is an experimental paradigm within learning theory known as *partial or intermittent reinforcement.* It is highly effective in producing persistent patterns of behavior that are difficult to extinguish or terminate (Amsel, 1958). Such intermittent maltreatment patterns have been found to produce strong emotional bonding in both animals and humans.

Intermittent Reinforcement and Traumatic Bonding
There is considerable evidence from both naturalistic and laboratory-based studies with animals that severe arousal, even when caused by an attachment object and especially when it is intermittently increased and reduced, provides a basis for strong emotional attachment. Scott (1963) reviewed the literature on critical periods for emotional attachment in animals and concluded that the evidence "indicates that any sort of strong emotion, whether hunger, fear, pain, or loneliness will speed up the process of socialization." Scott further states:

> The surprising thing is that emotions which we normally consider aversive should produce the same effect as those which appear to be rewarding. . . . An animal (and perhaps a person) of any age, exposed to certain individuals or physical surroundings for any length of time will inevitably become attached to them, the rapidity of the process being governed by the degree of emotional arousal associated with them. . . . If this conclusion should apply to our species as well as other animals . . . it provides an explanation of certain well known clinical observations such as the development by neglected children of strong affection for cruel and abusive parents, and the various peculiar affectional relationships that develop between prisoners and jailers, slaves and masters, and so on. (p. 189).

More recently, Rajecki, Lamb, and Obmascher (1978) have written a comprehensive critical review of emotional bonding in infants, in which they assess the major theories of infantile attachment, including those on both human and animal attachments (e.g., Bowlby, 1960; Lorenz, 1937). One criterion for the comparative evaluation of these theories was their relative ability to explain maltreatment effects. In reviewing the literature on maltreatment effects, Rajecki et al. found conclusive evidence for enhanced infant attachment under conditions of maltreatment in birds, dogs, and monkeys. Attempts to inhibit infants' bonding to abusive attachment objects were found inevitably to fail unless (1) they were persistent and consistently punitive and (2) an alternative attachment object existed.

Harlow and Harlow (1971) reviewed the research they carried out with infant monkeys, in which "evil surrogate mothers" were used as potential attachment objects. These surrogates would exude noxious air blasts, extrude brass spikes, hurl the infant to the floor, or vibrate so violently as to make the infant's teeth chatter. None of the above disrupted the bonding behavior of the infant monkeys. The authors concluded that, "Instead of producing experimental neurosis we have achieved a technique for enhancing maternal attachment" (p. 206). Similarly, Seay, Alexander, and Harlow (1964) note, "A surprising phenomenon was the universally persisting attempts by the infants to attach to the mother's body regardless of neglect or physical punishment" (p. 353).

When physical punishment is administered at intermittent intervals, and when it is interspersed with permissive and friendly contact, the phenomenon of traumatic bonding seems most powerful. Fischer (1955) attempted to inhibit the social responses of young dogs. One group was indulged (30 minutes of friendly and permissive contact with the experimenter each day), another punished (handled roughly or beaten for any approach response), a third intermittently indulged and punished, and a fourth kept in isolation. Using measures of human orientation to indicate the degrees of bonding shown by the dogs at 12 to 13 weeks of age, Fischer found that the indulged-punished group showed 231% of the human orientation of the indulged group. At 16 weeks, the indulged-punished group still showed the greatest amount of bonding of all four groups. As Rajecki and his colleagues conclude, "The data show that inconsistent treatment (i.e., maltreatment by and affection from the same source) yields an accentuation of attempts to gain proximity to the attachment object" (Rajecki et al., 1978, p. 425).

Intermittent Reinforcement Patterns in Domestic Violence

To what extent are findings based on animal studies applicable to humans? Rajecki et al. found no conclusive studies in the child abuse literature, but these consisted mainly of descriptive case studies; none had been designed to test hypotheses regarding the nature of emotional bonds. However, prima facie evidence suggests that a process similar to that found in animals may be the mechanism that maintains the strong bond formed by battered women for their batterers. Rounsaville (1978) speculates that "One feature that may weigh in favor of staying is the intermittent nature of the abuse. . . . Many [battered women] described highly pleasant periods of reconciliation between episodes. . . . This pattern was conducive to ignoring the problem or thinking of it as an aberrant, exceptional part of the relationship" (p. 17).

On the basis of over 120 detailed interviews with battered women, Walker (1979a) describes a cyclical pattern of domestic violence found in abusive spouse relationships that approximates the intermittent punishment-indulgence pattern used in animal research. Tension gradually builds (during *phase one*), an explosive battering incident occurs (during *phase two*), and a calm, loving respite follows (*phase three*). The battered woman's psychological reactions in each of the three phases, and the repetition of these phase-related responses, serves to "bind a battered woman to her batterer just as strongly as 'miracle glues' bind inanimate substances" (Walker, 1979a, p. xvi). The immediate reaction of the battered woman during the battering incident is "dissociation coupled with a sense of disbelief that the incident is really happening" (p. 62). This is followed by an emotional collapse indicative of extreme, aversive, and prolonged arousal similar to that experienced by disaster victims or victims of hostage takings (Flynn, 1986). The collapse is accompanied by inactivity, depression, anxiety, self-blame, and feelings of helplessness.

In all, the exaggerated arousal and subsequent feelings make the battered woman extremely vulnerable and dependent for some time after the battering incident. The emotional aftermath of a battering incident for the batterer, usually guilt and contrition, leads him to attempt to make amends via exceptionally loving treatment toward his partner. Thus, he becomes temporarily the fulfillment of her hoped-for fantasy husband. At the same time, his improved behavior serves to reduce the aversive arousal he himself has created, while also providing reinforcement for his partner to stay in the relationship.

Arousal theory in psychology (e.g., Berlyne, 1967; Zuckerman, 1979) postulates that mid-levels of arousal are considered optimal by organisms. Overload or underload triggers homeostatic behaviors that attempt to return the organism back to a mid-level. Stimuli associated with an increase in arousal during boring circumstances or a reduction in arousal that is too high (or aversive) tend to become conditioned reinforcers. For example, Kendrick and Cialdini (1977) hypothesize that the reduction of aversive arousal builds attachments to people present during this reduction through the mechanism of negative reinforcement; that is, interpersonal or emotional associations are made stronger by the removal or cessation of an unpleasant stimulus such as excessive arousal. In cases of battering, this mechanism of reinforcement could be especially strong due to the extremity of the aversive arousal caused by the battering incident and the subsequent reduction of that arousal in the form of pleasant contact during phase three of the cycle. When such negative reinforcement occurs intermittently over time, the reinforced response—which is for the woman to remain with the batterer—is strengthened.

Hence, two powerful sources of reinforcement exist in intermittently abusive relationships: the arousal-jag or excitement associated with an increase in arousal prior to violence and the relative tranquillity associated with the postviolence calm. Both are homeostatic in that they might operate to produce an optimal state of arousal. Both occur intermittently, creating a powerful reinforcement schedule. Thus, as the cycle repeats itself over and over again, the probability that the woman will leave the relationship becomes less and less (see also Solomon, 1980).

Walker has noted the profound effect this series of events and behavior can have on the battered woman. In her words,

> As they progressed from the end of phase two into phase three of the battering cycle, the change in those women I visited daily in the hospital was dramatic. Within a few days they went from being lonely, angry, frightened, and hurt to being happy, confident and loving. . . . These women were thoroughly convinced of their desire to stop being victims, until the batterer arrived. I always knew when a woman's husband had made contact with her by the profusion of flowers, candy, cards and other gifts in her hospital room (Walker, 1979a, p. 66).

During the third phase of the battering cycle, the batterer throws himself on his victim's mercy, reversing the power relationship between them dramatically. He places his fate in her hands; he will be destroyed—lost—if she doesn't rescue him by returning to the relationship. His behavior toward her, his pleas and his promises, are likely to relieve her fears and make her believe that she has control, that he will change his ways, that the violence will not recur. In other words, he reduces her aversive arousal initially caused by the build-up and battering phases of the cycle. As noted above, the psychological consequence of the power dynamics during the battering cycle serves to create and strengthen trauma-based emotional bonds between the man and woman, which make long-lasting separation difficult or impossible to achieve.

Traumatic bonding theory (Dutton & Painter, 1981) postulates that when a woman finally leaves an abusive relationship, her immediate fears may begin to subside and her hidden attachment to her abuser will begin to manifest itself. At this particular point in time, the woman is emotionally drained and vulnerable. At these times in the past the husband has been present, contrite, and (temporarily) loving and affectionate. As the fear subsides and the needs fulfilled by her husband increase, an equilibrium point is reached where the woman suddenly and impulsively decides to return.

For an empirical test of this theory, several factors would need to be assessed: (1) the strength of the woman's emotional attachment to her husband, (2) the intermittent nature of previous abuse, (3) postabuse positive reinforcement, and (4) the incrementally developed power imbalance that produces the attachment. Furthermore, emotional attachments of this nature should produce a constellation of beliefs about the causes of violence, and its avoidability in the future, which are both irrational (not based on past evidence) and which contribute to returning. Some assessment of these beliefs would also be required.

4.6 SOCIAL TRAPS: THE INCREMENTAL CHARACTER OF WIFE ASSAULT

A social trap, according to Platt (1973), is a situation in which behavior produces short-term payoffs and long-term costs. The long-term costs are obscured by the short-term payoffs, leading the person to perform behavior that is not in his or her long-term self-interest. From this perspective, an assaulted woman's beliefs and perceptions about the causes of her husband's violence become important as they help shape her private payoff matrix. For example, if she views the violence as originating in her husband and being out of her control, she may be less likely to attempt to modify her own behavior. A high percentage of initial wife assaults occur during the first year of marriage (Dutton & Painter, 1980; Rosenbaum & O'Leary, 1981)—a time when the woman is still experiencing the novelty and optimism of the new relationship. At this point in a marriage, the violence may appear to be an anomaly, out of keeping with the husband's character. Retrospective accounts indicate that at the time of the first assault, a majority of women blamed themselves for causing it (Dutton & Painter, 1980). This, combined with the relative lack of severity that usually characterizes the first violent incident (Wilt & Breedlove, 1977), the husband's postassault contrition, and his attempts to make amends and promises that it will not happen again, serve to both reinforce the belief that the violence is an isolated incident and the affective bonding processes described above. Hence, the traumatically established emotional bonds are strengthened *before* the victim realizes that the violence is not an anomaly and is likely to recur.

Repeated incidents of greater severity tend to shift the woman's cognitions from the belief that the violence will never happen again to the belief that the violence may recur unless the woman alters *her* behavior (Frieze, 1979; Walker, 1979a). With repeated incidents of violence and subsequent good behavior, the emotional bond is further strengthened. At the same time the woman still views the violence as avoidable. Only when she views it as unavoidable will she be strongly motivated to leave (Rounsaville, 1978; Porter, 1983). As the emotional bond strengthens and the duration of the relationship increases, the woman also comes to feel that she has more invested in the relationship and consequently more to lose if she leaves. These feelings and beliefs serve to preserve homeostasis and keep the woman in the relationship.

Furthermore, negative feelings of self-worth develop as a result of continuous assault (Rounsaville, 1978; Porter, 1983). These feelings, along with postassault depression (Rounsaville, 1978), develop the belief in the woman that she could not make it on her own or would not be attractive to other men. A consequent inertia develops about leaving.

In addition to all of the above consequences, many women fear that if they try to leave, the husband will find them and become even more violent. From this perspective, the entrapping features of the intermittent abuse become evident. It is for this reason that personality profiles do not predict who will become an assaulted woman. The dynamics of the social forces at work override personality features.

When assaulted women finally do leave an abusive relationship, it is because the severity of abuse has become so great that they fear for their lives or the safety of their children (Rounsaville, 1978).

4.7 PSYCHOLOGICAL AND ECONOMIC DETERMINANTS OF RETURNING TO ABUSIVE RELATIONSHIPS

Economic factors that could contribute to battered women returning to abusive relationships include an entire constellation of factors contributing to economic dependence on her husband. These range from macrosystem features such as male-female wage differentials to the woman's own job skills, employability, or number of dependents. Both psychological and economic explanations counter the notion that battered women remain in abusive relationships because of some disposition such as masochism. Instead, psychological and economic explanations determine which situational forces operate to trap women in abusive relationships. They differ, however, in the type of situational forces they see as entrapping.

Economic explanations view these forces as objective economic factors that are directly measurable: a low salary, poor employability, or dependents. Psychological theories focus more on the woman's subjective perception of her life alternatives, inside and outside of the relationship. Since these factors are subjective, their measurement requires a careful examination of the woman's perceptions, beliefs, attitudes, and anxieties. Some studies have examined directly why women remain in violent marriages, and we will review them here with a view toward comparing the relative weights of psychological or economic factors in a woman's decision to leave.

Rounsaville (1978) administered open-ended and structured interviews to 31 battered women (17 from a hospital emergency room and 14 from a mental health center). Rounsaville compared women in this sample who left their partners with ones who stayed and found that lack of resources (social class, social functioning, employment, and number of children) did not differentiate those who stayed from those who left. Rounsaville concluded that women who stayed in abusive relationships had resources that they overlooked or did not use.

Kalmuss and Straus (1982) measured wives objective dependency (employment, children five or younger, whether husband earned 75% of the family income) and subjective dependency (whether the wife perceived herself or her husband as being hurt more if their marriage were to break up) in a nationally representative sample of 1,183 marriages in 1976. They found a correlation of .147 between these two measures of dependency. Abuse was defined by items on the Straus *Conflict Tactics Scale* for the husband's behavior and by whether the abuse carried a high risk of serious injury. Kalmuss and Straus reported that "knowledge of a wife's level of objective dependency on her marriage appears to be a better predictor of whether her husband severely abuses her than is knowledge of her subjective dependency" (p. 283).

Strube and Barbour (1983) assessed objective and subjective economic dependence and objective and subjective commitment to a marriage in a sample of 98 physically abused women who had contacted a counseling unit associated with a county attorney's office. Counselors made an initial assessment of the dependence and commitment factors. A follow-up was made when the case was closed (one to 18 months later). The woman's status (in or out of the relationship) at this time constituted the dependent variable of the study.

Objective economic dependence was defined as the presence or absence of a job; *subjective economic dependence* was defined as the woman's stating economic hardship as a reason for staying in the relationship during the initial interview. *Objective commitment* was the length of time the woman had been in the relationship; *subjective commitment* was defined as the woman stating (during the initial interview) that she still loved her partner as a reason for staying. Sixty-two percent of the women in this sample had left their partner at follow-up (cf. the 40% reported by Snyder & Fruchtman, 1981). Objective measures accounted for 11.6% of the variance in relationship decisions; subjective measures accounted for 26.6% of the variance. The authors suggest that entrapment principles that involve subjective estimates of what has been already invested in a relationship be further studied.

A later study by Strube and Barbour (1984) obtained more elaborate objective demographic records from a sample of 251 abused women. In addition, social support availability and subjective reasons for remaining in the relationship were recorded. At the time of this initial assessment, all women were still in the relationship. Follow-up contact was made two to three months later, at which point 70.5% of the women had left their abusive partner. Strube and Barbour reduced their intercorrelated predictor variables to a set of eight variables via multiple regression. The variables with the greatest predictive power weights were employment ($\beta = .28$), economic hardship ($\beta = -.22$), love ($\beta = -.21$) and length of relationship ($\beta = -.16$). All eight combined variables, however, only accounted for 25% of the variance in decisions to stay or leave.

Smith and Chalmers (1984) interviewed 100 women in a Saskatchewan transition house in order to find out what conditions made it possible for women to leave an abusive relationship. They differentiated women who had left home many times (multiple leavers) from those who stayed away permanently after the first departure (single leavers). The single leavers had as their aim in leaving home a re-evaluation of the relationship or a desire to establish their own residence. The multiple leavers, however, had as their primary purpose escape from fear of their partners and effective stopping of their violence. Their departure typically was effective in this regard for a short-term period. These women usually returned when their partner promised to change their violent behavior or quit drinking. Smith and Chalmers pointed out that the woman's own hopes for her partner's change also influenced the decision to return.

This study suggests that homeostasis in some abusive relationships may accommodate successive leavings by one partner without a sustained intent to remain out of the relationship. This being the case, these women do not really change their mind when they return. Smith and Chalmers found that one-third of their sample permanently established their own residences.

Aquirre (1984) had interviewers assess 312 women in Texas shelters. All women were married and residing with their husbands immediately prior to entering the shelter. Aquirre's outcome measure was whether respondents reported at the time they exited shelters that they were returning to their husband. Aquirre examined the impact eight predictor variables had on this outcome, including the respondent's previous experience with violence, the number of injuries, issues experienced during the batterings, economic dependence on her husband, and four variables assessing her experience in the shelter. The only statistically significant predictor was the respondent's economic dependence (based on the respondent's own income level). However, Aquirre did not assess for psychological or relationship features. Thus, as with the studies reviewed above, his study does not constitute a test of economic versus psychological explanations for staying or returning to an abusive relationship. Furthermore, Aquirre's outcome measure is a measure of intent, not of actual staying or leaving.

4.7.1 Effectiveness of Current Studies

In a critical review of these studies, Painter (1985) pointed out that the samples of women used in these studies are typically from one source and may not generalize to women from other sources. Strube and Barbour (1983, 1984) and Gelles (1976) used women from counseling programs. Rounsaville (1978) drew his sample from a hospital emergency room and a mental health center. Other researchers (Aquirre, 1984; Okun, 1984; Porter, 1983; Snyder & Scheer, 1981) contacted women in shelters. Painter thinks that these populations of women may differ in important ways. For example, women in shelters may lack economic resources and come from more violent relationships.

Painter also pointed out the retrospective and static nature of the above studies. Women typically have already made a decision to leave or stay and are categorized according to that decision, although the decision process itself is fluid and dynamic. Painter suggested that a longitudinal study, despite its logistical difficulty, might be essential to avoid the retrospective "snapshot" nature of current research designs.

Finally, Painter criticized current studies for being merely descriptive, rather than explanatory, where relationship dynamics are concerned. These studies tell us the length of time the couple has been married, how soon in the relationship the violence began, and so forth, but they do not effectively assess relationship features such as interpersonal power, commitment (absolute and relative levels for each partner) or intermittency of abuse. In reviewing these studies, Painter reports that rates of women returning vary from 22% (Gelles, 1976) to 78% (Nielsen, Eberle, Thoennes, & Walker, 1979) in short-term follow-ups.

While the studies reported above present a mixed result in terms of evaluating economic versus psychological factors that entrap battered women, the range and depth of psychological factors has not been adequately measured in these studies. When one reads the psychological literature on victim experience, as described in Section 4.1, in the work of Flynn (1986), or Dutton and Painter (1981), and then turns to the empirical literature that uses simple bivariate reports (i.e., of who loses the most if a marriage breaks up or whether a women still loves her husband or not), this inadequacy is clear.

The majority of studies do not begin to tap the depth or complexity of the victim experience for a repeatedly assaulted woman. This experience produces strong emotional bonds that the woman herself may not understand or be able to verbalize. Transition house workers report the guilt and confusion of women who feel themselves being pulled back to a relationship that they know will have a negative outcome. Empirical studies to date have not assessed, in any but a superficial manner, the network of negative beliefs about the self and the implications of these beliefs for forecasting a life of dependence, strong positive associations with the husband, preoccupations and obsessive ruminating on a person who has been a salient force in someone's life. Nor have they assessed the emotional sequelae of the relationship termination such as anxiety, depression, and guilt about leaving.

Some conclusions can be drawn from the few replicated results that arise from these studies. First, most studies indicate that economic independence contributes to the likelihood of women leaving abusive relationships. Second, the longer the duration of the relationship at the time of the woman being interviewed, the greater the likelihood of the woman returning to the abuser. Whether this indicates commitment, investment, or something else is not clear. Third, neither abuse in childhood nor severity of violence in the current relationship are reliable predictors of relationship breakup. At the time of writing, all of these conclusions must be considered tentative.

4.7.2 Recommendations for Future Research

The ideal research design for answering these questions has not yet been implemented. Such a study would be longitudinal in nature, drawing women from a variety of sources, and would include a systematic assessment of relationship dynamics such as relative power, periodicity, time of onset of abuse, the woman's affective state (depression, strength of attachment to husband, or preoccupation with her mate), alternative support systems, and economic situation. These measures should be related to the woman's current life goals and subjective probability of achieving those goals in or out of her relationship.

Careful comparisons should be made to the difficulties of nonabused women in leaving relationships (see Kitson, 1982), and it should not be assumed that returning to a previously abusive relationship constitutes a failure. Some women may successfully implement strategies that stop their husbands from repeating the use of violence. Finally, a thorough assessment of the woman's beliefs about the causes of violence, her control over it, and its likelihood of stopping should be made. In the next section, we review literature on some of these beliefs.

4.8 BATTERED WOMEN'S CAUSAL ATTRIBUTIONS FOR VIOLENCE

In 1983, one of my graduate students, Carol Porter, interviewed 50 women in a shelter in San Jose, California, in order to ascertain how these women explained their husband's violence toward them. She was interested in the role this explanation might play in the long-term ability of these women to cope with the crisis of being assaulted, separated from their husbands, and forced to consider a traumatically imposed life change. Shelter counselors made individual, independent ratings of each woman's emotional state and ability to cope with her situation.

4.8.1 Self-Blame

Porter made a surprisingly correct and counterintuitive prediction in this study (which constituted her doctoral dissertation). She predicted that women who blamed themselves for the violence directed toward them would cope better and would be less likely to return to an abusive relationship. What makes this prediction so surprising is the conventional wisdom of therapists that self-blame by battered women acts to keep them in abusive relationships.

In a related study, Frieze (1979) interviewed assaulted and nonassaulted women about actual and hypothetical cases of wife abuse. For the hypothetical cases, 81% of assaulted and 79% of nonassaulted women attributed causality to the husband and only a small minority (16%, 20%) attributed it to the woman. However, when assaulted women were asked about an actual assault they had experienced, 50% attributed it to something *they* had done. Freize (1979) found that this tendency to attribute more causality to the self became greater when assault occurred more frequently. When assault was relatively rare, only 12% of women attributed it to themselves. But when it occurred frequently, 40% did so. Frieze (1979) suggested that when battered women internalize blame for abuse, their self-esteem is lowered, and greater depression and helplessness ensue.

Porter, however, was using a more elaborate notion of the function of self-blame that developed in social-psychological research on attribution. Wortman (1976) linked self-blame to the need for perceived control by speculating that victims may accept blame for their victimization because, in so doing, they generate a belief that if they are to blame for violence, they must have some control over it and hence can control its future occurrence. In other words, in order to be certain that we can control our future, we must accept responsibility for the past. For example, Bulman and Wortman (1977) found that there was a positive correlation between the degree of self-blame accepted by paraplegic victims of accidents and independent assessments of how well these victims were copying with their injury.

Porter distinguished between various types of self-blame, following a distinction made by Janoff-Bulman (1979). One level of self-blame is behavioral; that is, certain specific aspects of behavior are seen as having caused the violence. The second kind is characterological and views the violence as caused by a permanent, nonmodifiable aspect of character.

Janoff-Bulman found that depression following a traumatic event was related to characterological self-blame. Rape victims interviewed by Janoff-Bulman reported behavioral but not characterological self-blame. They blamed themselves for walking home alone at night but did not feel that they were raped because of the kind of person they were.

Porter suggested that behavioral self-blame might constitute an effective coping strategy for battered women since it would allow them to feel that future violence was modifiable. Assuming that they do not immediately return to an abusive relationship where the violence is not modifiable by them, behavioral self-blame could constitute a temporarily effective cognitive coping strategy by regenerating a belief in personal control. Characterological self-blame, on the other hand, leads to the belief that some unmodifiable aspect of oneself would continue to recreate victimization. The benefits from this coping strategy depend on the woman being out of the relationship. Furthermore, behavioral self-blame might be a functional transitional stage that might be later supplanted by a more interactive view of the cause of violence.

4.8.2 Self-Blame, Partner-Blame, and Contingency

Porter found that the more women blamed their partners, the less likely they were to describe themselves as calm, happy, or optimistic. Women who were rated by shelter staff as good copers were more likely to acknowledge a relationship between their own behavior or personality and their partner's violence. This finding, however, speaks more to a sense of contingency, rather than blame. That is, the women saw their husband's violence as contingent upon something they did but not upon something they blamed themselves for (see also Campbell, 1987). Furthermore, women who perceived this contingency between aspects of themselves and their partner's abuse were likely to perceive the abuse as unavoidable and less likely to return to the relationship.

In fact, perception of avoidability was the second strongest predictor of staying out of the relationship (the only stronger predictor was the duration of the abuse) and predicted more strongly than did the number of times the woman had previously left. Women who blamed their partners for the violence were *more* likely to return. One possible explanation for this blame-return relationship is that partner blaming is a by-product of anger, and anger connotes a strong, continuing emotional bond to the partner.

The distinction between contingency and blame is that women in this sample, while recognizing that their husband's violence was contingent upon something they did, felt positively about that particular aspect of their behavior. For instance, although a number of subjects reported that they felt their independence or tendency to be outspoken was related to the abusive behavior of their partners, they felt they were entitled to these aspects of themselves.

Porter did not find strong support for the characterological-behavioral self-blame distinction she had made, presumably because this distinction is blurred for chronic or repeated events. The prior literature (e.g., Janoff-Bulman, 1979) had concentrated on single victimizations. Porter concluded that even distinguishing characterological from behavioral self-blame is too imprecise. Battered women can blame themselves for a variety of reasons: for causing the abuse, for being unable to modify it, or for tolerating it and not leaving sooner. With self-blame having so many different meanings to different women, it is easy to see why it did not have a strong relationship to subsequent coping. On the other hand, the ability to perceive a contingency between one's behavior and abuse might have facilitated coping because, unlike blame, perceived contingency might be linked to a woman's self-concept and thus be more salient. A woman who viewed her partner's abuse as contingent upon positively valued aspects of herself was more likely to think well of herself and to describe her partner as insecure, jealous, or threatened by her.

Consistent with this speculation of Porter's is a study by Cohn and Giles-Sims (1979). The authors elicited attributions for cause of violence from the women when they first entered the shelter. Follow-up interviews at six months revealed that women who viewed assault as contingent on some aspect of their behavior were more likely to leave their husbands in the interim. Surprisingly, women who viewed the assault as caused by an aspect of their husbands' character were more likely to return.

The authors could offer no strong explanation for this latter finding. If replicated, it certainly would contradict attribution theory assumptions since it suggests a pattern of irrational behavior (returning to a situation where violence is likely and uncontrollable). Traumatic bonding theory, on the other hand, would have no difficulty in accounting for this group of women returning despite causal attributions to the husband. Since power imbalances, periodicity of abuse, and incremental increases in abuse were arranged so as to maximize the strength of traumatically established affective bonds, these would override the effects of rational attributions.

Campbell's (1987) study of 97 battered women and 96 nonbattered women with serious relationship problems also found that perception of interactive blame resulted in less troubled individuals, whether battered or not. Despite the tendency to believe that abused women usually concentrate blame on themselves, only 21.6% of the women in this study did so (which was not significantly different from the control group). Although self-blaming battered women were more likely to be depressed and have low self-esteem than external-blamers, the interaction of perceived stability of the relationship and self-blame with self-esteem suggests that self-blame when the victim perceives the situation as unchanging may be healthier for the individual than external blame in situations where the victim still hopes for change. Campbell's qualitative data suggests that accepting that the relationship was not going to change precipitated actions such as leaving or seeking an abuse injunction, with a resultant lessening of depression and increase in self-esteem, regardless of attribution of blame.

Finally, Porter speculated that battered women's assessments of blame might change over time. Many of her subjects had reported that they blamed themselves for the abuse until a point was reached where they truly believed they were doing nothing wrong. This point was reached for many women through counseling or through learning that many other women had similar experiences. This information reduced pluralistic ignorance (the belief that one's problem is particular to oneself), thus reducing attributions to the self as the problem.

An alternative view of the effects of blame and perception of contingency on returning to an abusive relationship is that blame connotes an emotional reaction and contingency perception connotes a letting go of this reaction. When we are angry (and still strongly emotionally involved), we tend to blame someone for relationship failure. Our blame reactions may be highly unstable, especially when the relationship failure is recent and emotions are quite strong. At this point, anger (blaming the other) and guilt (blaming the self) may alternate. Both, however, connote that a strong affective connection still remains. Hence, Porter's finding that women who blamed their partner were more likely to return is not so paradoxical.

With time and effective counseling, the emotional attachment to the partner may weaken, and as it does, blaming (and emotional reaction) may be supplanted by a less emotional appraisal of the causes of relationship problems. In the case of battered women, this would include perceptions of the contingency between aspects of their behavior (which they positively value) and their partner's violence. Porter's finding that self-blame altered over time might have masked a more general finding that all forms of blame diminish with time. Research in this area needs to pay close attention to the precise amount of time between relationship dissolution and data collection in order to clarify these blame/contingency distinctions.

CHAPTER SUMMARY

The overall picture that emerges from the literature on victimization is as follows: the immediate psychological consequences of being a victim of severe assault are (among others) depression, confusion, lack of motivation, anxiety, anger, and guilt. Yet there can be considerable variation in affect and actions following victimization. Sales et al.'s study of rape victims (1984) suggests that there are three categories of predictive factors that explain the differential reactions of victims of abusive incidents: (1) preassault factors (personality, drug and alcohol use, life stressors, absence of social support); (2) the severity of the violence; and (3) the victim's experience with the criminal justice system (while charging the assaulter reduces postassault symptoms, proceeding toward trial can exacerbate them).

It can be difficult for outsiders to appreciate why battered wives remain with their husbands. Masochism is often cited as an explanation: these women derive gratification from being abused. Yet there is no support for this belief. Its prevalence is an example of the tendency for people to attribute trait characteristics to others' problems (the fundamental attribution error) and to believe that harm only befalls those who deserve it (the "just world" hypothesis).

Why does a woman stay with an abusive husband? Various theories have been proposed at various levels. At the macrosystem (cultural) level, it is believed that women are socialized to feel responsible for marriage outcome and that self-worth is equated with marital success. Her traditional sex role as nurturer encourages her to rationalize her husband's problems as a sign that she is needed.

At the exosystem (community) level, researchers have investigated the role of social and economic resources on women choosing to remain in an abusive relationship. Gelles (1976) found that women with limited access to economic resources (e.g., little formal education, job skills, or employment opportunities) or who had young children were less likely to seek assistance or divorce when beaten. However, Rounsaville (1978) found that the availability of outside resources did not discriminate between victims who stayed or left an abusive relationship. He found, as did Gelles, that the severity and frequency of abuse were the best predictors of a battered woman's decision to stay or leave.

At the microsystem (family) level, several writers have suggested that the relationship between batterer and victim is characterized by unmet dependency needs. Each attempt to fulfill the other's unrealistic needs creates conflict that can lead to violence. To avoid such conflict and violence, the woman begins to organize her life around her husband, cutting herself off from outside support, and thus becomes trapped in the relationship.

At the ontogenetic (individual) level, the impact of parental role models has been clearly established. As with assaultive males, women who are victims of wife battering are more likely to have witnessed domestic violence as a child. Children who witness family violence not only learn specific aggressive behaviors, but are also more likely to believe that violence is a legitimate way to solve personal problems.

The theory of learned helplessness (Seligman, 1975) has also been suggested as an explanation for the tendency of battered wives to remain in their relationships. It proposes that when a woman believes she has no control over an unpleasant environment, she will lose all motivation to change her situation. However, this theory is contradicted by Campbell's 1987 study, which found that women who accepted the unchangeability of the relationship (regardless of who they blamed) were more likely to, for example, leave the relationship or seek an abuse injunction.

The theory of traumatic bonding (Dutton & Painter, 1981) links the tenacity and loyalty of assaulted women to special features within the abusive relationship rather than to inferred aspects of the woman's own personality or to her socioeconomic situation. This theory suggests that traumatic bonding occurs in situations of power imbalance and intermittent abuse. The maltreated woman perceives herself to be subjugated or dominated by her husband and becomes the recipient of a cycle of positive and negative behaviors over which she has little or no control. As a result, a strong emotional dependence is created that makes long-lasting separation difficult.

Why do battered women who have left their situation often return to their husbands? Economic approaches consider such factors as low salary, poor employment opportunities, and/or dependents. Psychological approaches focus on a woman's subjective perception of her life alternatives. Unfortunately, conclusive comparative studies of these two approaches have not yet been implemented. For now, it can be tentatively concluded that battered women are more likely to remain separated from their husbands if they are economically independent and if the relationship has been of short duration.

It is clear that battered women will only receive adequate care and attention if medical, social service, and criminal justice professionals understand the victimology of assault and relinquish stereotyped explanations for the victim's postassaultive behavior. The role of the criminal justice system in dealing with wife assault will be discussed in detail in Chapter 5.

ENDNOTE

1. Kalmuss (1984) reported an analysis of Straus et al.'s (1980) national survey data that demonstrated that witnessing father-mother violence increased the likelihood of daughters being both victims and perpetrators of violence in their own marriage (the same was true for sons). Kalmuss argues that intergenerational transmission of marital aggression is not sex-specific and questions the assumption that children would be more likely to model the same-sex parent. Kalmuss's analysis raises important questions about modelling effects. Why, for example, would some girls become victims and others become perpetrators of violence when both have witnessed father-mother violence? Observational influences may interact with other ontogenetically developed traits or habits to produce eventual behavioral outcomes of witnessing violence.

CHAPTER 5

The Criminal Justice Response to Wife Assault

The proper design of public policies requires a clear and sober understanding of the nature of man and, in particular, of the extent to which that nature can be changed by plan.
—J. Q. Wilson, *Thinking About Crime* (1983, p. 3)

Several results and conclusions from earlier chapters converge on the issues of police intervention in family violence. In Chapter 1 we learned that about 10.2% of women are assaulted by their husbands and about 6.8% are assaulted repeatedly (Schulman, 1979; Straus, Gelles, & Steinmetz, 1980). Of the women who are assaulted, about 14.5% call the police (Schulman, 1979; Straus & Gelles, 1985). Hence, about one in six assaults (using the Severe Abuse Index of the Straus *CTS* as the criterion) is reported to police. This report rate implies, first of all, that a limit is imposed on criminal justice effectiveness as a solution to wife assault. The criminal justice system cannot deal effectively with crimes that are both private and unreported.

As we shall see in Section 5.4, the single greatest impediment to a more effective criminal justice response to wife assault is the victim's failure to report the event to the police. If the assault is severe, and the victim is traumatized, then some of the psychological consequences of assault described in the last chapter may prevent the victim from taking effective self-protective actions. As we shall see in this chapter, however, many victims of wife assault do not define the event as a crime and may fail to report it to the police because of this non-criminal definition. Nevertheless, the one-in-six report statistic also suggests that, more often than any other outside agency, the police will come into contact with the greatest number of wife assaults, perhaps 14.5% of all committed assaults. If the state is to generate policy for diminishing the incidence of wife assault, such policy will need to focus on police procedure for intervention.

As a society we tend to dismiss the seriousness of violence between intimates. Shotland and Straw (1976) found that third-party perceptions about the seriousness of violence and the utility of intervention were strongly reduced by the knowledge that the violence occurred between intimates. Since the police share many of the perceptions and attitudes of the socializing culture (Rokeach, Miller, & Snyder, 1971; Dutton, 1986b), these perceptual issues may affect their choice of action in *clearing* domestic disturbance calls (i.e., disposing of the call through arrest or mediation or getting one party to temporarily leave [see Ford, 1987]). In this chapter, we will examine how police make such decisions.

We learned in Chapter 4 that when the situational determinants of a victim remaining with her abusive husband are unclear, third-party observers make victim-blaming attributions that may preclude their taking action to help her. We learned also from Chapter 4 that the immediate postassault trauma of victims might make them depressed, upset, confused, and uncertain about the efficacy of criminal justice action.

When we add to this the uncertainty that police feel when intervening in family matters, we begin to perceive the complexity of domestic dispute intervention from the police perspective. Police are charged with the responsibility of determining the best strategy (i.e., arrest, leave, mediate, etc.) for domestic disputes where assault may or may not have occurred, where the conflict might appear to have subsided, and where the victim may seem uninterested or opposed to charging her husband. Furthermore, the informal working knowledge of police may suggest that assaulted women inevitably fail to come to court, so that charging the male is believed by the police officer to be futile. Finally, since a real and unpredictable danger exists for the police officer in a small minority of domestic disputes, all these decisions have to be made with a certain amount of danger and anxiety present.

5.1 THE POLICE AND WIFE ASSAULT: EARLY STUDIES

Seminal psychological contributions to police intervention in family conflict were designed to improve the decision-making and communication abilities of police. Bard developed an experimental program with the New York Police Department in 1967 that was designed to diminish *iatrogenic violence,* that is, violence accidentally triggered by the police (mis)handling the conflict (Bard, 1971; Bard, Zacker, & Rutter, 1972). Bard held the pioneering view that police officers served a preventive function in that they could reduce the likelihood of future crime by proper handling of family conflict. His system trained officers how to use arbitration, mediation, and negotiation to manage crisis situations. The trained officers were then assigned to a high-crime precinct in the Harlem area of New York City and responded to all the domestic disturbance calls within it.

Bard established an ongoing case discussion system between the officers and psychologists for the duration of the two-year program. At the conclusion of the program, the project managers claimed that the training had produced decreases in injuries to officers and a reduction in the incidence of domestic disturbances (presumably by diminishing repeat calls). However, these claims have been disputed by others.

Liebman and Schwartz (1973) argued that Bard's data indicated a higher percentage of repeat calls than in a control district. Furthermore, family homicides and assaults increased in the experimental district and decreased in the control district. The highly publicized claim that injuries decreased for trained officers was based on no injuries to officers in the experimental district and one injury in the control district. The controversy over the Bard project highlighted the early issues that surrounded police intervention in domestic disturbances: Could such interventions be carried out so that the police would be safer and could the police decision about how to "clear" the disturbance call reduce future repeat calls?

5.1.1 Stereotypes in the Perception of Wife Assault

The furor over Bard's statistics obscured a second important outcome of Bard's project: the project furnished a huge data base on the characteristics of domestic disputes from the police perspective. A select group of 18 officers operating in biracial pairs reported the characteristics of 1,388 domestic disturbance calls in Harlem (Bard & Zacker, 1974). On these calls, an assault was alleged 36% of the time by the victim and confirmed by police judgment in 29% of cases. The most commonly reported immediate cause of conflict was infidelity. The police reported the use of physical force by citizens or by themselves in only 1% of 1,388 disputes studied. The alleged assailants appeared to have been drinking in 30% of the cases, but in only 4.3% were they judged by police to have been drunk. The police perceived alcohol to be primary in the origin of the dispute in only 14% of cases.

In order to generalize these findings, a second study was done in Norwalk, Connecticut, in 1972 (Zacker & Bard, 1977). Norwalk, in contrast to Harlem, is a white middle-class community considered to be socioeconomically representative of a large number of cities and townships in the United States. In 1972, from 4 PM to midnight, Norwalk (population in 1972 of 79,113) recorded 2,298 disturbance calls, or 6.3 per night. The data base for the study consisted of police self-reports for 344 disputes. Although 246 of these were for people in long-term relationships and 148 were for relatives, a specific category for husband-wife disputes was not reported.

Zacker and Bard (1977) reported that assaults occurred in one-third of these 344 disputes (44% of all disputes between relatives, 25% between nonrelatives) and were more likely between family members. Family disputes in Norwalk were more likely to be assaultive than family disputes in Harlem (44% vs. 30%). Again, alcohol was used by one or the other disputant 34.4% of the time and the attending officers reported that it was unrelated to whether or not an assault had occurred. Interestingly, Zacker and Bard noted that the Norwalk police had trouble believing this finding about alcohol and assault, even though it was based on their own data. Since Zacker and Bard did not report what percentage of disputes attended resulted in reports being filled out by police, there is no way to know if their sample suffers from selective attrition in police reporting.

This caveat notwithstanding, the work of Bard and Zacker provided some interesting systematic data on domestic disturbance at the police level: that assaultiveness was higher in a middle-class white area than it was in a working-class black area—a contradiction of the stereotyping of family disturbance. Also, the durability of police working knowledge (e.g., that alcohol causes most domestic disturbances)—in the face of contradictory evidence that they themselves collected—suggests that mere reporting of the facts in police training will not persuade police when those facts contradict the dogma of police ideology (Dutton, 1986b).

5.1.2 Can Police Prevent Repeat Family Violence?

A second prominent study of police response to domestic disputes was conducted for the Police Foundation in 1977 by Marie Wilt (in Detroit) and Ron Breedlove (in Kansas City). This study began by analyzing the arrest records of homicide and assault participants for the years 1970 and 1971. The characteristics of the homicides, aggravated assaults, and the participants were analyzed based on interviews by police and project personnel and on Distur- bance Profile Cards filled out by officers responding to domestic disturbances. In addition, the number of police responses to the address of participants in a homicide and/or assault for the two years prior to the arrest were recorded. Data from the Disturbance Profile Cards indicated that the best predictors of homicide/assault were the presence of a gun in the household, a history of prior disturbances, and the presence of alcohol. Unfortunately, the police return rate for these cards was only 5%, making the generalizability of these findings ques- tionable. Analysis of the data for prior police response indicated that 90% of the homicide and 85% of the aggravated assault participants had at least one prior police response to their address and 50% of both homicide and aggravated assault participants had five or more police responses.

The Wilt and Breedlove study was cited as indicating the potential of police preventing domestic disturbance calls, since the possibility of avoiding the subse- quent violent crime might have been realized if the police had acted more ef- fectively on the prior calls. However, as we shall see below, what is considered to be more effective is debatable.

Also, the Wilt and Breedlove study was retrospective in nature, working back from a crime-identified sample. Hence, it does not tell us what percentage of police responses to domestic calls do not result in repeat violence. We are, in effect, looking only at the interventions that subsequently had an undesirable outcome. In determining police policy, prospective studies that examine long-term effects of police practice are required to establish the incidence of desirable/undesirable outcomes as a function of the mode of intervention.

5.1.3 Policy Changes and Training

An examination of the impact of policy on the actual practice of responding to domestic disturbance calls was made by Levens and Dutton (1980). Baseline measures of police practices were obtained by researchers who analyzed 174 hours of taped calls from citizens to police to determine categories for these calls. Figure 5.1 demonstrates these categories and the percentages of calls falling into each category.

Police officers were requested to fill out research reports on each family dispute they attended. Police time and contact records were examined for all relevant police activity, and field observations were made of a subset of dispute interventions. Baseline data were collected for a six-month period (January–June, 1975). At the end of this period, the chief of police announced a more aggressive policy of intervention for family disputes, including intensive training for recruits, in-service training for veteran officers, and training of dispatch communications personnel. Follow-up data were collected in July–August, 1976, at which point 40% of the street force had received training.

Baseline measures indicated that 17.5% of all calls to police were for family disputes and 13.5% were specifically for husband-wife disputes. These calls generally increased in frequency toward the end of the week and were greatest from 7 P.M to 1 A.M.

Analysis of police dispatch records yielded a subsample of 283 domestic disputes (i.e., involving family, neighbor, landlord, or tenant) and 96 husband-wife disturbances for which police presence was requested. Surprisingly, police attended only 47.9% of these calls. Callers who did not receive police service were told their problem was not a police matter or were given quasilegal advice. Police dispatch probability was analyzed by type of information given by the caller. Mention of weapons increased the dispatch probability to .78, mention of violence to .61, mention of alcohol to .59. Dispatch probabilities were unaffected by time of day or availability of officers.

Levens and Dutton concluded that the low-dispatch probabilities reflected a negative attitude held by police toward domestic dispute intervention. Data on 117 domestic dispute requests taken in 1976 after the policy change showed a substantial increase in police willingness to respond, with a dispatch probability of 78.6%, significantly higher than the 47.9% obtained in the 1975 measure.

FIGURE 5.1 Telephone requests for police assistance and breakdown of dispatches into service and law enforcement

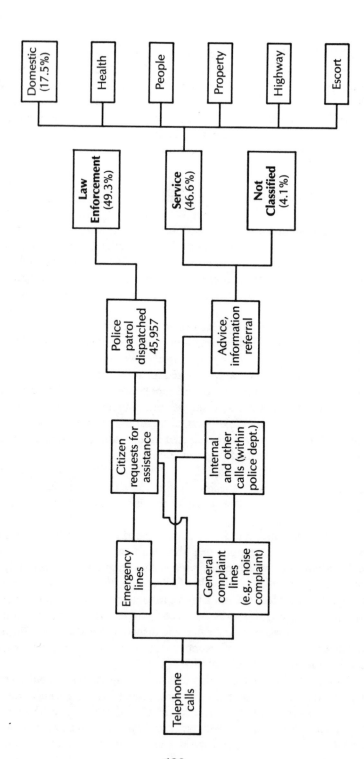

Source: Levens and Dutton (1980)

Apparently, the policy change had an effect on the likelihood of dispatching cars.

In order to ascertain whether the effects of training and policy change influenced the police handling of the calls, observational and self-report measures of what police did when they attended the call were combined (Dutton, 1981a; Dutton & Levens, 1977). Training significantly increased the use of mediation and referral techniques and made police less likely to remove one party for the evening. There were no differences in arrest rates (which were around 6% of all calls attended) between trained and untrained police. The use of arrest as a strategy of choice for police handling of husband-wife disputes has been a topic of some controversy. More recent research on the police and domestic disturbances has focused on the decision criteria that determine whether or not the police will arrest an alleged assaultive husband.

5.2 POLICE DECISIONS TO ARREST FOR WIFE ASSAULT

Is there a prima facie case for police arrest on domestic disturbance calls? We know from the Bard and Zacker (1974) study that police witness assaults at 29% to 33% of the domestic disturbances they attend. Furthermore, the victims of these assaults are disproportionately (95%) women (Berk et al., 1981). The women victims are injured in 36% of all domestic disturbances attended by police and require medical attention 17% of the time (Jaffe & Burris, 1982). Clearly, then, domestic disturbance calls do present a category of calls for police service with a high violence potential. We also know from the Schulman (1979) and Straus, Gelles, and Steinmetz (1980) surveys that the likelihood of repeat violence is high (66% without police intervention). Furthermore, in a study that we will review below, Sherman and Berk (1984) found that recidivist assault within six months has a 28% to 37% likelihood when police attend and do not make an arrest.

Combining these findings, a case can be made for police arrest for putative wife assault. If one objective of the criminal justice system is to prevent recurrent violence, the means of handling husband-wife disputes is important, because such disputes constitute a source of considerable repeat violence. This being the case, it is instructive to examine studies that have attempted to determine how police decide whether or not to arrest on domestic disturbance calls.

Essentially, three types of methodology have been used to examine such decisions. The first has involved having police specify how they would respond to hypothetical scenarios. A second has been to reconstruct arrest decisions from information on police reports. The third has been to examine police behavior under real intervention conditions.

5.2.1 Hypothetical Scenarios _____

Loving and Farmer (1980) used the first method, giving questionnaires to 130 police officers of assorted ranks from 16 police agencies. Police responded that they would make an arrest in domestic violence situations if a crime had been committed or if the likelihood of recurring violence was high. In rating the importance of factors influencing their decision to arrest, they mentioned the following in decreasing order of importance: commission of a felony, serious injury to the victim, use of a weapon, use of violence against the police, likelihood of future violence, previous legal action against the assailant, previous injury to victim or damage to property, and an alcohol- or drug-intoxicated assailant. Factors that would lead police to refrain from making an arrest—in decreasing order of importance—were a refusal by the victim to press charges, the victim's tendency to drop charges, and lack of serious injury. Of course, as Loving and Farmer point out, there is no way of knowing, on the basis of this study, whether these factors would be given similar weight under actual intervention conditions. The risk of officers providing what they perceive to be socially desirable responses pervades studies of this sort (see, for example, Rosenthal, 1969).

Waaland and Keeley (1985) devised simulated police reports (71 descriptions of cases) containing seven informational cues: the man's occupational status, history of wife assault, assailant's behavior toward the officers, extent of the victim's injuries, drinking by the assailant, drinking by the victim, and verbal antagonism of the assailant by the victim. With the exception of occupational status, three levels of each cue were presented in 56 unique combinations (order of information was randomized with a few restrictions). Twenty-six patrol officers in Oregon were asked to make judgments of both the husband's and wife's responsibility for the incident and to assign one of four possible legal outcomes for the offender.

Waaland and Keeley found that officers believed an abusive husband to be more responsible than his wife, but the judgment of this responsibility varied widely among officers. Victim antagonism and victim drinking influenced police judgments of responsibility, but judgments of responsibility did not influence police decisions to arrest. Decisions to arrest were most strongly influenced by victim injuries (which accounted for 85% of the variance in composite arrest decisions). The assailant's behavior toward investigating officers and his assaultive history made smaller but significant contributions to arrest decisions.

Waaland and Keeley considered the social desirability issue in their study, noting that officers report basing their intervention decisions primarily on legal information (i.e., extent of victim injuries). Not coincidentally, the state of Oregon had adopted legal standards for domestic intervention at the time data were collected. These new legal standards may have influenced officers to appear to be going by the book. Interestingly, despite the high probability of social desirability influences, very low arrest rates were obtained in this study. Although

36% of the victims were depicted as severely injured, half the officers did not prescribe arrest under these conditions. Multiple bruises and blackened eyes were not considered sufficient causes for legal action, although such evidence explicitly defines unlawful assault under Oregon law.

Not all studies that use a hypothetical example seem to suffer from socially desirable responding. Ford (1987) provided such a hypothetical example to 439 law enforcement officers in Indiana and correlated their self-reported likelihood of arrest to a variety of attitudes and stereotypes about victims of wife assault. Ford's hypothetical example contained sufficient grounds to establish probable cause (in the opinion of judges, prosecutors, and defense attorneys). Only 20% of officers, however, indicated a greater than 50/50 chance that they would arrest under these circumstances. Since the state policy mandated arrest where reasonable and probable grounds existed, this 20% rate certainly does not represent police providing a researcher with the procedurally correct answer. Factors that contributed most heavily to the police disinclination to arrest were police perceptions that the couple was in a continuing relationship and that the woman had not made a serious effort to leave (and their belief that she should take action on her own to leave). In weighing the conflicting stories given by the hypothetical man and woman at the scene, the notion that "if things were as bad as she says, why doesn't she leave?" influenced police perceptions of whether probable cause existed. Police who were most likely to report they would arrest tended to do so because of the perception that the violence would recur.

5.2.2 Observational Studies

The obvious method to circumvent the social desirability issues raised by hypothetical studies is direct or indirect observation of actual police practice. Indirect observation means the examination of police records and the reconstruction of their arrest decision through multivariate analysis of the information provided on the records.

Berk and Loseke (1980) used this method to examine 262 official police reports on domestic disturbance interventions and generated a multiple regression model to predict whether police would arrest or not in these reported cases. The variable that had the greatest weight in predicting whether or not the police would arrest was the victim's willingness to sign a citizen's arrest warrant. The next most powerful predictors were (1) alcohol use or intoxication by the male and (2) allegations of violence by the victim. Neither injuries to the victim nor property damage had any significant effect on arrests. In addition, when the victim was the person who called the police, arrest rates dropped. Berk and Loseke do point out that the injuries variable approached significance ($p = .08$) and that a more sensitive measure of severity of victim injuries may have produced a significant result. They concluded that police intervention decisions do not appear to center on the collection of evidence for proof of legal violations, but rather are the outgrowth of a subjective theory that the officer forms about the causes of the domestic dispute.

To a certain extent, this subjective theory begins to develop before the officer arrives at the scene. It is fueled by personal beliefs about male-female violence and by the dispatcher's descriptions of the current situation. Berk and Loseke suggest that when the police arrive they begin to look for signs that verify their theory of what caused the conflict. The researchers propose, as have others (Dutton, 1981a; Bennett-Sandler, 1975), that police intervention decisions are not pure products of legal requirements or departmental policy, but rather are the result of an admixture of personal attitudes and informal occupational norms that combine with more formalized policy. Hence, altering police intervention practice would require not only specific policy directives but changes in recruitment and training that have attitudinal objectives and are buttressed by support from prosecutors and judges (Dutton, 1986b).

Direct observational methods on the whole tend to support these conclusions. Furthermore, they avoid a weakness in the indirect observational technique. Police reports that provide the data base for such techniques may be after-the-fact reconstructions of incidents intended by the police officer to justify actions that he or she has already taken, rather than accounts of what actually occurred in the encounter.

An early field observation of police intervention was conducted by Black (1979) on data collected in 1966. Field observations of 108 domestic dispute interventions involving married couples revealed that, although 65 cases involved violence, only 13 arrests were made. Black reported that police acted more coercively with black and working-class couples and in a more conciliatory fashion with white middle-class couples. However, his data may not represent contemporary police practice.

Worden and Pollitz (1984) examined direct reports of trained observers who witnessed 167 domestic disturbances in 24 different police departments as part of a Police Services Study conducted at Indiana University. Worden and Pollitz corroborated results from Berk and Loseke's indirect study. Both studies found that probability of police arrest increased substantially with the woman victim's promise to sign a warrant, with the male's appearance of having been drinking, and with the woman's allegations of violence. Both studies also found that arrest did not increase if one disputant had been injured. Worden and Pollitz also confirmed the findings that disrespectful behavior toward the police increases the likelihood of arrest. Observers coded citizens' behavior into categories such as apologetic, sarcastic, disrespectful, and hostile. The disrespectful category increased the probability of arrest by .43.

Worden and Pollitz also attempted to relate police attitudes to their arrest decisions. They divided police into crime fighter and problem solver categories on the basis of their agreement or disagreement with the item "police should not have to handle calls that involve social or personal problems where no crime is involved." Agreement with this item had little effect on arrest decisions, since arrest was infrequent in any case.

Smith and Klein (1984) asked trained civilians to ride on 900 patrol shifts and observe 5,688 police-citizen encounters in 24 metropolitan U.S. areas. Of these, 433 involved an interpersonal dispute where the dispute was in progress when the police arrived. For methodological reasons, 100 of these cases were omitted, leaving a data base of 333. It should be pointed out that these were not all husband-wife or even male-female disputes. For these 333 cases, arrests were made by police 15.3% of the time. The main determinants of arrest in this study were (1) the complainant's statement that they wanted an arrest, (2) the demeanour of the offender, (3) whether the offender had been drinking, and (4) the socioeconomic status (SES) of the area where the house was located. The arrest rates by SES were as follows: high status: 5.5%, middle status: 1.9%, low status: 21.2%.

Among factors that had no effect on the decision to arrest were (1) the race of the parties involved, (2) whether or not one party was injured, and (3) whether weapons were involved. Arrest was less likely in domestic disputes compared to nondomestic disputes, but the difference was not significant. The authors concluded that the police appeared reluctant to arrest in both domestic and nondomestic disputes.

Hence, both hypothetical situation studies and direct observational studies of police decision making in domestic disturbances come to the same conclusion: that subjective and irrelevant factors play too great a role in the police decision to arrest or not to arrest. By irrelevant we mean factors that are unrelated to preventing future crime. Ford's (1987) finding that police hold stereotypes about victims of wife assault is one example. Others include the apparent lack of weight given to a victim's injuries by police, and the indifference toward ascertaining whether the assault is an isolated incident or part of a continuing series of violent incidents. If habitual assault is occurring, the likelihood increases of future violence, victim injury, and repeat demands on police service. From a decision-making perspective, information about these factors seems essential. On the other hand, the man's demeanor toward the police is relatively irrelevant to recidivism and is probably given too much weight by police. The police decision about arrest versus other alternatives initiates a chain of criminal justice policy decisions about wife assaulters. The objective of arrest decisions is to prevent wife assault from recurring. How might this objective best be achieved? What constellation of decisions by police, prosecutors, and judges might operate to reduce recidivist assault? To these questions we now begin to formulate an answer by discovering what is commonly done in cases of wife assault. We will begin by reviewing available empirical studies that bear on the criminal justice response to wife assault.

5.3 THE OBJECTIVE PROBABILITY
OF BEING DETECTED AND PUNISHED

5.3.1 The Probability of Wife Assault
Being Reported to Police

First let us consider the probability of detection, given that wife assault has occurred. We will refer to this as p (detection of event). That is, given that an event of wife assault occurs, what is the probability that it will be detected by the criminal justice system? Recall from Section 1.1 the telephone victim survey conducted by Schulman (1979) using the *Conflict Tactics Scale*. In this survey, Schulman found that only 17% of severe violence categories on the *CTS* (N-R) or assault events were reported to the police (9% of the K-R events were reported). While the Schulman survey had the advantage of utilizing a fairly precise measure of the abusive action (the *CTS*), the data base was not large (consisting of 332 incidents of severe violence occurring to 156 women). Furthermore, since all the data were collected in Kentucky, report rates to police may have been idiosyncratic to that specific jurisdiction.

However, the recent national survey by Straus and Gelles (1985) of 6,002 households avoided such regionalism. In this survey, Straus found that the police were called for only 4.9% of 553 violent incidents (items K-R on the *CTS*) and for 10% of 147 severe violence incidents (N-R). Hence, Schulman and Straus and Gelles found that only 17% and 10%, respectively, of severe violence items were reported to police. These items are commensurate with de facto police criteria (e.g., kicking, hitting with fist, or worse) for arrest for assault. For the purpose of calculating the objective probability of wife assault being detected by police, we shall use a weighted mean of the Schulman and Straus and Gelles samples (weighted on the basis of their severe assault data bases of 332 and 147, respectively). The resulting rate of reporting to police was 14.5%.

5.3.2 Probability of Police Attendance

However, police response is not always forthcoming for all reported events. In the Levens and Dutton (1980) study reported above, 47.9% of all husband-wife dispute calls were being attended. This finding was quite surprising given the violence potential of such calls. The Bard and Zacker (1974) study, cited above, discovered that assaults occurred in 29% of 1,388 family disputes attended in Harlem and 33% of 2,298 disputes in Norwalk, Connecticut. The Levens and Dutton finding, however, was consistent with a variety of other studies

Note: Portions of Section 5.3 are reprinted from Donald G. Dutton, The criminal justice response to wife assault, *Law and Human Behavior,* 1987, 11(3). By permission of Plenum Publishing Co.

(e.g., Parnas, 1972; Fields & Fields, 1973; Jaffe & Burris, 1982) indicating an indifferent police response to wife assault.

In a variety of Canadian provinces and U.S. states, the police response to wife assault has become more aggressive as a result of pressure from women's groups and lawsuits (see, for example, Bard, 1978; Lerman, 1981). Levens and Dutton (1980) found that the attendance rate by the police force for domestic disturbances was 78.6% —after training and policy changes were instituted. Unless a police department has an explicit policy of attending every dispute call and computerized monitoring of all calls and dispatches, detection will be compromised. The p (detection/event) will be determined by the report rate multiplied by the attendance rate. For example, if we accept a report rate of 14.5% (based on the Schulman and Straus & Gelles surveys) and apply the Levens and Dutton (1980) attendance rate of 78.6% (for 1976), the resulting p (detection/event) is (14.5% × 78.6%), or 11.5%. While this involves combining data from different jurisdictions (and we have no way of knowing how representative these jurisdictions are), those data sources represent an estimate using the best empirical studies available on the victim's likelihood of reporting and the police's likelihood of attending.

5.3.3 Probability of Police Report

One could argue that p (reporting) × p (attending) do not yet constitute detection, which requires that an event be formally registered in a system. For the criminal justice system, this registration takes the form of a police report. If police view a family dispute as not serious and feel overworked with report writing, the likelihood of that event being recorded will be low. Only through reconstructing calls for service, police dispatches, and subsequent reports would it be possible to determine whether police attended but failed to write a report.

Levens and Dutton (1980) performed this type of analysis and concluded that police wrote reports on 16.5% of the family dispute calls they attended. Given Bard and Zacker's (1974) finding that assaults occurred in 29% to 33% of family dispute calls attended by police, this suggests a further failure to officially detect an event because the police overlook the assault or consider it unworthy of a report. The effect on p (detection/event) is to further lower p (detection) by a factor of (16.5/31), which represents the percentage of events reported over an estimate of the total number of attendances where an event occurred. Hence, p (detection/event) equals the p (reporting) × p (police attending) × p (report being issued) or 6.1% (14.6 × 78.6 × 16.5/31).

It could be argued that a police report is not necessary for subsequent criminal justice action to occur. Police have frequently advised women to initiate legal proceedings on their own by laying a charge with a prosecutor or justice of the peace (Field, 1978). However, the likelihood of self-initiated charges proceeding is extremely slight. Fields and Fields (1973) examined 7,500 requests for prosecutors to issue warrants for wife assault in Washington, D.C. Less than 200 were issued. Parnas (1973) found that of 5,057 self-initiated requests for warrants, only 323 were issued. Some studies (Hogarth, 1980) also revealed a Catch-22 for putative complainants: no proceedings would be initiated as a matter of policy by justices of the peace without a police report. The Fields and Fields and Parnas studies suggest a p (warrant/request) of only .04. If we assumed that every woman who called the police when assaulted by her husband and who did not receive assistance in the form of police attendance and a formal report continued on her own to initiate proceedings, detection (in the form of a formal warrant) would still be only marginally improved (1.1 of all reported events). Hence, if we combined police-initiated and self-initiated formal reports, p (detection/event) would be 6.5%.

The relevance of this 6.5% figure is that it gives us a rough indication of the percentage of wife assaults that are publicly recorded by the police. In other words, in 92.8% of assaults against wives, the assault remains a private event—with respect to the criminal justice system. No punishment will occur via the state. We turn our attention now to the next step in the criminal justice system.

5.3.4 Arrest for Wife Assault

P (arrest/detection) refers to the action taken by police when attending family dispute calls. Again, the evidence shows a winnowing process whereby most attended calls do not result in arrest. Arrest rates vary in the observational studies done on police.[1] Black (1979) estimated an arrest rate of 26% for assaults between husbands and wives; Meyer and Lorimer (1979) estimated a 5% rate in a study in Colorado; Emerson (1979) produced a 6% estimate in Los Angeles. Levens and Dutton (1980) found that police arrested in only 6% of all family disturbance calls where they attended. Worden and Pollitz (1984) found an average arrest rate of 10% in 24 U.S. cities. A combined weighted estimate of the arrest rate in these studies is 7.3%.

Of course, not all domestic disturbances result in assaults. Two ways of estimating whether prima facie evidence exists for an assault are (1) by estimating the percent of victims injured in domestic altercations (although accidents may happen, the accidental nature of the injury is probably best decided by the court) or (2) by direct observation. Bard and Zacker (1974) used direct observation to estimate an assault rate of 29% (of 1,388 domestic disturbances in Harlem). Zacker and Bard (1977) estimated 33% in Norwalk.

Jaffe and Burris (1982) found a 3% police arrest rate, despite 36% of women being injured and 17% of the victims requiring medical attention as a result of the altercation. Berk, Berk, Loseke, and Rauma (1983), in a study of 262 husband/wife domestic disturbances to which the police were called, found that the woman was injured in 39% of the calls (the man was injured in 3%, both parties in 4%).

Based on these studies, prima facie evidence for wife assault occurs in about 34.5% of domestic disputes attended by police. Given the arrest rate of 7.3% based on the cumulative studies reported above, a discrepancy exists between the percentage of cases where prima facie evidence for arrest exists, and arrests are made. The probability of an arrest being made — given that police detected prima facie evidence for arrest — is 21.2%. Since we estimated the probability of detection to be 6.5%, the probability of arrest would be 1.4% (see Figure 5.2).

The Effects of Arrest

Jaffe, Wolfe, Telford, and Austin (1986) examined police records and conducted interviews with wives of men arrested for wife assault. Their interviews included CTS assessments of the men's use of violence for a one-year period prior to and following arrest. When police charged a man for wife assault, significant decreases in postcharge violence occurred, whether measured by the number of new contacts the man had with police in the ensuing year, or by his wife's report (using the CTS) of his use of violence. Specific violent acts against wives were reduced by two-thirds for the year following arrest, compared to the year preceding arrest. Unfortunately, Jaffe et al. did not specify the exact nature of contacts with police, so we do not know whether re-arrest occurred.

Sherman and Berk (1984) provided some evidence that recidivism may be reduced for men who are arrested. They assigned 314 cases of misdemeanor wife assault attended by the Minneapolis police to randomly assigned treatments of arrest, separation, or mediation. The recidivism rate of arrested men was significantly lower (13% repeated assault on police reports, 19% repeated assault

FIGURE 5.2 Conditional probabilities at each step of the criminal justice process

p (detection/event)	= 6.5%		
↓			
p (arrest/detection)	= 21.2%	p (arrest/event)	= 1.4%
↓		↓	
p (conviction/arrest)	= 53%	p (conviction/event)	= 0.8%
↓		↓	
p (punishment/conviction)	= 52%	p (punishment/event)	= 0.4%

Source: Dutton (1987b)

based on interviews with wives) than men who received other resolution treatments for a six-month period following the event. Corresponding recidivism rates for separation and mediation were 26% (28%) and 18% (37%) as reported by police and wives, respectively.[2] Sherman and Berk did not report whether the trial had completed or was pending for the arrested men during this period, how many couples had separated, or whether the assaultive males knew their wives were being interviewed every two weeks by social scientists.

What makes the Sherman and Berk evidence impressive (apart from the randomized design) is that the reduced recidivism rate (if we accept that it was not produced by these unreported factors) seems to have largely been produced with repeat offenders. Eighty percent of the victims in their study had been previously assaulted at least once by the suspect in the prior six months. This result suggests that for the 6.7% of all men estimated to be repeat offenders without police intervention (Schulman, 1979; Straus et al., 1980), a possibility of recidivism reduction exists (at least for a six-month period) in that only 19% will again assault their wives if arrest occurs. Hence, only 1.27% (6.7 × .19) of all men appear to be incorrigible wife assaulters who repeatedly assault their wives, even after arrest (see Figure 5.3).

5.3.5 Conviction for Wife Assault

Given that an arrest is made, will the case wind up in court? Schulman (1979) reported that 17% of 322 severe assault cases were reported to police.

FIGURE 5.3   The victim survey data on recidivism

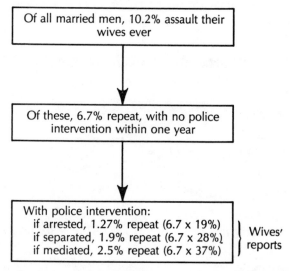

Sources: Schulman (1979), Straus et al. (1980), and Sherman and Berk (1984)

Of these 17% (56), police made an arrest in 41% of the cases. Hence, 7% (23) were arrested. Schulman reported that 6% (20) went to court. Lerman (1981) reported the data from the Seattle City Attorney's Office Project where 1,116 wife assault charges were filed between 1978 and 1980. All of these cases came before the court. Jaffe et al. (1986) reported that 667 wife assault charges were laid by the London, Ontario, police (or the victim) in the years 1979, 1981, and 1983. Of these, 630 came before the court. The conclusion from these three independent studies is that we can essentially treat p (court/arrest) as equal to 1.00.

Could these incorrigible repeat wife assaulters be made less likely to repeat wife assault by court punishment? Much has been written about the unwillingness of courts to convict for wife assault (Field, 1978; Parnas, 1973; Lerman, 1981). Parnas's (1973) study indicated that p (conviction/arrest) was practically zero in Chicago's Court of Domestic Relations. The most frequent disposition was summary dismissal for failure of the complainant to appear or dismissal at the complainant's request. When cases were heard, the most common disposition was a blank, fake peace bond. Neither party received a copy and the consequences for violation were not explained.

In recent years, court policy has changed in many jurisdictions and prosecutors have developed practices to maximize victim cooperation (Dutton, 1981a; Lerman, 1981). Empirical studies of court dispositions, however, have usually been performed in jurisdictions with exceptional awareness about wife assault. These jurisdictions have developed experimental programs that have included court-outcome studies as a component of evaluation.

For example, the Domestic Violence Unit in Westchester County, New York, over a one-year period (1979–1980), brought 355 cases before the court and obtained a 50% conviction rate (Lerman, 1981). The Battered Women's Project in the Seattle City Attorney's Office, over a two-year period (1978–1980), brought 1,116 cases before the court and obtained a 57% conviction rate (Lerman, 1981).[3] The Family Consultant service in London, Ontario, brought 67 cases before the court in a four-month period in 1981, obtaining a 52% conviction rate (Burris & Jaffe, 1983). Muller and Dutton (1982) examined 175 cases before a Vancouver, British Columbia, family court in 1982. In all, 35% were found guilty. As Tble 5.1 demonstrates, the combined estimate of p (conviction/arrest) for these four jurisdictions is .53.

However, conviction in many cases led merely to a discharge or probation. If we consider incarceration or fines as determining punishment and less punishing outcomes as probation, suspended sentences, and batterers' therapy, Seattle punished 57% of guilty offenders, London, Ontario, punished 40%, and Vancouver Family Court punished only 11.5%. (Family courts tend to be more lenient [Burris & Jaffe, 1983]). As Table 5.2 demonstrates, p (punishment/conviction) is thus only about .52 (a weighted mean based mainly on the Seattle data).

TABLE 5.1   The probability of conviction given arrest has occurred

Jurisdiction	Year	N	Guilty	p (conviction)
Westchester, NY	1979–80	355	178	.5
Seattle, WA	1978–80	1,116	636	.57
London, Ont.	1981	67	35	.52
Vancouver, B.C.	1982	175	64	.35
		1,713	910	

weighted overall p =   .53

Sources: Data from Lerman (1981), Jaffe and Burris (1982), Muller and Dutton (1982)

TABLE 5.2   The probability of punishment given conviction has occurred

Location	n guilty	n punishment	p
Seattle, WA	638	366	.57
London, Ont.	57	23	.40
Vancouver, B.C.	61	7	.11
	756	396	

weighted p =   .52

Sources: Data from Lerman (1981), Burris and Jaffe (1983), Muller and Dutton (1982)

If we accept these data as providing rough estimates of p (conviction/arrest) and p (punishment/conviction), respectively, and keeping in mind that p (arrest/event) is approximately 1.4%, it would follow that p (punishment/event) would be .53 × .52 × .014 = .004 (see Figure 5.2). For every 100 wife assaults, about 14 are reported, 6 are detected, 1.5 arrests are made, .75 men are convicted, and .37 men are punished with a jail sentence or a fine. However, since the conviction and punishment data are drawn mainly from the Seattle program, they may overrepresent p (punishment/arrest).

Furthermore, punishment is rarely severe; average sentences for first convictions typically involve probation with conditions attached (Lerman, 1981). This punishment rate of 0.5% is lower than the percentage of men who constitute incorrigible wife assaulters, suggesting that criminal justice policy to deal with this latter population might involve increased arrest rates, better identification of incorrigible offenders, and special sentencing for this group designed to reduce their recidivism.

If aggregate reduction in recidivism is the goal of policy, what happens in court is relatively unimportant compared to the police response. Courts are limited by police arrest rates, and as long as only 21.2% of cases where prima facie evidence for assault result in arrest, the courts will encounter a much smaller population of potential recidivists and have a correspondingly smaller impact on aggregate reduction of recidivist assault.

5.4   WIFE ASSAULT VERSUS OTHER CRIMES

Is it possible to determine whether the criminal justice response to wife assault is less aggressive than for other crimes? Certainly, at first glance, the studies we have just reviewed reveal a strong filtering effect where the majority of detected assaults do not result in arrest or conviction. Based on the observational studies of police intervention into domestic disputes, the finding that police arrest in only 24% of the cases where prima facie evidence for arrest exists suggests that the arrest option may be underutilized by police. This is especially noteworthy since some evidence now exists (Jaffe, Wolfe, Telford, & Austin, 1986; Sherman & Berk, 1984) that arrest decreases recidivist assault.

Comparison of the winnowing effect of the criminal justice system response to wife assault with other crimes is complicated by some methodological issues. Both the National Criminal Justice Survey and Canadian Urban Victimization Survey compared reporting rates to police for spouse assaults and other crimes (see Section 1.1). The NCJS found that the reporting rate was higher for spouse assault (54.8%) than for other assaults (44.9). Similarly, the CUVS found report rates for spouse assault to be 36%, while that for stranger assaults was 22%, for sexual assault 26%, and for robbery 44%. If we accept the caveat that much spouse assault may not be perceived by the victim as crime, the resulting reporting figures do not suggest an underreporting of spouse assault. As we have described above, both the NCJS and CUVS surveys were crime surveys and required the respondent to perceive an aggressive action by their spouse as criminal. Not all violent acts by a spouse are necessarily defined as crime by the victim.

In a U.S. national victim survey reported by Hood and Sparks (1970), the overall report rate for 121 crimes was 49%. The only strong result to appear from these data is that victims seem more willing to report crime in the United States than in Canada. The overwhelmingly most frequent reason for not reporting spouse assault given on the NCJS survey was that it was a private matter (70.9%); only 9% reported fear of reprisal. Obviously, the criminal justice system can do very little about unreported crimes. When crimes are reported, however, some interesting comparisons develop.

Hood and Sparks (1970) found that police responded to 77% of reported crimes, while Levens and Dutton (1980) found police responded to only 53.8% of family dispute calls where assault was a possibility. This difference of course may reflect merely a police tendency to respond after the fact rather than an underresponse to family violence. However, on 145 calls monitored by Levens and Dutton, where violence was reported as having already occurred, the police response rate was still only 61%. After a policy change, however, the attendance rate on domestic dispute calls increased to 78.6%.

Hood and Sparks (1970) found that police made arrests in 20% of the cases where they attended and decided that a crime had been committed. Our review of observational studies of police handling of family disputes concluded that police made arrests in 24% of cases where evidence of a crime (assault) existed to a third-party observer.

Hood and Sparks (1970) found that trials resulted in 42% of the arrested cases, while our review of three independent studies of arrests for wife assault concluded that virtually all of them came to trial. Hood and Sparks (1970) found that 52% of cases coming to trial wound up in convictions, while our review found that 53% of wife assault cases before the court resulted in convictions.

What can we conclude from this? First, the winnowing effect of the criminal justice system for wife assault cases does not appear to be appreciably different than for other crimes. Given that the event is reported, the police are about as likely to attend (78.6% vs. 77%), arrest (24% vs. 20%), and obtain a conviction (53% vs. 52%) for wife assault compared to other crimes. This is not to argue that the police response to wife assault is sufficient—to the contrary it is highly subjective and errs in a lenient direction—but merely to point out that available evidence suggests that police do not single out wife assault as less actionable. The well-known police dislike of handling domestic disturbances (Dutton, 1981c) does not appear to lead to their performing differently than in other crime situations.

The main impediment to a more comprehensive handling of wife assault by the criminal justice system is the tendency of victims to view the assault in noncriminal terms. When the assault is viewed as a crime by the victim (i.e., the assaults reported on the NCJS and CUVS surveys), criminal justice action is comparable to other crimes. However, when we examine the aftermath questions of surveys on family conflict rather than crime (Schulman, 1979; Straus, Gelles, & Steinmetz, 1980; Straus & Gelles, 1985), we see that the tendency to report potentially arrestable assaults is low: Schulman found a 17% report rate for severe aggression items on the *CTS* and Straus (personal communication, 1986) found a 10% report rate in his 1985 national survey (only 27/533 of severe aggression actions were reported to police).

5.5 RECIDIVISM REDUCTION

Looking at aggregate data on all assaulters, the largest contributor to the prevention of recidivist wife assault is some constellation of extralegal factors that prevents one-third of men who have assaulted their wives from repeating the act within a year. We can speculate that these factors might include feelings of guilt or remorse, as reported by some men in treatment for wife assault (Dutton, 1986b), but might also include the wife's reaction to the assault. Many men volunteer for treatment groups because their wives have threatened to leave if assault recurs (Dutton, 1986a).

The Sherman and Berk (1984) and Jaffe et al. (1986) studies reported above suggest that arrest per se reduced recidivism, although the population of assaultive males who come to the attention of the police is probably only about 14.5% of the entire population of wife assaulters (Schulman, 1979; Straus & Gelles, 1985). Nevertheless, from the perspective of social policy, the police are the outside agency that encounters the greatest number of assault offenders and victims. All further criminal justice contact, whether through courts, probation, or court-mandated treatment groups, reaches a much smaller population of putative recidivists than do the police. As we shall see in the next chapter, court-mandated treatment for wife assaulters appears to reduce recidivism (Dutton, 1987b). However, only half the men who appear in court are convicted and even fewer have mandatory treatment attached as a condition of their probation.

Thus, from the perspective of reducing recidivism, treatment groups show initial indications of success but reach a much smaller target population. If one wanted to reduce recidivism most effectively, the simplest means might be to increase arrest rates up to the level reported for prima facie evidence for assault in observational studies. The main argument against increased arrest rates has been the danger of flooding the courts, with consequent plea bargaining to lesser charges (Wilson, 1983). However, this would probably have little effect in cases of wife assault where, as we have seen, severe penalties are rare and probation is the most frequent outcome of conviction.

Fagan (1987) has argued that the central mechanism that precludes recidivism is an equalization of power in the male-female relationship. Citing data from his own study and from a study by Lee Bowker (1983), Fagan points out that fear of divorce and fear of relationship loss were mentioned more frequently as factors that enabled batterers to desist than was fear of legal sanction. Furthermore, Bowker's subjects (battered women) reported that social disclosure of the assaults worked as well as legal intervention in getting their husbands to stop their assaultive behavior.

Cessation, Fagan concludes, occurs when legal or extralegal factors diminish power imbalances[4] in the family and raise the costs of repeat assault for the husband. When wife assault is disclosed to informal groups or to police, a variety of psychosocial mechanisms are initiated:

1. The victim may discover that assault is more common than she formerly believed, and as a consequence, may stop blaming herself for the assault (see Section 4.8).

2. The husband may learn that others consider his assaultive behavior as illegal or unacceptable.

3. The husband may learn that his wife has the power to disclose his unacceptable behavior to others who can sanction or punish him.

Whether or not the husband fears re-arrest, these psychosocial factors may reduce recidivist assault. Clearly, studies (such as Sherman & Berk, 1984) that assume deterrence to be the operant mechanism when reduced recidivism occurs are overlooking the potential impact of these alternative psychosocial mechanisms. What is required to illuminate this issue are some longitudinal studies of the cognitive systems of victims and offenders before and after arrest and treatment.

5.6 DETERRENCE

Can the criminal justice system deter wife assault through more aggressive responding? *Deterrence* refers to the state's ability to diminish the incidence of a prohibited action through legal threats by making the cost of the action greater than any benefits that derive from the action (Andenaes, 1974; Blumstein, Cohen, & Nagin, 1978; Ehrlich, 1975; Zimring & Hawkins, 1973). While considerable disagreement exists in the literature about whether criminal justice deterrence of violent crime has or has not been demonstrated by crime incidence studies (National Research Council [U.S.], 1978; Wilson, 1983; Phillips & Hensley, 1984; Gibbs, 1985), some agreement exists as to the minimal conditions for criminal justice to serve as a deterrent. The efficacy of legal threat in deterring prohibited actions requires that the criminal justice system generate perceived certainty, severity, and swiftness of punishment (Wilson, 1983). Furthermore, where gains from the prohibited action are great (as in illegal drug sales) or where the action is impulsive and not reasoned, deterrent effects are unlikely (Wilson, 1983).

General deterrence refers to a state's ability to control or minimize the incidence of a prohibited act in a general population (e.g., the total number of wife assaults in a specific jurisdiction and time period). *Specific deterrence* refers to a state's ability to prevent or minimize recidivism in a population that has already committed at least one prohibited act. If states publicized new, more severe punishments for wife assault and large-sample victim surveys revealed a diminution in first-time offenders after the crackdown, then claims for a general deterrence effect of the crackdown could be made. If actual procedures for rendering swift and certain punishment demonstrated to first-time offenders that the state was treating their prohibited action more seriously than they expected, with an ensuing decrease in their rate of recidivism, specific deterrence could be claimed. Clearly, for general deterrence to occur, the probability of the assault being detected by the authorities must be high enough to generate the belief in the general population that ensuing punishment is highly probable.

5.7   SUBJECTIVE CONTRIBUTORS TO RECIDIVISM REDUCTION

As our review above demonstrates, detection of wife assault is a low probability in an objective sense. However, deterrence research for other crimes has begun to focus on subjective perceptions of likelihood of punishment (Gibbs, 1985; Williams & Hawkins, 1984), although no research of this sort has yet been reported with wife assaulters.

It is obviously difficult to ascertain the subjective perception of the wife assaulter with regards to the probability of his being punished. It is reasonable, based on the Schulman (1979) and Straus et al. (1980) surveys, to conclude that through some admixture of socialization and general deterrence, the majority of men (89.8%) do not assault their wives (see Figure 5.3). Furthermore, of the 10% of men who do assault their wives once, 33% to 37% (3.3% of all men) do not repeat within a year (Schulman, 1979; Straus et al., 1980). Since only 14.5% of women in the Schulman and Straus and Gelles samples who reported being assaulted called the police (Schulman, 1979), the 33% to 37% cessation rate is probably due to factors other than concern about punishment by the criminal justice system.

Guilt, remorse, shame, or related emotional reactions (see Martin, 1977; Walker, 1979a) produced by the assaultive event or the victim's threat to leave the relationship if assault recurs could account for the drop in recidivism. If this is so, we must also account for the failure of these mechanisms in the 6.7% of men who are repeatedly assaultive. We shall return to this consideration below. The possibility of desistance (Fagan, 1987) or reduced recidivism, in any event, would be restricted to this very small percentage of men who are repeat wife assaulters and who are most likely to come to the attention of the criminal justice system.

We do not know, at present, whether men arrested for wife assault do not repeat because of fear of re-arrest or whether the original arrest serves a didactic function of demonstrating to them that wife assault is unacceptable behavior. Data is required on the subjective perceptions of men arrested for wife assault, including their projections of the likelihood of re-arrest should they repeat assault and a determination of the extent of their self-punishing reaction to the assault. The impact of these data on eventual likelihood of repeat assault would be highly instructive.

A first step in this direction is represented by some data presented by Dutton and Strachan (1987b) who asked a sample of 27 men starting a treatment program for wife assault to estimate the likelihood and the severity of a variety of consequences if they were to reoffend. The resulting sanction weights (likelihood × severity) were compared to similar estimates made by nonviolent, violent (to their wives), and repeatedly violent men obtained in samples by Williams and Carmody (1987) and Kennedy and Dutton (1987). Men who had not been arrested for wife assault estimated extremely low probabilities of criminal justice intervention in a hypothetical future assault (e.g., 2.6 out 10 where 10 meant certain arrest). Similarly, the perceived severity of criminal justice intervention was slight. This result maintained regardless of whether the men had been violent or not, or whether they had been repeatedly violent. In contrast, the men in the Dutton and Strachan sample who had been to court an average of four months prior to filling out the questionnaire reported triple to quadruple the sanction weights of all other men. The experience of being arrested and convicted clearly had a strong impact on these men's perceptions of future sanctions. Curiously, not only the sanction weights of criminal justice system intervention were inflated but also the sanction weights of potential spousal actions such as divorce or separation if a future assault were to occur (See Table 5.3).

Carroll (1978) examined subjective judgments about crime opportunities by having offenders and nonoffenders make verbal judgments about whether or not they would commit a crime where each crime opportunity was described in terms of (1) the probability of success, (2) the money obtained if successful, (3) the probability of capture, and (4) the penalty if caught. Carroll found that subjects made "simple and perhaps unidimensional" analyses of these crime opportunities and exhibited strong individual preferences in their choice of a dimension on which they based their decision. Of course, the nature of the experimental task employed by Carroll lent itself especially to rational weighing of costs and gains.

Johnson and Tversky (1983) demonstrated that generating fear, anxiety, or worry produced increases in perception of risks related to that emotion or

TABLE 5.3 Sanction weights derived from arrest and nonarrest repeat offenders

| | Williams & Carmody | | Kennedy & Dutton | | Dutton & Strachan |
	nonviol.	repeat viol.	nonviol.	viol.	arrested
partner would retaliate	6.7	8.7	10.5	6.8	21.4
partner would call police	n.a.	n.a.	15.9	6.6	54.5
arrest	19.0	17.9	17.0	6.8	64.7
partner would divorce	29.6	25.3	30.4	19.1	52.2
social condemnation	47.7	34.0	46.2	33.6	40.5
lose self-respect	n.a.	n.a.	61.6	48.9	58.3
n =	1,533	93	344	44	27

affect. They related this finding to the availability bias (Kahneman & Tversky, 1973) that describes the inflated causal weight given to dramatic, but infrequent, events. Slovic, Fischoff, and Lichenstein (1982), for example, found that people overestimated the likelihood of causes of death that were dramatic and sensational (e.g., homicide, fire) and underestimated unspectacular events that are given less media attention (e.g., suicide, drowning). This developing literature in social cognition suggests that subjective factors in risk perception may have relevance in criminal justice settings where subjective risk may relate to deterrence.

Wilson (1983) has also raised an objection to an exclusively objective approach to evaluating the criminal justice system's capacity to deter, questioning the assumption made by such an analysis about a person's knowledge or estimate of being caught. Wilson describes how recidivist offenders frequently belong to a criminal subculture that has extensive informal knowledge of criminal justice system operation. They know, in effect, how to beat the system.

One could argue, however, that subjective estimates of the likelihood of punishment could also operate in the opposite direction. For example, a placebo effect of the criminal justice system could operate if objective probabilities of punishment were low but potential law breakers believed otherwise. As Wilson points out in his discussion of the Sherman and Berk (1984) study, short-term deterrence for the arrested husbands in that study may have occurred because a sudden, conspicuous change in police behavior acted as a salient cue for an aggressive criminal justice system response. Since few of the men in this group were subsequently punished with fine or incarceration, the police action of arrest, in and of itself, may have provided a salient signal for future system intervention.

Chambers (1979) provides data consistent with this position in an elaborate long-term study of factors that maximized the likelihood of divorced fathers making child support payments. By comparing a variety of counties in Wisconsin and Michigan with different collection practices and penalties for nonpayment, Chambers concluded that high jailing rates made little difference in collections, except when potential offenders believed they were likely to wind up in jail. That subjective belief appeared to arise from the conjunction of two factors: (1) jailing of others and (2) a collection agency integrated with enforcement that repeatedly warned men about the high likelihood of their own confinement if they missed payments. This combination seems to have signalled or cued men to an aggressive enforcement response. The warnings in the Chambers study, however, were notices of arrearage that specified legal steps that would be taken against the man if he did not comply. Could arrest per se serve the same kind of signal function for wife assaulters, even when incarceration for wife assault is rare?

Sherman and Berk (1984) reported that 31% of their sample of wife assaulters had prior arrests for crimes against persons (only 5% for wife assault). Unfortunately, they did not analyze for the impact of prior history on subsequent likelihood of recidivism. (Were the 19% of arrested males who again assaulted their wives males with the greatest prior contact with—and thus the least fear of—criminal justice intervention?). If we bear in mind that only 6.7% of men repeatedly assault their wives (Schulman, 1979; Straus et al., 1980), then clearly these recidivist assaulters should be the target of criminal justice intervention.

Sherman and Berk (1984) reported that in their sample of wife assaulters, 80% had assaulted their wives in the previous six months but only 5% had been arrested for it. Once arrested, however, only 19% repeated the assault in the next six months. Considering these aggregate data, arrest may function to signal increased state interventions above and beyond any objective probability of future detection, arrest, or punishment. Furthermore, arrest may serve a didactic function of indicating that the state considers wife assault to be a crime. Clearly, research is required that relates subjective estimates of punishment to likelihood of recidivism.

There are two methodological problems with the Sherman and Berk data that further weaken their claim for a direct effect of arrest on deterrence. They did not report for the sample of 161 women who participated in their follow-up interviews whether some had separated from their assailant after police intervention. Sherman and Berk claim that "we can think of no good reasons why differential underaccounting (of repeat violence by men in the arrest vs. the separation and mediation treatment groups) should materialize" (p. 269). Sherman and Berk base this argument on a failure to find differences among the three treatment conditions in the victim's willingness to be interviewed. They do not report, however, whether arrested men or their victims are differentially more likely to leave the relationship.

A second problem concerns whether or not the men know that their wives were reporting repeat violence every two weeks. If they were aware of this procedure, the combination of arrest and perceived surveillance could have served to produce a drop in recidivism that might not have occurred with arrest alone. Because these men had been arrested once and their wives were being interviewed every two weeks about repeat violence, they may have overestimated their chances of being arrested again (compared to men in the other treatment conditions). However, even if this alternative interpretation is correct, it suggests a method to decrease recidivism: arrest and set up intermittent monitoring of convicted men and their wives. Indeed, one may view the Sherman and Berk (1984) data as demonstrating a strong main effect for surveillance. Even separation (for the evening) and mediation conditions produced large drops in recidivism. Based on police records and wives' reports, only 26% (28%) of separated men and 18% (37%) of mediated men repeated assault.

Apart from these methodological difficulties, we do not know from the Sherman and Berk data whether the recidivism reduction observed for the arrested group is due to deterrence or to some other factor. As described above, arrest also serves to teach that an act is considered wrong by society. These other functions of law could lead to recidivism reduction whether or not men believed punishment for repeat assault to be likely. Only research on the subjective estimates of consequences for future assault would disentangle these explanations.

Some, but not all, wife assaults are impulsive acts, performed in states of high physiological and emotional arousal (Dutton, Fehr, & McEwen, 1982). By definition, such actions do not fall under the rational self-interest assumptions of deterrence theory. However, many wife assaults are deliberate and the result of careful choice by the assaulter of time, place, and parts of the body to be injured (Gelles, 1975), indicating that the rational process is not always absent. That recidivism reduction may occur with some wife assaulters is supported by the Sherman and Berk (1984) study that indicated that 81% of assaultive males could monitor and control their assaultive behavior for a six-month period postarrest (regardless of whether arrest or arrest plus suspected surveillance caused the effect). The remaining 19% need further incentive and assistance to monitor and control their behavior.

5.7.1 Role of Court-Mandated Treatment   ——————————

At present a variety of court-mandated treatment groups have developed to provide such assistance based on social learning notions of development and maintenance of aggressive behavior patterns (Bandura, 1979). Bandura (1979) describes in detail the psychological mechanisms that allow reprehensible conduct to recur. (We reviewed these in detail in Section 2.5.) While arrest may challenge all of these mechanisms of self-justification, they are further confronted through court-mandated treatment. Indeed, a primary objective of such treatment (as we shall see in Chapter 6) is to directly undermine such cognitive, habit-sustaining mechanisms in assaultive males (Ganley, 1981; Dutton, 1981c).

A second objective of such confrontation is to challenge the belief held by some convicted wife assaulters that their arrest was unjust. To the extent that a wife assaulter believes that (1) his wife's injuries were minimal or (2) she was to blame for the conflict or (3) his use of violence was justified, then he is more likely to view his subsequent arrest and conviction as unjust. Most treatment formats (Eddy & Myers, 1984; Browning, 1984) confront these beliefs as well.

A third objective of treatment is to enable wife assaulters to improve their ability to detect the warning signs of their own violence (e.g., increased arousal, anger) and to develop a more elaborate set of behaviors for managing previously violence-evoking situations. The empirical question for such treatment is whether these improved cognitive and behavioral abilities, when linked with the belief that future assault will lead to punishment, can decrease recidivism for a treatment population.

5.7.2 Power and Beliefs

Men who repeatedly assault their wives gain from their use of violence both personal feelings of power (Novaco, 1976) and a feeling of having gained control of a conflict that felt unmanageable prior to the violence (Sonkin, Martin, & Walker, 1985). These are not the type of economic gains typically considered by deterrence theory. For most men, these gains are expensive, since they are obtained through the use of reprehensible conduct (Bandura, 1979) that is not acceptable (Stark & McEvoy, 1970) and that erodes the quality of the marital relationship. It is indicative of the power of these informal social controls that most men eschew wife assault and only a small group repeat the act. For these repeaters, arrest and surveillance serve to reduce their recidivism rate (Sherman & Berk, 1984), and court-mandated treatment seems to lower the likelihood of repeat assault (Dutton, 1987b) below that level generated by arrest and conviction alone.

Nevertheless, our assessments of the impact of criminal justice interventions with wife assault remain rather piecemeal, and solid conclusions await a more systematic long-term study. In particular, subjective belief systems of offenders need to be scrutinized as an important mediator between objective system change and subsequent recidivism rates. Specifically, we need to know more about the impact of various intervention strategies on perception of risk of arrest and under what psychological circumstances that perception may govern the behavior of the assaulter.

CHAPTER SUMMARY

In this chapter we have reviewed the literature on the police response to domestic disturbance calls. Since the police come into contact with family violence more than any other government agency, they have the potential for making the greatest impact on detection and cessation of future violence. In reviewing these studies, we found that about one-third of all husband-wife domestic disturbances lead to an assault occurring and, somewhat contrary to the beliefs of the police themselves, alcohol was only a causative factor in about 14% of domestic disturbances attended by police.

Police decisions to arrest on domestic disturbance calls seem to give too little weight to victim injuries and too much weight to the demeanor of the alleged assailant. However, given that the assault is defined by the victim as a crime and reported, criminal justice processing of the case is similar to other crimes. One could make the point, given the aggressor-victim relationship (being under the same roof, in a continuing relationship), that perhaps the criminal justice response should be more aggressive, since the likelihood of repeat violence is higher than for assaults between strangers.

We have argued in this chapter that some qualified support exists for deterrence of future assault through the police use of arrest and have further suggested that coupling arrest with mandatory treatment is a promising policy strategy for greater reduction of recidivism. We turn now to a description and analysis of treatment for wife assault.

ENDNOTES

1. Estimates of arrest rate obtained through victim interviews or police reports vary even more and seem less reliable than observational studies. Roy's (1977) survey of women in crisis centers revealed that 90% reported no arrest by police when requested. Schulman (1979), however, in his victim survey, found a 41% arrest rate by police reported by victims (with an additional 16% rate of police obtaining a warrant). Schulman's estimate is based on a rather small *n* of 76 incidents, however. Bell (1985) found that 45% of 128,171 domestic disputes reported to Ohio police between 1979 and 1981 resulted in injuries or death to the victim. Offenders were arrested in only 14% of these cases. Bell's data base was incidents reported to police (and sheriffs) and although it is not clear from his methodology section, these incidents were presumably recorded on a report form which he then sampled. Bell's data are consistent with the observational studies described (albeit more extreme in the discrepancy between injured victims and arrests). Similarly, Berk and Loseke (1980) reported a 38.5% arrest rate for 262 domestic disturbances reported by police. When their entire unrefined sample is considered, however, the arrest rate drops to 14%. Since selection factors influence what incidents get reported by police, we believe that observational studies constitute the best measure of incidence of victim injuries.

2. It appears difficult to reconcile this drop in recidivism with the Wilt and Breedlove (1977) finding (Section 5.1) that 90% of subsequent felonious wife assault charges in Kansas City occurred in households visited at least once by police (who merely separated the assailant and victim on the prior occasion). Wilt and Breedlove's study has been interpreted as evidence that recidivism with increasing severity is likely when mere separation occurs, whereas Sherman and Berk's study (1984) shows a steep drop in recidivism based solely on separation. Wilt and Breedlove's data, however, are retrospective, working backwards from a pool of eventual felonious wife assault cases. It therefore cannot generate a baseline estimate of recidivism. On the other hand, Sherman and Berk's data,

with the ambiguous nature of the two-week follow-up interviews, may underestimate recidivism rates when the assailant does not suspect surveillance by authorities.

3. Police and other criminal justice professionals occasionally argue that aggressive prosecution of wife assault is futile because the victim will not cooperate with the prosecution. There is a kernel of truth to this complaint. The court study by the Battered Women's Project of the Seattle City Attorney's Office (Lerman, 1981) found that 596 wife assault charges led to 495 convictions (an 83% conviction rate) when the victim cooperated. When the victim did not cooperate, the conviction rate fell to 27.5% (143/520). What this statistic does not tell us, however, is what role the criminal justice system can play in generating victim cooperation. Dutton (1981a), in reviewing innovative court programs for wife assault, found that in jurisdictions where the prosecution operated to maximize protection of the victim (such as in Santa Barbara, California) and to dispell her fears and confusions about the criminal justice process, victim cooperation with the prosecution was 90%.

4. Coleman and Straus (1985) found that violence was greatest in husband-dominant and wife-dominant families, less in shared-responsibility families, and least in egalitarian families. Fagan's power-equalization hypothesis might work for families that were husband-dominant before police intervention, but it does not explain intervention effects on wife-dominant families.

CHAPTER 6

The Treatment of Wife Assault

People are not born with preformed repertoires of aggressive behavior. They must learn them.
—A. Bandura, *Psychology of Crime and Criminal Justice* (1979, p. 200)

In the last chapter we presented court-mandated treatment of wife assault as making an essential contribution to the criminal justice objective of reducing recidivism. Treatment, it was argued, provides a means through which repeat wife assaulters can learn alternative skills for conflict management, improve their ability to detect and express anger, and have the negative consequences of their violence made salient to them. The means by which the latter cognitive shift occurs is through direct therapeutic challenge to the cognitive mechanisms (e.g., minimizing, rationalizing, denying responsibility) that support reprehensible conduct (Bandura, 1979). We described these mechanisms in Chapter 2 and reported in Chapter 3 an empirical study that described their use by wife assaulters. We have argued that the didactic function of arrest may be to provide a major challenge or confrontation to these cognitive mechanisms. In this chapter we will examine how therapy extends the process of reframing the assaulter's interpretation of anger-inducing events.

6.1 TREATMENT PHILOSOPHY

In order to devise a form of therapy to be used as a condition of probation for men convicted of wife assault, certain sets of requirements must be met. First, the therapeutic form will have to have a philosophical base that is compatible with criminal justice philosophy. If, for example, criminal justice philosophy emphasizes personal responsibility for action, a treatment philosophy with a similar orientation is recommended.

In some areas of human conduct, a division exists between legal philosophy stressing individual responsibility and social science explanation stressing situational determinism (see Fincham & Jaspars, 1980; Dutton, 1981b). Social learning theory, while acknowledging the formative role of situational events in shaping habit patterns, nevertheless stresses choice and responsibility for individual action. The therapist, then, must repeatedly challenge statements by the client that his violence was caused by an external force (his wife's behavior being a typical example), a short-term situational occurrence (being drunk), or an uncontrollable predisposition (a bad temper, uncontrollable arousal, a drinking problem). In each case the therapist reminds the client that his wife did not force him to hit her, that other men get drunk and do not become violent, and that the client may have been violent when sober, or drunk and nonviolent. The point of this exercise is to get the client to acknowledge that his violence has elements of choice involved in it and that he has greater ability to control the violence than he formerly acknowledged.

Figure 6.1 represents an event-anger-aggression model that demonstrates the points of choice where therapeutic modification of clients' perceptions is aimed. Figure 6.1 demonstrates a conceptual model for the event-aggression link that is influenced by the learning process in four ways:

1. The appraisal of the event as maliciously intended or threatening seems to be a learned process (see Section 2.3).
2. The affective reaction to the consequent arousal may be shaped by sex-role socialization or other learned factors.
3. The mode of behavioral expression of anger represents a learned habit.
4. The choice of a target for abuse seems also to be a learned tendency.

Descriptions of therapy with assaultive males (e.g., Ganley, 1981; Gondolf, 1985a; Sonkin, Martin, & Walker, 1985) outline the variety of techniques that are used in treatment groups to generate the learning of new perceptions and behaviors. These include having the men keep anger diaries in which they log the *instigators* (i.e., events that made them angry), an analysis of the violent event in the group, a discussion of emotional reactions to specific behaviors of others (or empathy building), and relaxation exercises while imagining anger-provoking situations.

While the emphasis and form of these therapeutic practices may vary from group to group, the objective that they serve remains constant: they demonstrate to the clients how their use of violence is a learned behavior sustained by their own perceptions. This presents the possibility of learning alternative behaviors with less destructive consequences. Many men come to treatment for assaultive behavior with the belief that their violence is immutable. Having a therapist confront their interpretation of their wives' motives, their denial of emotions other than anger, and their refusal to use other behaviors to express anger grad-

FIGURE 6.1   Cognitive mediators of instigator-aggression relationship

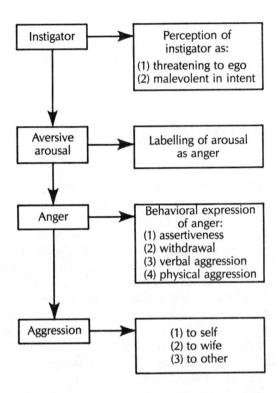

ually develops their perception that alternatives to violence are possible.

Clinical descriptions of men who are directed by the courts for such treatment (Ganley, 1981; Sonkin et al., 1985) underscore the need for highly structured, confrontative techniques. These men are described as cognitively rigid and unassertive, with strong tendencies to externalize blame for their behavior. They rarely have experience in psychological treatment groups (unless involved in alcohol treatment programs) and typically have had little interest in considering the possibility of personal change. Hence, highly directive treatment and the provision of motivation builders to clients is required.

Since many court-directed treatment programs are short term in nature (i.e., 3 to 6 months), therapeutic priorities must be selected carefully. It is unlikely, for example, that a man socialized into a macho working environment is going to embrace a feminist view of male socialization during weekly treatment sessions, especially when he returns to a work milieu that is philosophically contradictory to a feminist perspective (*cf.* Ptacek, 1984). However, demonstrating to a wife assaulter that his sex-role expectations may differ from his wife's and teaching him skills to negotiate these differences are not necessarily incompatible with his social milieu. Accordingly, we favor anger-management techniques that can be adapted to a variety of social milieus rather than attempts to generate ideological change that may be incompatible with the client's background and needs. It is important for therapists, if they have strong personal feelings about social change, to separate their roles as therapists and change agents. Otherwise, they may not be operating in the best interests of their clients.

6.2 COGNITIVE-BEHAVIORAL THERAPIES FOR ANGER

Cognitive-behavioral therapies are based on three fundamental assumptions: (1) that cognition affects behavior, (2) that cognition may be monitored and altered, and (3) that behavior change can be generated through changing cognitions (Dobson & Block, 1987). Stemming from a growing body of literature in the 1970s emphasizing the role of cognition in anxiety (Lazarus & Averill, 1972) and depression (Beck, 1976), and from a dissatisfaction with the results of long-term psychodynamically oriented psychotherapy (Eysenck, 1969; Rachman & Wilson, 1980), cognitive behavioral treatment began to be applied to a wide variety of affective and behavioral disorders (Dobson & Block, 1987). These included problems with self-control (Mahoney & Thoreson, 1979), anxiety (Meichenbaum, 1977), depression (Beck, 1976), and anger (Novaco, 1975).

Novaco's (1975) application of cognitive-behavioral therapy to anger management focused on the interrelationship of autonomic and cognitive determinants. As described in Chapter 2, Novaco also pointed out the positive functions served by anger arousal: it energizes behavior and serves expressive functions (advertising potency and determination) and defensive functions (overrides feelings of anxiety, vulnerability, and ego threat). If anger serves this variety of functions, therapy must include alternative means for clients to satisfy each function. This is not always easily accomplished in short-term therapy. For example, if a client's anxiety and vulnerability increase as a result of his learning to reinterpret his anger in these new emotional terms, the client may need to learn strategies for dealing with these alternative—and male sex-role dissonant—feelings. Therapeutic time may not permit this, however. A less ambitious therapeutic objective may be the development of awareness in the client that other feelings can be mislabelled as anger.

Novaco's (1975) anger management treatment was designed to alter clients' anger-enhancing cognitions. To this end, Novaco focused on

1. Changing clients' perceptions of the aversive stimulus or incident from a personal affront to a task that requires a solution

2. Teaching clients to use their own arousal as a cue for nonaggressive coping strategies
3. Increasing clients' perceptions that they are in control of themselves in provoking circumstances
4. Teaching clients to dissect provocation sequences into stages, with self-instructions for managing each stage
5. Teaching relaxation techniques to enable clients to reduce anger-arousal.

If we refer back to Figure 6.1, Novaco's techniques would apply to all four learned aspects of the stimulus-response chain. In social learning terms, anger-management attempts to modify both the perception of the instigators to aggression and the cognitive regulators of aggression.

In order to achieve the five objectives above, Novaco first assessed the impact of various provocations on clients by means of an anger inventory (Novaco, 1975) containing 90 statements of provocation incidents. Clients rated on a five-point scale how angry they would feel if that incident happened to them. Analysis of reactions to the anger-inventory items generated provocations that were role-played with clients. Novaco (1975) reported that his treatment techniques successfully allowed subjects to lower self-report anger scores and physiological indices associated with anger (i.e., systolic and diastolic blood pressure and galvanic skin response scores). In addition, subjects demonstrated improved scores on interpersonal reactions to provocation (i.e., constructive action scores increased while verbal and physical antagonism scores decreased).

While these results are promising, they were obtained under role-play conditions that lend themselves to subjects occasionally cooperating to verify experimental hypotheses (Orne, 1969). However, even if these *demand characteristics* (that cue subjects to the nature of the experimental hypotheses) were involved in Novaco's assessment, they still demonstrate that when angry clients want to lower their anger they can do so. They can effectively improve their affective, physiological, and interpersonal responses to provocation. Novaco also tried to offset the artificial nature of role-played provocations by conducting direct experience laboratory provocations (unsuspected personal affronts that would be perceived as real-life provocations). However, given that his subjects were wired for physiological measurement, the deceptive nature of this design is questionable.

Novaco reports comparisons of various partial treatment groups (e.g., groups concentrating on cognitive control alone, relaxation training alone, etc.) in an effort to ascertain which components had the greatest effect on improving anger management. Subjects themselves reported the most important aspect of treatment was task orientation when faced with a provocation. Task orientation requires clients to define the situation as one requiring a solution rather than an attack and directs attention away from internal stimuli associated with anger.

The automatic perception of a provocation as a personal affront begins to change as clients learn that not becoming demonstrably angry does not mean that they have to give up their position or back down—that is, that increased assertiveness is possible when anger is controlled.

6.3 TREATMENT GROUPS FOR WIFE ASSAULTERS

The development of treatment groups to specifically work with wife assaulters was pioneered by Anne Ganley (Ganley & Harris, 1978; Ganley, 1981). Ganley developed her treatment program from a social-learning orientation (similar to that developed in Chapter 2) focusing on improving the poor conflict-resolution skills learned by wife assaulters in their family of origin. In such families violence is often the only means of dealing with conflict-generated anger, listening skills are poor, verbal problem-solving skills are poor, and emotional self-disclosure is equated with loss of control. As a step toward rectifying these deficits, Ganley included assertiveness training as part of her treatment model.

Ganley viewed battering as a learned tension-reducing response that occurred in the family setting because that was the safest place to aggress without punishment and because batterers held stereotyped views of the man as being the absolute ruler at home. Ganley described the tendency of batterers to deny or minimize their violence and to externalize it by holding others responsible and culpable for their own moods and outbursts. She recommended confrontation as a therapeutic strategy for dealing with these forms of neutralization of self-punishment. She also developed a highly structured treatment format that stressed personal accountability to each participant. Exercises such as maintaining an anger diary emphasized the need for personal responsibility in constant monitoring of anger.

Batterers also tended to express emotions such as hurt, anxiety, excitement, sadness, guilt, humiliation, and helplessness as anger. Ganley's treatment program develops a batterer's motivation to change by helping the batterer identify the negative feelings about his violence. Anger diaries, one of which is depicted in Figure 6.2, help the man to identify the instigators of his anger, and his physical and cognitive responses to anger. Men list the "triggers" (instigators) of their anger (what another person did or said to anger them), how angry they became (on a 10-point scale), how they knew they were angry (physiological responses, etc.), their "talk up" (what they said to themselves to increase their anger), and their "talk down" (what they said to themselves to calm themselves down). Men list the "triggers" as objective recordings of events. They are taught to be specific, not to make assumptions about the other's motive, and to record only what was seen or heard.

This exercise forces wife assaulters to analyze how frequently they impute negative motives to others and the extent to which these assumptions generate anger. Comparisons of the "trigger" and "talk up" columns emphasize the subjective quality of their anger responses (since the "talk up" column generally contains blaming statements that serve to increase the man's self-generated anger). "Talk down" or anger-decreasing statements have to be taught to most men. These statements contain the acknowledgement that the man is feeling angry. They serve to both improve his ability to detect anger cues and to generate self-control through changing his self-statements from external blame to acknowledgment of internal feelings. For a complete description and examples of anger diaries, the reader is referred to Sonkin and Durphy (1982) or to Sonkin, Martin, and Walker (1985). When men are successfully participating in treatment groups and consistently completing anger diaries, the diaries are used as a step to assertiveness training.

Bower and Bower (1976) develop assertiveness by getting clients to verbalize a DESC script. DESC is an acronym for *describe, express, specify,* and *consequences.* Clients are asked to describe which behaviors in the other bother them, to express how these behaviors make them feel, to specify what new behaviors they want, and to express the positive consequences for the other person if they perform these behaviors. This assertiveness exercise becomes a first step in teaching clients to negotiate interpersonal differences.

The bridge from the anger diary to the DESC script is built as follows: The "triggers" from the anger diary (specific acts or statements) provide the describe portion of the DESC script. The specificity learned in keeping an anger diary helps the man to focus his verbal statements on a behavior rather than a predisposition of the other person. The "talk down" column (statement of feeling) then becomes the express part of the DESC script. Hence, the anger diary provides the first half of an assertive statement, often an improvement in communication without the specify and consequence portions. These latter steps teach the man to assert what changes he wants and what changes he is willing to make himself as a consequence.

As a result, they develop a problem-oriented or negotiation approach to the communication of anger. After rehearsal and practice in the treatment group, men are encouraged to continue with couples communication therapy. It should be emphasized that we recommend such treatment only when the use of violence by the man is under control. The couples communication aspect of treatment is designed to improve the conflict climate of the wife assaulter's primary relationship, once his wife no longer feels at risk for further violence.

While anger recognition and improved communication skills provide the essence of treatment for assaultive males, other issues also constitute an important adjunct to this treatment. Since the treatment is for male-female violence, the role of sex-role socialization in setting the stage for violence is important. Male socialization narrows the range of acceptable emotions (Fasteau, 1974; Pleck,

FIGURE 6.2   Anger diary based on a DESC (describe, express, specify, and consequences) script

Anger Diary

Name_____

Date_____

Date of Event	Trigger	How Anger Known	Rating (1-10)	Self Talk Talk-Up	Self Talk Talk-Down
Nov. 17	WIFE KEPT BOTHERING FRIEND OF SON BY REPEATEDLY ASKING HIM QUESTIONS ABOUT A BOOK HIS FATHER WROTE	STARTING FEELING MORE UP TIGHT THE MORE SHE WENT ON.	4	WHY DOESN'T SHE LEAVE THE POOR KID ALONE. WHY DOESN'T SHE JUST SHUT UP AND WATCH THE MOVIE LIKE EVERYONE ELSE.	I FEEL ANGRY ABOUT THE WAY SHE'S TREATING THIS KID BUT MAKING A SCENE ABOUT IT IN FRONT OF THE KIDS WILL ONLY BRING ME DOWN TO HER LEVEL.
Nov. 18	WIFE CONTINUALLY NAGGING AT ME + POINTING HER FINGER IN MY FACE	NECK + BACK FELT TENSE + HAD EMPTY FEELING IN GUT.	7	THIS BITCH IS PUSHING ME TO THE LIMIT ONCE AGAIN. WHY CAN'T SHE BACK OFF AND TRY TO WORK THINGS OUT QUIETLY.	I FEEL REALLY MAD BUT I WON'T LOOSE CONTROL. I BETTER GET AWAY FOR AWHILE AND HOPE THINGS COOL DOWN.
Nov. 19	WIFE NOT HELPING WITH ANYTHING AROUND THE HOUSE BECAUSE SHE SAYS SHE IS SICK.	FELT UNUSUALLY NERVOUS + UP TIGHT	3	THE ONLY REASON SHE FEELS SO SICK IS BECAUSE SHE DRANK ALL WEEKEND AND NOW I HAVE TO PAY FOR IT ONCE AGAIN BY HAVING MORE WORK TO DO.	I'M GETTING ANGRY AGAIN FOR THE SAME OLD REASON HER DRINKING. DON'T LET IT GET TO YOU. THINGS WILL HAVE TO IMPROVE OR OUR RELATIONSHIP WON'T LAST.

FIGURE 6.2 (*continued*)

Anger Diary

Name _____

Date _____

Date of Event	Trigger	How Anger Known	Rating (1-10)	Self Talk	
				Talk-Up	Talk-Down
Nov. 30	Finding out wife had gone out and not come home all night	Felt my adrenalin start to flow and started moving around house at a quick pace	4	She's done it again. Gone out without as much as a note or phone call to say where she is. That bitch doesn't give a shit about my feelings.	This isn't the first time or I might really get worried. I'm sure she will show up tomorrow so I might as well go back to bed. Actually I feel relieved that she isn't here.
Dec. 1	Wife started yelling at me — why didn't you leave me a note to say where you were. Called me an asshole, etc. Then told me not to touch the frying pan to make dinner because everything belonged to her. Saw bottle of rum on counter.	Entire body became tense and stomach got very upset.	9	That fucking bitch. How dare she question + talk to me like this when she disappeared last night without an explanation. She's drunk and I'm fed up with her—period.	Time out! Get out of here now she's pushing me beyond my control. Get away from her now!
Dec. 2	Barging in house drunk late at night and started yelling not to come near her then smacked me with her hand right in the left eye.	Muscles became tense + face became hot.	7	What a fucking nerve. I've no intention of going anywhere near her just go to bed and pass out. I don't want anything to do with you	I'm furious with her but I'm not going to retaliate or I'll be the one to pay for all this shit she's causing.

Source: Provided by a client in the assaultive husband's project

1981) and occasionally creates unrealistic expectations about family roles that provide a source of chronic conflict (Coleman & Straus, 1985). Treatment should address these issues and attempt to develop empathy for the victim. One way of developing empathy is to have assaultive males describe their own experiences as victims of parental abuse. Exploring the feelings connected to these experiences in a group context and explicitly relating the feelings to their wives' experiences as victims can serve to strengthen empathy by making salient the negative consequences of violence for the victim.

Treatment should also include an attempt to get males to think about power in a different way. A man typically enters treatment thinking about power vis à vis his wife in an adversarial fashion. His gain is his wife's loss and vice versa. We attempt to encourage him to view power in interdependent terms: that by diminishing his wife, he loses a vital partner. And by accepting her empowerment, he also gains. We do this by making salient the personal losses the man sustains as a result of violence toward his wife (her emotional and sexual withdrawal, mistrust, chronic anger toward him, etc.). By yoking the couple's gains and losses repeatedly in treatment, the concept of power interdependence becomes more salient. An objective of feminist therapy is thus achieved by a means consonant with the values of the dominant socializing culture.

Finally, since treatment for assaultive males usually occurs in a group setting, group process issues (Yalom, 1975) are also important. Assaultive males are described in most clinical texts as isolated (Ganley, 1981; Sonkin et al., 1985). They frequently feel anxious about describing personal problems and feelings in front of other men. Therapists have to do considerable bridge building by explicitly connecting the experiences of men in the groups in order to establish some camaraderie and a sense of safety for self-disclosure. On the other hand, the therapist must not allow group cohesiveness to generate mutual protection in the service of denial and minimizing. Therapists must use confrontation carefully, making it clear that it is necessary for learning new conflict-management skills in order to avoid the feeling these men frequently have of being attacked or judged negatively.

6.4 INDIVIDUAL VERSUS SYSTEMS APPROACHES TO TREATMENT

Considerable controversy surrounds the choice of a treatment approach for wife assault. Treatment programs for assaultive males view violence as a response learned by an individual during his ontogenetic development. The habit of reacting to conflict with violence is seen as a predisposition of that individual. The therapeutic implication is that the individual aggressor must be treated first to learn how to control his use of violence prior to couples therapy or family systems therapy that teaches the family to deal more constructively with conflict. Since couples therapy frequently includes negotiation and mediation aspects, a woman who feels threatened and unsafe cannot negotiate without preserving a power imbalance that makes true negotiation impossible.

A view of wife assault that assumes assaulters ontogenetically learn the use of violence makes the prediction that assaultive males would be violent across relationships and that such behavior would manifest itself whenever a set of instigators appeared. In Section 2.3, we discussed a study by Kelley and Stahelski (1970) that suggested that conflict generation is a predispositional social orientation in some people that occurs transsituationally. Rounsaville (1978) reported that 39% of assaultive males in his study (n = 31) had a prior violent relationship (this finding, however, was based on interviews with the women).

Kalmuss and Seltzer (1986) present data from the 1975 national survey (Straus et al., 1980) that address the question of whether predispositional or family systems perspectives more adequately describe the transrelationship incidence of spouse abuse. Kalmuss and Seltzer compared intact families (both spouses married for the first time), remarried families (one or both spouses divorced, but no children from prior marriages), and reconstituted families (one or both divorced and children from prior marriages). Predispositional explanations would predict, Kalmuss and Seltzer argue, that individuals who are violence-prone would manifest violence transsituationally. Since divorced couples are approximately 10 times as likely to have used violence (Levinger, 1966) than nondivorced, predispositional explanations would predict increased violence rates for remarried families over and above intact families.

Family systems approaches view structural stress as a major contributor to violence and hence would predict reconstituted families to be more violent than intact or remarried families (on the assumption that the complex structure and the role confusion would increase the likelihood of violence). The national survey data tended to support a predispositional view: contrasts in incidence of violence between intact and remarried families were significant; contrasts between remarried and reconstituted families were not. Hence, Kalmuss and Seltzer conclude that structural variables do not increase the likelihood of spouse abuse, while an inferred predisposition toward violence (based on the status of being divorced) does.

Kalmuss and Seltzer controlled for exposure to violence in the family of origin and found that their results persisted. Remarried adults who observed no physical aggression between their parents are still almost twice as likely to be involved in spouse abuse as are similar adults in intact families. They suggest that behavioral repertoires that include violence may not necessarily be rooted in early childhood experiences but may originate in the adults' first marriages.

Family systems approaches (Giles-Sims, 1983; Neidig & Friedman, 1984) view wife assault from an interactive (microsystem) rather than an intrapsychic

perspective. The rules of the family system that define what behavior is acceptable, the power imbalances of that system, and the personal resources of individual members that provide a basis for exchange are viewed as major contributors to family violence. Giles-Sims (see Section 1.6) acknowledges (1983,
p. 33) that "victims may inadvertently be reinforcing the violent behavior," a
perspective supported in the child abuse literature by the interactive studies of
Patterson and his colleagues and reviewed in Chapter 2.

Patterson, Cobb, and Ray (1972), for example, observed parents' reinforcement of the violence of their highly destructive boys. Parents were not aware
of reinforcements they provided, and Giles-Sims suggests that the same may
be true for battered women. Pagelow (1984) describes how some of these reinforcers include a low likelihood of retaliation, an acceptance by the weaker partner of battering as a proper response to stress, and a rigid traditional ideology
(that the woman shouldn't leave the marriage no matter how destructive it is
and that she has a responsibility to save the man from his own excesses). All
of these reinforcers lead, in effect, to the assaultive male avoiding punishment
for his violence.[1]

Neidig and Friedman (1984) begin their description of their couples treatment program with the statement that "abusive behavior is a relationship issue
but it is ultimately the responsibility of the male to control physical violence."
Their view is that approaches that attribute total responsibility to either party
lead to blaming which only compounds the problem. It does so, according to
these authors, by beginning a chain of retributional strategies by the victim and
the aggressor whereby each tries to get even for the other's most recent trans-
gression. A systems approach avoids blaming by getting couples to think of the
causes of violence from a circular-feedback perspective rather than a linear one.
This leads to constructive interventions in the escalating process, which permit
each partner to accept a portion of the responsibility.

Having said that, however, Neidig and Friedman assign "ultimate responsibility to the male for controlling violence," a recognition that both parties are
not equal in physical strength. To some readers this may suggest an artificial
separation of responsibility from blame, a topic that we touched on in Section
4.8. If a man is responsible for his violence, then why is he not to blame if he
acts violently? One answer may be that his violence occurred in a state of high
arousal when he perceived no alternatives to the actions he took.[2] In therapeutic
terms, a couples approach and an individual approach have a fundamental
disagreement: the couples approach tries to reduce blame of the individual who
aggresses and the individual approach tries to increase his responsibility.

The decision of whether an individual or a couples approach to therapy
is best may depend on the client. If a man has a history of violence in several
relationships with women, he may be a conflict-generator capable of creating
the system pattern observed by the systems therapist in his current relationship.
As some therapists have noted (Richter, 1974), single persons are capable of

generating entire interaction patterns within families on the basis of their individual pathology. Richter describes how a paranoid personality who holds power in a family can generate a shared paranoia in the entire family system. We recommend obtaining detailed social histories of clients prior to embarking on a systems approach, especially in view of the Kalmuss and Seltzer (1986) findings reported above. If a male batterer has a history of violence with women that predates his current relationship, couples treatment may not be advisable. Where the violence and conflict seem specific to the present relationship, such treatment may be more successful.

6.5 ARE TREATMENT GROUPS EFFECTIVE?

The last decade has seen a proliferation of court-mandated treatment groups for men convicted of wife assault. Browning (1984) and Eddy and Meyers (1984) provide descriptive profiles of 24 Canadian and 54 U.S. treatment programs for assaultive males. Both reviews outline referral processes, treatment procedures, and funding issues for such programs; both agree on the need for an evaluation of treatment effectiveness.

Treatment groups for wife assaulters originated from public pressure on the criminal justice system to respond more effectively to the problem of wife assault (e.g., through the U.S. Commission on Civil Rights and Standing Committee of Health, Welfare and Social Affairs, Canada). As Dutton (1981a) pointed out, the hopes for such groups were twofold. First, the groups were seen as a means of improving protection for women who opted to remain in a relationship with a husband who would not seek treatment voluntarily. Second, by providing a viable sentencing option for judges, treatment groups could create a salutory ripple effect throughout the criminal justice system by making judges more willing to convict, prosecutors more willing to proceed with cases (where they perceived their chances of gaining a conviction as having improved), and police more willing to proceed with charges that they perceived as being actionable by prosecutors. Clearly, both of these hopes were based on the expectation that treatment groups would be effective.

Furthermore, since incarceration for a first offense of wife assault is unlikely (Lerman, 1981; Dutton, 1987b), treatment groups represent an addendum to probation that could provide convicted men with a means for managing anger (see Novaco, 1975). The hazard of treatment groups lies in their offering false hope. If men remain at risk for violence despite treatment, then their wives may be imperiled while falsely believing that the man is cured. Offender treatments for other behavioral problems have had mixed results (Shore & Massimo, 1979; Gendreau & Ross, 1980). Clearly, there is a need to assess the effectiveness of court-mandated treatment for wife assault.

Attempts at assessing treatment programs have not been as systematic or thorough as one might expect. Given the potential stake in these programs from a policy perspective, a thorough evaluation seems obligatory. Deschner (1984) evaluated the effects of teaching anger-control skills to nine groups of battering spouses. She reported data on 58 clients (32 women and 26 men) who completed intakes and at least four treatment sessions. Treatment included training in anger recognition, time-out procedures, cognitive techniques, and assertiveness training. Pre-post anger measures were taken using anger self-reports to imagined anger-arousing scenes. The postmeasures were taken four months after treatment completion. Clients also completed the *Taylor-Johnson Temperament Analysis* (1980) that assesses transitional moods.[3]

Deschner reported that anger-control training was effective in increasing battering couples' anger-management skills and reducing the intensity and frequency of their disputes. However, as Deschner pointed out, these results were all based on self-report data and may have been biased by the client's wish to please the researchers. Clients want to believe that the treatment in which they have just invested time will be successful, and they want the therapist to believe this as well. Separation of the evaluator from the therapist becomes an important component of an effective evaluation design.

Maiuro, Cahn, Vitaliano, and Zegree (1986) also reported results of an anger-control program for batterers conducted at Harborview Hospital in Seattle. This program also had a cognitive-behavioral basis with techniques based on Novaco's work. The evaluation compared 63 batterers with independently documented histories of domestic violence (who were treated for 18 weeks) with 26 untreated controls (wait-listed for treatment) matched to the batterers on demographic variables and general level of disturbance. The pre-post measures included the *Buss-Durkee Hostility Inventory* (Buss & Durkee, 1957), the *Hostility and Direction of Hostility Questionnaire* (Caine, Foulds, & Hope, 1967), the *Beck Depression Inventory* (Beck, 1967), assertiveness scales, and anger-aggression scales completed by their spouse. Maiuro et al. reported significant differences between groups on all measures. The wait-list controls showed no decreases, while the treated men showed significant decreases on the anger/hostility measures, the depression measure, and the spouse-based ratings of anger and aggression. The treatment group also evidenced significant increases in assertiveness compared to the control group. Maiuro et al. concluded that specialized anger-control treatment could be effective in modifying psychological and behavioral variables related to battering.

Saunders and Hanusa (1984) reported evaluation data on 25 men who completed 20 sessions of a cognitive-behavioral treatment comprised of assertiveness training, relaxation training, and cognitive restructuring. Saunders and Hanusa reported decreases in threats from female competence and depression but no significant drop in anger-scale scores. Actually, there was a decrease reported in pre- and postanger scores (on a modified version of the Novaco anger scale).

When social desirability scores (attempts by the subject to look good in their responses, measured by the Marlowe-Crowne *Social Desirability Scale*) were used to adjust anger scores, however, the significant differences disappeared. This emphasizes once again the problem with relying exclusively on self-report measures of treatment effectiveness.

Pirog-Good and Stets (in press) evaluated group success by surveying leaders of treatment groups for batterers in the United States and reporting recidivism rates for 72 such programs. They found from their survey that, of every 100 men who enroll in treatment programs for batterers, 60 complete the program. Of these 60, 42 to 53 do not return to battering in the year following treatment. Thus, the success rate in absolute terms is 79%. However, this study has two major problems associated with it. One is that the recidivism measure was not systematic but "based on the educated estimates of (program) administrators." These personal estimates, as the authors admit, can be unreliable. The second problem is that no controls exist; hence, we do not know what percentage of nonrecidivists would have stopped battering without treatment.

6.5.1   What Constitutes Effective Treatment?

The effect size of treatment (Rosenthal, 1983) for wife assaulters can be established by estimating what percentage of men would not repeat assault *without* treatment. Schulman (1979) and Straus et al. (1980) reported that single events of severe violence occurred for about 33% of couples reporting physical assaults and repeated events of assault occurred for the remaining 66%. As far as determining the effectiveness of treatment, the following implications may be drawn from these surveys:

1. If a posttreatment evaluation period is one year or less, 33% of treated men would be expected not to repeat assault even without treatment.
2. Since frequency rates vary greatly, some comparison should be made between posttreatment behavior to each man's individual pretreatment frequency of violence rate.
3. For posttreatment evaluation periods of more than one year, additional means of generating baseline incidence will be required.

The Straus et al. and Schulman samples pertained to men who may have assaulted only once and who may or may not have had criminal justice contact, whereas most treatment for wife assault follows arrest and conviction (as we saw in Chapter 5) and a history of wife assault (see Table 6.1). The Sherman and

Note: Portions of Section 6.5.1 are reprinted from Dutton, D. G. (1987a). The outcome of court-mandated treatment for wife assault: A quasi-experimental evaluation. *Violence & victims* ·*1*(3). Used by permission of Springer Publishing Co., New York.

Berk (1984) study reported an attempt to evaluate the specific deterrence effect of arrest for misdemeanor wife assault with men who did have criminal justice contact. Their six-month follow-up of 161 domestic disturbances—where police contact occurred—indicated an overall recidivism rate of 28.9%, and a 19% rate for men who were arrested. Despite the interpretative problems described in Chapter 5, the Sherman and Berk study allows us to estimate expected recidivism with surveillance (e.g., probation) after criminal justice intervention. Specifically, if a treated population has been arrested prior to treatment, we might expect a 19% recidivism rate in the first six months.

Jaffe, Wolfe, Telford, and Austin (1986) monitored prearrest and post-arrest assaultive behavior of males through both interviews with their wives and examination of police files. This was part of an evaluation of changes in police response following a policy directive mandating arrest for wife assault. Jaffe et al. found substantial postarrest reductions in violence directed toward wives both in wives' own reports and the police records.

A major problem in assessing the effects of wife assault treatment has been the lack of a baseline measure of recidivism for a matched group of untreated offenders. In the absence of randomized designs, the next-best comparison group is a group of males demographically similar to the treated group, with similar arrest patterns prior to arrest, and (if available) similar patterns of frequency of wife assault. Since we know something of the demographics and arrest records of the Sherman and Berk and Jaffe et al. samples, they can provide important additional comparison groups against which we can judge the effectiveness of a treated group.

In order to estimate the recidivism rate for men arrested and convicted of wife assault but not treated, Dutton (1987a) scrutinized police records of a group of 50 men for up to 3 years post conviction. During the same period, records for 59 men arrested, convicted, and treated for wife assault were examined. Demographic comparisons with the Sherman and Berk and Jaffe et al. samples with the untreated and treated Dutton (1987a) samples in this study are presented in Table 6.1

The treatment program consisted of four months of court-mandated group therapy that included cognitive behavior modification, anger management, and assertiveness. Men in the evaluated treatment program met in groups of eight for 3 hours each week. Three measures of use of violence against wives were obtained in this study. First, police information records were examined, which showed all court appearances including convictions. These records constitute the official recidivism rate for the treated and untreated groups. To provide longitudinal pre-postassessments of the use of violence by treated men, other measures of wife assault were obtained by having men in treatment and their wives independently fill out the Straus (1979) *Conflict Tactics Scale* (Form N) for a period prior to and following treatment.

The *CTS* measures were only obtainable, however, for men who had

TABLE 6.1 Characteristics of treated and untreated groups

		Sherman & Berk (1984)	Jaffe et al. (1986)	Dutton (1987a) Untreated	Dutton (1987a) Treated
	n =	205	61	50	50
$\bar{X}$ age		32.0	n.a.	34.4	34.6
$\bar{X}$ years education		n.a.	n.a.	10.8	11.2
% unemployed		60%	37%	48%	45%
$\bar{X}$ of prior assaults[a]		n.a.	n.a.	.80	.88
$\bar{X}$ of prior nonviolent crimes		n.a.	n.a.	4.04	2.64
% with prior assault		31%	24%	28%	27%
% with any prior offense		59%	n.a.	62%	60%
Assault on wife in six months prior to arrest		80%	80%[b]	80%	80%
Recidivism Rate:					
within 6 months		13%[c]	n.a.[d]	16%	4%
within 2.5 years		n.a.		40%	4%[e]

[a]prior to assault leading to current court appearance, offender-victim relationship not specified.

[b]80% had police record for spouse assault, but time period was not specified in Jaffe and Wolfe.

[c]13% based on police report; 19% based on interview with wives.

[d]Jaffe et al. did not measure arrest per se, but number of contacts with police. For this measure, men in their postarrest group average 1.6 contacts with police within one year of arrest.

[e]4% based on police report; 16% based on interview with wives.

undergone treatment. Hence, they provide pre-postdata on the rate of assault, but they do not allow us to attribute unambiguously any changes to treatment per se. Diminution of the use of violence could be due to arrest, or arrest and conviction, or arrest, conviction, and treatment, or maturation, or regression toward the mean (Campbell, 1969). While the use of both official recidivism and self-report measures partially offsets the problems of interpretation associated with either one alone, it does not yet constitute an ideal evaluation design, as we will discuss below. Both the treated (n = 50) and untreated (n = 50) males in this study had been convicted of wife assault and had similar histories of assault. The untreated group had a total of 40 prior assaults; the treated group had 44 prior assaults (prior to the assault that led to their present conviction).

The decision to include men in treatment is made primarily by their probation officer and secondarily by the therapist. Considerations for the probation officer often include mundane issues such as whether a convicted man has employment that makes the treatment location accessible. Other men are untreated simply because their probation order expires before a space in the treatment group is available. Therapists base treatment decisions on the man's willingness to participate, although even recalcitrant men are often taken on a trial basis. For the 50 untreated men in the Dutton (1987a) study, 42 were not treated due to practical considerations and 8 were rejected by the therapists as unsuitable for treatment. In trying to match the treated and untreated groups, however, we can say with confidence that they are similar both demographically and in their preconviction record of violence. However, systematic psychological assessment was not performed, so we cannot rule out potential differences between groups on psychological profiles. For purposes of this study, treated men were defined as those who had completed treatment; untreated were defined as men who had been interviewed for the group but who had completed fewer than four sessions of treatment. The postinterview follow-up period was assessed in 1985 and varied from 3 years for men who had been interviewed in 1982 to six months for more recent intake interviews ($\overline{X}$ = 2 years).

Results of Police Data

The untreated group repeated assaults in 20/50 cases; the treated group in 2/50 cases. This difference was statistically significant ($p < .001$, $\chi^2 = 18.9$, $df = 1$). In other words, treatment improves the nonrecidivist success rate from 60% to 96%, according to the police records.

Furthermore, it is instructive to note that for the untreated group, 9/20 recidivist assaults were of an extremely serious variety, classified as assault causing bodily harm. This typically indicated the use of a weapon and/or extreme injuries to the victim and comparable to the term *aggravated assault.* However, a note of caution must accompany this apparent escalation in severity of crimes. It is not clear from police records whether it reflects an actual increase in severity of assault or a refusal of the prosecution to plea bargain to lesser charges when the offender is a repeat offender (see Repucci and Clingempeel, 1978).

Sherman and Berk (1984) reported that 13% of their arrested group (n = 54) generated new police reports of wife assault within six months. Our untreated group generated new police reports 16% of the time (8/50) within six months. This increased to 40% over the entire posttreatment assessment period.

Self-Reports and Wives' Reports

Sixty-four percent of treated men were married throughout treatment and follow-up (n = 37). These men and their wives were administered Form N of the Straus *Conflict Tactics Scale* (Straus, 1979). Data on men's pretreatment conflict resolution were collected by having the men fill in a *CTS* for violence for a period of one year prior to their arrest and conviction. Their wives filled out a *CTS* within five weeks of the beginning of their husband's treatment that also assessed violence occurring during the preceding year. Posttreatment data were collected by having men and their wives independently fill out a *CTS* at a point ranging from 6 months to 3 years after treatment completion ($\overline{X}$ = 2 years). Wives filled it out without the husband present. All data were then adjusted to yearly rates.

Each spouse was asked to rate the frequency with which each item or conflict tactic was used both by them and by their spouse in the time period specified. The frequency scale ranges from zero (never) to 6 (more than 20 times). Using Straus's regular scoring system, which involves summing the frequency ratings over the items, a range of scores from zero to 48 is possible for all violence items and from zero to 30 for severe violence items. Means for husband and wife ratings of annual rates of husband's use of violence are presented in Table 6.2.

Results of Self-Reports and Wives' Reports

For this subsample of 37 couples, both husbands' self-reports (t = 8.2, p < .01, df = 36) and wives' reports of husbands' violence (t = 10.7, p < .01, df = 36) show significant pre-postdrops. Treated husbands still used acts of severe violence an average of 1.7 times a year (wives' report), down from an

TABLE 6.2 Husbands' and wives' mean ratings of husbands' annual use of violence before and after treatment

		Subscale Range	
		Pretreatment Scores	*Posttreatment Scores*
	Dutton (1987a) Sample		
Husband's rating (of	Verbal Abuse (0–36)	23.9	12.8
own violence)	All Violence (0–48)	13.4	4.6
(*n* = 37)	Severe Violence (0–30)	5.5	1.1
Wife's rating (of	Verbal Abuse (0–48)	28.3	13.9
husband's violence)	All Violence (0–30)	21.3	6.1
(*n* = 37)	Severe Violence	10.6	1.7

	Jaffe, Wolfe, Telford, & Austin (1986) Sample[a]		
		Prearrest	*Postarrest/ No Treatment*
Wife's rating (of	Verbal Abuse (0–48)	18.32	13.56
husband's violence)	All Violence (0–48)	24.17	9.19
(*n* = 61)	Severe Violence	n.a.[b]	n.a.[b]

[a]Jaffe et al. used a modified version of the *CTS*. Their raw data have been transformed to simplify direct comparisons.
[b]See Table 6.3 for percentages reporting use of Severe Aggression items.

average of 10.6 times a year. Thirty-one of the 37 wives (84%) reported no acts of severe violence since termination of treatment. Intercorrelations of husbands' and wives' reports of husbands' use of violent acts improved significantly from a pretreatment score of .63 to a posttreatment score of .81 ($t = 9.6, p < .01$, $df = 36$) (see Browning & Dutton, 1986).

Reports of use of verbal aggression were similar to use of severe violence. Overall rates of use of verbal aggression dropped after treatment based on both husbands' reports ($t = 11.2, p < .01, df = 26$) and wives' reports ($t = 13.8$, $p < .01, df = 26$). However, 8 wives reported increases in verbal aggression.

The results of this study constituted a first step toward a conclusive assessment of long-term effects of treatment for wife assault. Clearly, the design could offer only tentative conclusions in this direction. While police reports, self-reports, and wives' reports of male violence all showed significant posttreatment drops, a variety of problems exist with the interpretation of these results.

Police reports typically overlook the *chiffe noire* for wife assault since only a small percentage of all wife assaults end up in charges being made (see Chapter 5). However, this small percentage of assaultive males still places a considerable demand on police and court resources in most jurisdictions. A 36% reduction in recidivism for the charged group would constitute a substantial conservation of criminal justice resources. Self-reports run the risk of being self-serving by underreporting violence (Browning & Dutton, 1986). Men who have been convicted of wife assault once may be especially loath to report new assaults to interviewers because of anxiety about re-arrest. Wives' reports of husband violence might suffer from a similar unwillingness on the wives' part to involve their husbands once again in the criminal justice system or to admit that the therapy group failed. Interviewers were careful to explain to wives that their reports of husbands' posttreatment violence would not generate criminal justice action and that therapy was not expected to terminate all husband violence. However, there is no way of knowing if this was universally believed.

Even if one accepted that an amalgam of police, self-report, and wife-report data generated rough indices of husband violence, other interpretative problems existed with the design. Since men were not allocated at random to treatment and no-treatment conditions, we could not attribute differences in outcome to treatment per se. Although the treated and untreated groups were roughly matched on demographic factors and pretreatment arrest patterns for violence, other systematic differences between the groups could exist.

The untreated group, for example, had a higher number of arrests for nonviolent crime (although not for violent crime). This suggests an alternative interpretation of the differences in recidivism between treated and untreated groups. The drop in recidivism for the treated group might have been due not to treatment per se but to some combination of arrest, conviction, and treatment. The lesser impact of arrest and conviction on the untreated group may have been due to their more extensive criminal justice experience. However, although the average number of prior arrests was higher in the untreated group, a low and nonsignificant correlation of this factor with eventual recidivism made it an unlikely contributor to group differences.

The present study also lacked a comparison of treated and untreated men in terms of psychological profiles. Again, however, the ability of psychological profiles to predict likelihood of recidivism is low (Megargee, 1970; Monahan, 1976; Repucci and Clingempeel, 1978; Haynes, 1985; Stone, 1985) and unlikely to generate a difference of the magnitude found in the study.

Interestingly, none of the treated husbands used violence during a wait-list period between the intake interview and the onset of treatment (based on both self- and wife's reports). This period varied from a few weeks up to three months. This suggests that, at a point where criminal justice action (court conviction) is still salient and further scrutiny of use of violence (treatment) is anticipated, assaultive males can monitor and control their use of violence. This finding suggests (as do the Sherman and Berk results) that surveillance is a useful means of diminishing the rate of wife assault. Viewed from this perspective, treatment becomes a means of instilling self-surveillance when long-term surveillance by the criminal justice system becomes a practical impossibility.

Comparison of the present results with the Jaffe et al. (1986) study is also illuminating, since it allows an assessment of the effect of arrest plus treatment with arrest per se (although one must use extreme caution when dealing with different sample populations and interview contexts—see Tables 6.1 and 6.2). Jaffe et al.'s postarrest untreated group yielded verbal abuse scores of 13.56 and physical aggression scores of 9.19 on the *CTS* (based on their wives' reports). The verbal abuse score is quite similar to that generated by the Dutton post-treatment men (13.9), but the Jaffe et al. prearrest scores were quite lower than those generated by the Dutton group (18.3 vs. 28.3).

Postarrest scores for all violence (the physical aggression subscore on the *CTS*) were 9.19 for the Jaffe et al. untreated postarrest group and 6.1 for the Dutton posttreatment group. Jaffe et al. did not report severe violence subscores. Table 6.3, however, demonstrates the percentages of men using severe violence in the two studies. This analysis suggests that the aggregate subscores for all violence reported in Table 6.2 may be somewhat misleading. Treated men in Table 6.3 use significantly less severe violence than Jaffe et al.'s arrested-untreated group ($t = 10.2$, $p < .01$, $df = 121$). The greatest differences occur for the most severe items. A cautious conclusion is that treatment further reduced the incidence of wife assault beyond the reduction caused by arrest per se.

More Evaluations of Treatment Programs

Since the initial outcome study (Dutton, 1987a) reported above, several other attempts have been made to evaluate treatment groups for wife assaulters. Shepard (1987) used a behavior checklist that assessed both psychological and

TABLE 6.3   Percentages of wives reporting husbands' use of severe violence in the Jaffe et al. (1986) and the Dutton (1987a) study

	Jaffe et al. Prearrest	Dutton Prearrest	Jaffe et al. Postarrest Untreated	Dutton Postarrest Posttreatment
	(n = 73)	(n = 50)		(n = 50)
Kicked	57.2%	59.6%	22.9	12.8%
Hit	45.2%	46.1%	18.0	10.1%
Beat up	63.0%	61.0%	24.6	0%
Threatened	24.7	28.2%	9.8	0%
Used weapon	4.1%	5.1%	1.6	0%

physical abuse and that contained some items in common with the *Conflict Tactics Scale*. This instrument (among others) was given to the men at the beginning of counseling (intake), after three months of counseling, after another three months of counseling and educational groups, and three months after program completion. Their wives completed these scales as well. Using this measure, Shepard found that 70% of the women reported no physical abuse at follow up (*n* = 77), and only 40% reported no psychological abuse at this time. Shepard had no matched control group. The major reduction in physical abuse came during the first three months of the program, suggesting that brief therapy of this sort is as effective as more protracted intervention.

Edelson, Syers, and Brygger (1987) and Edelson and Gruszknski (1988) reported data evaluating the Domestic Abuse Project in Minneapolis, which constitutes the largest (in terms of sample size) evaluation project performed to date. Follow-up data were obtained using the *Conflict Tactics Scale* at six months after treatment completion. Edelson and Grusznski assessed three cohorts of men who completed treatment and compared them to drop outs for repeat violence. Based on reports of female partners of men in cohort 1, 67% (*n* = 18) of the men who completed counseling were completely nonviolent (compared to 54% of men who dropped out of the program). Of the 33% who had used violence after treatment, 26% used direct violence (defined as grabbing, shoving, wrestling, slapping, carrying, restraining, spanking, or anything more severe); the other 7% used threats of violence.

Cohort 2 data provided by the men's partners revealed that, of 42 men completing treatment and still with partners, 67% were both nonviolent and nonthreatening at follow-up, 26% used direct violence against their partners at least once, and 7% used severe violence (defined as choking or strangling, physically forcing sex, punching or kicking, burning, beating, threatening with a weapon, using a weapon). These men also used significantly less violence (as reported by their partners) than did a group of men who had dropped out of the program.

Cohort 3 data indicated less treatment success with only 59% of men completely nonviolent. Edelson and Grusznski compared men's self-reports with their wives' reports and found the greatest discrepancy in the use of threats: the men reported themselves as nonviolent while their wives reported the men as using threats of violence against them. Edelson and Grusznski conclude that while the groups appear successful at eliminating violence, it is still too early to determine which clients benefit the most and which type of treatment works the best.

A less optimistic conclusion was reached in an outcome evaluation by Douglas and Perrin (1987). Two samples (n = 20, 34) of court-ordered batterers were interviewed six months after completion of a diversionary treatment program for first-time offenders. Program completers self-reported a 20% rate of recurrence of violence and a 15% rate of rearrest. However, police records indicated a rearrest rate of 15% for violent crimes. Of those subjects who were rearrested for violent crime, only 33% self-reported recurrence of violence. Although it is not known if these were wife assaults, this result represents no improvement on the Sherman and Berk recidivism rate of 19%.

How can we reconcile these various results? The Edelson et al. and Shepard studies reported 67% to 70% success rates while the Dutton study reported 84%. The difference here seems to lie in the criterion measure. For example, Edelson et al. counted pushing and restraining as actions that constituted treatment failure, while Dutton counted only those actions that had a higher probability of leading to arrest or generating injury. Since many treatment programs for wife assaulters are court related, criminal justice officials who fund the programs are mainly interested in success as defined by their system (i.e., no recidivism).

From a therapeutic standpoint, however, a diminution of other forms of abusive behavior (such as threatening or verbal abuse) clearly is also highly desirable. The main difference seems to be between the Douglas and Perrin finding of a 15% recidivism rate for treated offenders and the Dutton finding of a 4% rate. At least three major differences exist between these two studies: different populations, different treatment programs, and diversionary (arrest plus treatment) versus court-mandated (arrest, conviction plus treatment) treatment. A tentative conclusion is that men take treatment more seriously after conviction. Dutton and Strachan (1987b) found that men in treatment rated the actual court appearance as the most severe event that happened to them after the assault. Further research is needed to clarify these issues, but at present it seems fair to conclude that court-mandated treatment has been fairly successful at preventing repeat violence.

Clearly, a serious need exists for a design through which men convicted of wife assault are assigned at random to treatment or nontreatment conditions. Judges occasionally attach public service conditions to probation orders, and a case could be made for participation in an evaluation study as a condition of probation for untreated men. Occasionally, neighboring jurisdictions do or do not refer men to mandatory treatment and might constitute an essential comparison. In addition to a randomized design to circumvent the cumbersome matching made necessary in this study, a thorough psychological assessment of all men should be made. With a large stake in the outcome of treatment groups for wife assaulters, we need to know the conditions under which they are successful.

Given the limited success of other forms of offender treatment (Shore & Massimo, 1979; Gendreau & Ross, 1980), some criminal justice officials are generally skeptical about the success of treatment for wife assaulters. They tend to view a false dichotomy between treatment and law-and-order approaches to violence, when in actuality both have the same objective: to prevent repeat violence. As we saw in Chapter 5, incarceration for first-time wife assaulters is extremely rare unless the assault was extremely violent and caused serious injury. Although 33% to 60% of these men will probably not reoffend (Schulman, 1979; Straus, 1977a; Sherman & Berk, 1984), proponents of treatment groups have argued that wife assaulters require therapeutic intervention to alter habitual methods of dealing with conflict through the use of violence (Ganley, 1981).

The results of the Dutton (1987a) study, although preliminary, tend to support this view. If the results of the Sherman and Berk (1984), Jaffe, Wolfe, Telford, and Austin (1986), and Dutton (1987a) studies can be replicated, it would argue strongly for arrest/treatment combinations to diminish recidivist wife assaults. Through this model, arrest serves both a didactic and deterrent function to show the man that wife assault is unacceptable and will be punished by the state. The treatment group then provides the opportunity for the man to learn new responses to the interchanges with his wife that formerly generated violent behavior. In this sense, treatment and law-and-order approaches operate symbiotically to reduce future violence.

CHAPTER SUMMARY

In this chapter we have developed a treatment philosophy for wife assaulters that holds men responsible for their use of violence and helps them to analyze and control their anger. We have traced the development of such a cognitive-behavioral treatment program and reviewed evidence for its success, both with men with general anger problems and with wife assaulters.

We have examined the controversy over treating individuals as opposed to family systems and have argued that, since the empirical evidence suggests that individuals with conflict-generating habits transfer these habits from one family to another (Kalmuss & Seltzer, 1986), family systems approaches may occasionally err by emphasizing the current family system while disregarding the history of past relationships of the family's individual members. Detailed historical assessment might allow the detection of individual conflict-generators whose intrapsychic problems manifest themselves interpersonally in the contemporary family. Ignoring this possibility unfairly makes other family members share responsibility for the intrapsychic pathology of one dominant member.

Feminist therapy tends to err in the other direction, viewing all male violence as systematic domination of women. Feminist therapy calls for resocialization of men in treatment even though this resocialization may be at odds with the man's primary socializing milieu and world view. If this is the case, the resocialization in treatment is unlikely to compete effectively. Feminist therapists seem to believe that because men have greater objective sociopolitical and economic power, their violence therefore is always used in the protection of this power. In my therapeutic experience, assaultive males frequently feel completely powerless despite economic and sociopolitical power. That they earn more money than their wives is irrelevant to them. That they feel incapable of living up to the economic demands of raising a family, winning an argument with their wife, fulfilling a life goal or earning as much as a relevant comparison person is more salient to their view of themselves as powerless. Clearly, there is a vast discrepancy between objective power and subjective feelings of powerlessness (see Becker, 1973; Ng, 1980).

Anger management-assertiveness treatment falls philosophically into a middle ground between family systems and feminist approaches. It uses a philosophy of personal responsibility that is compatible both with criminal justice philosophy and the values of the broader culture in which it is nested. In that sense, it is a conservative approach, seeking to change individuals to fit systems rather than seeking social change. It is an essentially pragmatic approach, a band-aid that requires buttressing by other therapeutic forms and by constant action for social change.

We have presented a quasiexperimental review of the outcome of one such treatment program and a review of other, similar programs. What is sorely needed is a repeated, randomized evaluation. If such an evaluation reaffirmed the results of the current studies, we would argue strongly for arrest-treatment strategies to reduce recidivist assault.

ENDNOTES

1. This perspective raises, of course, the thorny issue of who has the responsibility of punishing the male for his violence. Perhaps a less problematic question is whether the victim is responsible for her own future safety. If one answers

in the affirmative, then she is responsible for self-protective actions such as leaving or taking refuge. For a variety of reasons (described in Chapter 4), these options are not always easily available for battered women.

2. If he does not live up to his responsibility, we tend to hold him culpable; he is to blame. We make a negative judgment about his lack of responsibility. As therapists we try to teach increased self-control and responsibility for violence to clients. The limit of personal responsibility is one's perception of choice. If a battered woman perceives that her husband will kill her if she leaves, we do not blame her for staying in an abusive relationship. She does not perceive that she has a choice. This may also be true for the assaultive male: he may not perceive that he has a choice. Altering his perceptions makes that choice more visible, and hence increases his responsibility.

3. Male clients in Deschner's study reported posttreatment decreases in dominance on the Taylor-Johnson scale, while female clients reported greatest decreases in depression.

CHAPTER 7

The Future

*When we profess to believe in deterrence and to value justice, but
refuse to spend the energy and money required to produce either,
we are sending a clear signal that we think that safe streets, unlike
all other great public goods, can be had on the cheap. We thereby
trifle with the wicked, make sport of the innocent, and encourage
the calculators. Justice suffers, and so do we all.*
                    —J. Q. Wilson, *Thinking About Crime* (1983, p. 260)

How will the current generation of children deal with conflict in their marriages
when they reach adulthood? Will they be more violent than contemporary adults?
Will incidence rates for wife assault increase during the next decade? Two lines
of analysis converge on these questions. One line examines the demographic
structure of society to predict how violence rates may increase or decrease as a
result of baby booms and other demographic factors that affect the structure
of contemporary and future society. In Section 7.2 we will consider this
perspective.

A second line of analysis examines the effects of current family dysfunction on the probability of dysfunction in the next generation. We know, for
example, that approximately 40% of today's children will witness their parents
divorce by age 16 (Bumpass, 1984). Levinger's (1966) analysis of court records
for divorce applicants found that 36.8% of the wives cited physical aggression
by the husband as one complaint. Even among nondivorced families, we know
from the surveys reported in Chapter 1 that 8.7% to 12.6% of families report
acts of severe abuse. How does the witnessing of abuse affect a child? What prog-
nostications can we make about the adult conflict-resolution behavior of these
child witnesses?

7.1 EFFECTS OF OBSERVING VIOLENCE ON THE CHILD WITNESS

In the 1975 U.S. national survey, Straus, Gelles, and Steinmetz (1980) describe
what they call the social heredity of family violence—that is, the learning of

violence in the family of origin. In order to ascertain whether such learning occurred, Straus et al. compared husbands whose parents had not been violent toward each other to husbands who reported at least one incident of violence between their parents. Men who had seen parents physically attack each other were almost three times more likely to have hit their own wives during the year of the study. In fact, about one out of three had done so (35%) compared with one out of ten (10.7%) of the men with nonviolent parents. These statistics were virtually identical for women. Women whose parents were violent had a much higher rate of hitting their own husbands (26.7%) compared to daughters of nonviolent parents (8.9%). The scale of violence toward spouses rose steadily with the violence these people observed between their own parents. Sons of the most violent parents had wife-beating rates 1,000% greater than sons of nonviolent parents, and daughters had a 600% greater rate.

Straus et al. argue that the family of origin is the place where people experience violence first and learn the emotional and moral meaning of violence. For most, this experience occurs through being a victim of violence;[1] for others it is the observation of parental violence. Straus et al. describe the unintended lessons of such violence:

1. That those who love you are also those who hit you
2. That hitting other members of the same family is morally acceptable
3. That violence is permissible when other things don't work

Being hit as a teenager clearly makes people more prone to spouse assault: people who experienced the most punishment as teenagers had spouse-beating rates four times greater than those whose parents did not hit them. Straus et al. concluded by reporting a double-whammy effect: When people both experience violence from a parent themselves and witness parent-parent violence, they are five to nine times more likely to be violent than people who experience neither type of violence.

Rosenbaum and O'Leary (1981) obtained comparison data for 20 maritally dysfunctional couples (receiving therapy for problems related to marital violence) with a group of 20 nonviolent couples. The authors reported that abusive husbands were more likely to have been victimized by parental physical abuse and to have witnessed parental violence. They did not report covariation between the two. The significant between-group difference for witnessing violence occurred regardless of whether the wives' reports of husbands' family backgrounds or the husbands' self-reports were used.

Kalmuss (1984) reviewed prior studies on effects of observing father-mother violence and found mixed results, which she attributed to methodological inconsistencies in the research. Some studies, for example, examined attributional consequences (i.e., cognitive means of interpreting or making sense of violence) of witnessing parental violence (Ulbrich & Huber, 1981) rather than effects on violent actions per se. Others failed to distinguish behavioral effects due to victimization from those due to witnessing and failed to disentangle the two dependent behavioral variables involved: likelihood of aggression and likelihood of victimization.

Furthermore, effects of parent-parent aggression may be contingent upon the role of the same-sex parent. If children model the behavior of the same-sex parent, we would expect sons to show increased aggression when they witnessed father-mother aggression. We would expect daughters who witnessed such aggression to be at increased risk for victimhood. These effects should be reversed for mother-father aggression. Using the data from the 1975 U.S. national survey (Straus et al., 1980), Kalmuss established that 15.8% of her respondents had witnessed parental hitting and 62.4% had themselves been hit by parents while in their teens.

By correlating these responses with CTS scores for their adult relationships, Kalmuss was able to generate the following findings: witnessing parental hitting and being hit as a teenager are both related to severe husband-wife (and wife-husband) aggression. However, for both types of aggression, the stronger effect comes from witnessing parental hitting (which doubles the odds of husband-wife aggression). As with the Straus et al. (1980) study, Kalmuss reports a double-whammy effect: The odds of husband-wife aggression increase dramatically when sons both observe and are victimized by parental aggression.

7.1.1 Modelling of Aggression

Kalmuss concludes that two types of modelling occur for parental aggression. *Generalized modelling* communicates the acceptability of aggression between family members and increases the likelihood of *any form* of family aggression in the next generation. *Specific modelling* occurs when individuals reproduce the particular types of family aggression to which they were exposed. *Intergenerational modelling,* Kalmuss concludes, involves more specific than generalized modeling in that severe marital aggression is more strongly related to witnessing than to being victimized by parental aggression.

It is not clear how Kalmuss arrives at the conclusion that witnessing involves more the specific than the general modelling mechanism, especially given a further finding from her study that there is no evidence for sex-specific learning of aggression. Exposure to fathers hitting mothers increases the likelihood of both husband-wife and wife-husband aggression in the next generation. Neither is specified by sex; that is, both sons and daughters are more likely to be victims and perpetrators when they have witnessed parental hitting. This latter finding is consistent with social learning findings that challenge the notion that children are more likely to imitate same-sex parents (Bandura, 1973; Hetherington, 1965).

As Kalmuss points out, however, her study has two limitations: first, as with most studies of this sort, it is based on retrospective accounts, which respondents may reconstruct to justify current use of marital aggression. Second, the data report on only one member of a current relationship. It is not known whether the results would change as a function of the current partner's experience with parental violence.

A later study by Kalmuss and Seltzer (1986) partially rectified this latter problem. In this study (cited in Chapter 6), Kalmuss and Seltzer examined continuity in the use of violence across relationships (first and second marriages) and concluded that evidence supported the notion that individual characteristics, rather than current family structure, better accounted for use of violence. They also concluded, however, that a repertoire of marital violence was not necessarily rooted in early childhood experience but frequently originated in the first marriage and maintained itself in new relationships.

How can we sum up these findings? The weight of evidence, it seems, suggests that witnessing violence in the family of origin strongly increases the odds of using violence in the adult relationship. This learning is not sex-specific but occurs about equally for men and women and independently of the sex of the aggressor parent. Self-taught aggression also occurs and carries over from the relationship in which it was learned to new relationships.

7.1.2 Immediate Effects of Witnessing Parental Violence

We do not know, of course, whether the modeling effects described above are examples of simple imitation or whether witnessing parental violence produces other negative psychological consequences that act as mediating variables for adult aggression. The research of Jaffe and Wolfe, for example, has indicated a variety of adjustment problems for children who witness violence.

Wolfe, Jaffe, Wilson, and Zak (1985) evaluated behavioral problems of 198 children from violent and nonviolent families. The *CTS* was used to assess violence and the Achenbach *Child Behavior Checklist* to assess the children's behavioral problems. Half of the children were from transition houses. Interviewers established via interviews with the mother whether the children had witnessed the violence, but the study did not report scales for extent of exposure. Amount of violence had significant effects on diminished social competence and behavioral problems, but this effect was mediated by maternal stress. Over one-quarter of the children assessed had behavioral problems falling into the clinical range on the measurement instrument. These children tended to have been exposed to a higher frequency of violence and to have experienced more negative life events. Additionally, the maternal stress variable accounted for 19% of the variance in child behavior problems.

Jaffe, Wolfe, Wilson, and Zak (1986a) reported that adjustment problems seemed more severe for boys than for girls exposed to parental violence. Boys displayed a higher degree of both externalizing symptoms (e.g., argumentativeness, bullying, temper tantrums) and internalizing symptoms (e.g., withdrawal, attention deficits). General social competence was impaired and all the above problems were significantly associated with the degree of violence witnessed. Girls from abusive homes were described as internalizing symptoms related to depression and anxiety. Boys also showed heightened signs of inadequacy, dependency, anxiety, and depression. The authors raised the question of whether these behaviors were modelled by abusive fathers in addition to violence.

Jaffe, Wolfe, Wilson, and Zak (1986b) compared victims of child abuse with children who had witnessed parental violence (defined as having been in visual or auditory range of the parents during conflict where violence occurred at least once in the previous year). The profiles of behavioral problems in the two groups were quite similar. *Child Behavior Checklist* scores indicated that witnessing parental violence was as harmful as experiencing physical abuse. However, as the authors point out, common factors existed for both groups, such as family stress, abrupt home changes, inadequate child management, and parental separations. Also, the abused and the witness samples may have had as much as a 40% overlap. However, they conclude that exposure to family violence is a major factor determining children's problem behavior.

Interestingly, some of the problem areas identified by Jaffe et al. (1986b) for this sample of children from violent homes, such as exaggerated dependency and impulse control problems, have also been identified as common in populations of wife assaulters (Ganley, 1981). Further research is required in order to establish whether these psychological sequelae of witnessing violence mediate the intergenerational transmission of violence.

7.2 DEMOGRAPHIC TRENDS

Turner, Fenn, and Cole (1981) developed a social-psychological analysis of violent behavior that begins with the social learning analysis that we have developed above (see Chapter 2). Social learning analyses attempt to explain the development and maintenance of violent habits in *individuals*. To predict changes in incidence rates in *aggregates*, Turner et al. combined their social learning analysis with a demographic analysis.

They argue that certain demographic groups are at risk for various violent crimes. Homicide, for example, is most frequently committed by males between the ages of 16 to 24 (modal age = 21). When structural changes occur in a population, the relative proportion of males falling into this age category can fluctuate. As the number of males falling into the 16- to 34-year category increases, the homicide rate should increase. In North American society, a postwar baby boom saw increases in the birth rate for each year from 1947 to 1957, when the birth rate began to decline. Hence, 1957 is a peak year that represents the zenith of the birth rate and the beginning of a disproportionately large age cohort that is 30 years old in 1987, 40 in 1997, and so on. Other factors being equal, we should witness increases in crimes associated with high risk-age groups as this disproportionately large cohort matures. As the baby boom reaches and passes the age of risk for specific crimes, the rate for that crime should rise and then fall.

Turner et al. provide demographic analyses of marriage, divorce, homicide, and unemployment that suggest increases in youth violence are greatest when (1) a relatively high proportion of the population falls into the high-risk age category and (2) an economic downturn occurs, generating a feeling of relative deprivation in this group. Historically, the last two periods of relative deprivation (1930–1935 and 1970–1975) demonstrated increased probabilities of homicide.

Turner et al. (1981) reason that young males, ceteris paribus, are more likely to have socially learned responses of aggression in response to aversive stressors. Economic downturns occurring just when these males are expected to enter the labor market constitute a major aversive stressor. Hence, population demographics interact with economic indicators, learned behaviors to stress, and age-relevant social expectations (to get a job), to influence rates of violence. When unemployment is high in general, or when a high percentage of young males are forced out of the labor market by trends such as women re-entering this market, a situation is created where a large group exists who (1) are likely to have learned aggression as a response to stress and (2) are currently experiencing economic stress. When a relatively high proportion of males in the high-risk age category exist in conjunction with these other two factors, violence rates climb. Turner et al. claim that from 1925 to 1970, homicides (rate/100,000 population) are related to fluctuations in relative deprivation and to changing birth rates.

If we examine the demographic profile of wife assaulters based on a variety of studies (Rounsaville, 1978; Dutton & Browning, 1984; Jaffe & Burris, 1982; Sherman & Berk, 1984) where the subject populations come from differing sources (e.g., the criminal justice system, wives in shelter houses, self-referred, etc.), the median age for wife assaulters seems to be 31. This means that if we assume marriage rates to be fairly steady, the peak year for wife assault, according to a demographic analysis, should be 1988. That is the year that the greatest number of at-risk males would be married. According to Turner et al.'s analysis, the peak of wife-assault incidence in 1988 would be preceded by an increase in wife assault caused by (1) annual increases in the proportion of at-risk males and (2) increases from 1975 to 1985 in the marriage rate.

In the next section, we will examine some comparative data from two U.S. national surveys conducted in 1975 and 1985 in order to test this demographic prediction of increased rates of wife assault.

7.3 A COMPARISON OF THE 1975 AND 1985 U.S. NATIONAL SURVEYS

In 1985 Straus and Gelles again supervised a U.S. national survey of family violence. A national probability sample of 6,002 households was obtained through telephone interviews conducted by Louis Harris and Associates (Straus & Gelles, 1985). The sample criteria were broadened in this survey to include not only married or cohabiting couples but any household with an adult over 18 who was divorced or separated in the two years prior to the survey. The response rate for this survey was 84%. For the sake of comparability, Straus and Gelles (1985) compared data from a 1985 subsample of 3,520 married/cohabiting couples with their 1975 sample.

As we noted in the previous section, a social demographic analysis would lead to a prediction of an increase in wife assault between 1975 and 1985 as the number of males in the at-risk age of 31 increases (up to a peak in 1988). However, husand-to-wife violence declined from 1975 to 1985. Rates of husband-wife violence on the Physical Violence Scale of the *CTS* dropped from 12.1 to 11.3, and rates on the Severe Violence Scale dropped from 3.8 to 3.0 (a 21% decrease). There was a slight (nonsignificant) increase in wife-husband violence. Hence, the data appear to contradict the prediction made by social demographers.

However, prior to disconfirming social demographic theory we should consider some alternative explanations derived from the 1975 to 1985 results. Straus and Gelles (1985) point out that the 1975 survey was a face-to-face interview and the 1985 survey was a telephone interview. Studies comparing telephone to in-person interviewing (Groves & Kahn, 1979) indicate that major differences in results rarely occur as a function of the method used. However, Straus and Gelles speculate that respondents would feel freer to report the issue of family violence to an anonymous telephone interviewer. This should lead to increases in reporting and, hence, if we accept Straus and Gelles's argument, suggests that the obtained decrease may have been even larger than what appeared in the data (to offset the expected increase generated by the shift in the method). Unfortunately, we do not know for certain what the effect of the shift in method may have been. One could also speculate that if rapport is established in an in-person interview, freedom to report may increase. We have found in interviews with wives of clients for court-mandated therapy that incidence reporting increases once trust and rapport are established.

A second methodological difference is that the telephone survey produced a 20% higher completion rate than the 1975 in-person survey. If we assume that people who refuse to participate may be more violent, then the telephone survey screened out fewer violent people and correspondingly should have produced increased incidence rates. Again, if this is true, the decline obtained may underrepresent the true decline.

Unfortunately, these suspected methodological differences are based on speculation. At this point, the safest conclusion may be that the 21% decrease found in the 1985 survey is far larger than could be accounted for by methodological differences in person and telephone surveys (Groves & Kahn, 1979). This being the case, why might wife assault have decreased in the last decade, contrary to the prediction of social demographers? In the next section we will offer a possible answer.

7.4 FROM SOCIETAL INDICATORS TO INDIVIDUAL PATHOLOGY

Attempting to predict how an individual will behave based on aggregate socioeconomic or demographic indicators has been termed an *ecological fallacy* by Dooley and Catalano (1984). In extending the work of psychologist Barbara Dohrenwend, Dooley and Catalano have examined the impact of aggregate indicators in unemployment, economic stress, and so forth on individual pathology. Their interest was sparked by uncritical linking of unemployment rates with increases in suicide, homicide, and psychiatric admissions.

In reviewing the literature on panel studies that address the issue of change in symptoms over time as a function of job loss or length of unemployment, Dooley and Catalano found very mixed results. Typically, job loss is followed by an increase in symptoms (e.g., health or mental health problems). However, several studies found no clear effects and some found counterintuitive improvements. The majority of studies that did find worsening of symptoms found relatively modest associations between economic stressors and symptoms. Catastrophic outcomes such as suicide or psychiatric admission were extremely rare.

Dooley and Catalano devised a cross-level approach to studying the issue that allowed them to divide the variability in an individual-level disorder measure into several possible sources: (1) pre-existing individual characteristics (age, sex, social economic status, etc.), (2) noneconomic stressful life events, (3) stressful economic life events, and (4) the economic environment at the aggregate level as well as all interactions between 1, 2, 3, and 4.

Dooley and Catalano conducted a series of trend surveys by telephone over a five-year period with a minimum of 500 respondents per survey. In total, over 8,000 respondents answered their questionnaire from 1978 to 1982. The surveys included comprehensive measures of stressful events and symptoms at two different times for each subject. The impact of the economy on symptoms was extremely moderate, to say the least. The best predictor of symptoms at Time 2 was symptoms at Time 1. And when the variance in Time 2 symptoms accounted for by Time 1 symptoms was partialed out, economic life events accounted for only 1% of the remaining variance. Dooley and Catalano concluded that the economy is related to symptoms by more than one pathway. A poor economic climate has a small direct effect on symptoms primarily for those in the work force. It also has a small indirect effect by creating an increase in the number of undesirable economic events for middle-status persons. These undesirable economic events are fairly strongly related to symptoms.

The implications of Dooley and Catalano's analysis for wife assault are as follows: Demographic and economic factors probably are not good predictors of wife-assault incidence rates. More sophisticated causal models need to be developed that identify variables that may moderate or enhance the impact of sociodemographic or economic variables on assaultive behavior. At present we have not empirically established what such moderating variables might be, although our hunch is that two candidates would be ontogenetically learned conflict-resolution habits and microsystem features as reviewed in Chapters 1 through 3. With regard to microsystem features, the increase of women in the work force suggests a trend toward diminished economic inequality between men and women, and as Coleman and Straus (1985) have shown, relatively egalitarian marriages tend to be less violent.

Straus and Gelles (1985) make the argument that raising public consciousness about family violence may also lead to decreased incidence. They argue that child abuse, which shows the greatest increase in public acceptance as a serious social problem, also shows the greatest decrease in incidence from 1975 to 1985. This increased awareness both influences the personal definition of what constitutes unacceptable behavior and the perceived consequences for transgressions. This latter factor, discussed in Chapter 5, includes the subjective perception of punishment and, by implication, notions of general deterrence. Publicity surrounding new police policy for wife assault has occurred in many U.S. states and Canadian provinces during the last decade. To date, no systematic assessment of the impact of this policy on the perceptions and behavior of at-risk males has been made, although such an assessment is clearly important.

At present, two surveys (1975 and 1985) are not sufficient to declare a trend. One would like to see further decreases reported in a 1995 survey. Nevertheless, given the enormous difficulties involved in generating social change, the 1985 results may be cause for cautious optimism. In 15 years, family violence has infiltrated public consciousness as a legitimate social problem. That phenomenon, in and of itself, may serve to make battered women feel that they are not alone (and not the cause) of their husbands' violence.

In 1982 a man in our treatment group appeared on local television and described his problem with violence toward his wife. By so doing, he helped the process by which a private behavior becomes identified as a public problem.

It is clear from contrasting surveys of crime victims with conflict tactics surveys that many victims of wife assault still do not define the violence committed on them as criminal nor requiring state intervention. The assumption made by many battered women that husband-wife violence is particular to their relationship leaves them with a sense of personal blame for their own victimization. Publicizing wife assault as a social problem diminishes this tendency toward self-blame by victims. It brings wife assault out of the closet, allowing both victims and aggressors to accept wife assault as a problem behavior capable of modification. This process diminishes the terrifying isolation that constitutes the everyday existence of both victims and aggressors.

A LAST WORD

We attempted in this book to develop a perspective on wife assault that is essentially a social-psychological one. We presented some paradoxes about men who assault their wives: that although they have some features in common (e.g., strong motives for power, poor assertiveness, exaggerated anxieties about control and intimacy), they also present great variation in their individual etiologies. And although they are aggressors, they are also victims—victims of their past exposure to violence and their present alienation from themselves.

We have attempted to apply these same standards to the analysis of battered women: They are not masochistic; they do not remain because they enjoy being victimized by violence.

Women use violence as much as men do (but with a less destructive effect), and the same social factors—particularly observation of parental violence—influence the use of violence in both women and men. Extreme power imbalances in current adult relationships make both men and women more violent. Male violence is by far the greater social problem because it has more severe consequences, but in explaining the development of violent behavior, the same rules apply, with the same results.

This conclusion will not sit well with people who hold tightly to some currently popular perspectives on wife assault. The notion that all male violence serves to maintain patriarchy, for example, overlooks both variation in male use of violence and the use of violence by women. Feminism has long argued that socialization shapes the behavior of males and females, and we have argued in this book that social factors shape both male and female violence. Both males and females learn to be violent through observation, and both can react violently to power imbalances in primary relationships. The overwhelming weight of evidence supports the view that violence in intimate relationships is a learned phenomenon.

Police and criminal justice officials may feel I have been too critical of their practices but police arrest rates for wife assault are too low and arrests are made for the wrong reasons. If the police want to be professional in their orientation to their job they must consider factors that achieve objectives (such as diminishing recidivist violence) rather than personal factors (the demeanor of a husband on a disturbance call) in their decision making.

Arrest-treatment combinations are not a complete solution to the problem of wife assault, but they are probably the best solution we currently have. Arrest remains the primary means available to the state to keep wife assaulters from denying that they have behavioral problems with consequences for others. Treatment should logically extend the wife assaulter's recognition and provide the means for change. It should also be based on a philosophy that is consistent with criminal justice views of personal responsibility if it is to be integrated into the criminal justice process. Treatment also should recognize the flexibility (or lack thereof) of the cultural parameters within which attitude and behavior change can be effected for each individual (e.g., community, type of work, etc.).

Treatment programs should try to obtain objectives that include nonviolent expression of anger, recognition that intimate relationships require an interdependent orientation toward the distribution of power, and recognition that assaultive behavior will impact on children. Most assaultive males feel a sense of guilt about their use of violence and do not want their children to be violent.

Finally, we have tried to convey a sense of the enormous amount of research still needed in the area of wife assault: We need to know more about the attributions made by aggressive males about the actions of others and how these attributions fuel anger and violence. We need to know for whom therapy is (or is not) effective and how subjective perceptions and beliefs of assaultive males both sustain their habits of violence and provide a means for change. This research requires collaboration among psychologists, sociologists, and criminologists and should be integrated around a common practical theme: how best to stop wife assault.

ENDNOTE

1. Straus et al. (1980) report that physical punishment of children is commonplace and seems to have been consistently so (based on retrospective reports) for the last two generations. Grandparents seem to have hit parents as much (37.3%) as those parents hit their children.

References

Abelson, R. P., & Levi, A. (1985). Decision making and decision theory. In G. Lindzey and E. Aronson (Eds.), *Handbook of Social Psychology* (3rd ed.). (Vol. 1). (pp. 231–310). New York: Random House.

Adler, A. (1966). The psychology of power. *Journal of Individual Psychology, 22,* 166–172.

Allen, J. G., & Hamsher, J. H. (1974). The development and validation of a test of emotional styles. *Journal of Consulting and Clinical Psychology, 42*(5), 663–668.

Allen, V., & Greenberger, D. (1978). An aesthetic theory of school vandalism. In E. Wenk & N. Harlow (Eds.), *School crime and disruption.* Davis, CA: Responsible Action (International Dialogue Press).

Amsel, A. (1958). Role of frustrative non-reward in non-continuous reward situations. *Psychological Bulletin, 55,* 102–119.

Andenaes, J. (1974). *Punishment and deterrence.* Ann Arbor: University of Michigan Press.

Anderson, T. W. (1958). *An introduction to multivariate statistical analysis.* New York: John Wiley & Sons.

Aquirre, B. E. (1984). *Why do they return? Abused wives in shelters.* Paper presented at the Second National Family Violence Researchers Conference, Durham, NH.

Bandura, A. (1973). *Aggression: A social learning analysis.* Englewood Cliffs, NJ: Prentice-Hall.

Bandura, A. (1977). Self-efficacy: Towards a unified theory of behavioral change. *Psychological Review, 84,* 191–215.

Bandura, A. (1979). The social learning perspective: Mechanisms of aggression. In H. Toch (Ed.), *Psychology of crime and criminal justice.* New York: Holt, Rinehart & Winston.

Bard, M. (1971, January). Iatrogenic violence. *The Police Chief.*

Bard, M. (1978). The police and family violence: Practice and policy. In U.S. Civil Rights Commission, *Battered women: Issues of public policy.* Washington, DC: U.S. Government Printing Office.

Bard, M., & Zacker, J. (1974). Assaultiveness and alcohol use in family disputes: Police perceptions. *Criminology, 12*(3), 281–292.

Bard, M., Zacker, J., & Rutter, E. (1972). *Police family crisis intervention and conflict-management: An action research analysis* (Report No. NI 70-068). New York: U.S. Department of Justice.

Baron, R. A. (1971a). Magnitude of victim's pain cues and level of prior anger arousal as determinants of adult aggressive behavior. *Journal of Personality and Social Psychology, 17,* 236–243.

Baron, R. A. (1971b). Aggression as a function of magnitude of victim's pain cues, level of prior anger arousal, and aggressor-victim similarity. *Journal of Personality and Social Psychology, 18,* 48–54.

Bateson, G. (1972). *Steps to an ecology of mind.* New York: Ballantine.

Baum, A., Fleming, R., & Singer, J. E. (1983). Coping with victimization by technological disaster. *Journal of Social Issues, 39*(2), 119–140.

Baum, A., & Singer, J. E. (Eds.). (1980). Applications of personal control. *Advances in Environmental Psychology* (Vol. 2). Englewood Cliffs, NJ: Lawrence Erlbaum Associates.

Beck, A. T. (1967). *Depression: clinical, experimental and theoretical aspects.* New York: Harper & Row.

Beck, A. T. (1976). *Cognitive theory and the emotional disorders.* New York: International Universities Press.

Becker, E. (1973). *The denial of death.* Glencoe, IL: Free Press.

Bell, D. J. (1985). *Domestic violence victimization: A multiyear perspective.* Paper presented at the American Society of Criminology Meeting, San Diego, CA.

Belsky, J. (1980). Child maltreatment: An ecological integration. *American Psychologist, 35*(4), 320–335.

Bennett-Sandler, G. (1975). *Structuring police organizations to promote crisis management programs.* Paper presented at the Symposium on Crisis Management in Law Enforcement, National Conference of Christians & Jews and California Association of Police Trainers, Berkeley, CA.

Berk, R. A., Berk, S. F., Loseke, D. R., & Rauma, D. (1983). Mutual combat and other family violence myths. In D. Finkelhor, R. J. Gelles, G. T. Hotaling, & M. A. Straus (Eds.), *The dark side of families: Current family violence research.* Beverly Hills, CA: Sage.

Berk, S. F., & Loseke, D. R. (1980). "Handling" family violence: Situational determinants of police arrest in domestic disturbances. *Law & Society Review, 15*(2), 317–346.

Berlyne, D. E. (1967). *Arousal and reinforcement.* In D. Levine (Ed.), *Nebraska Symposium on Motivation* (pp. 1–132). Lincoln: University of Nebraska Press.

Bettelheim, B. (1943). Individual and mass behavior in extreme situations. *Journal of Abnormal and Social Psychology, 38,* 417–452.

Bigelow, R. (1972). The evolution of co-operation, aggression and self-control. In J. K. Cole and D. D. Jensen (Eds.), *Nebraska Symposium on Motivation* (pp. 1–58). Lincoln: University of Nebraska Press.

Black, D. (1979). *Dispute settlement by the police.* Unpublished: Yale University.

Bland, R., & Orn, H. (1986, March). Family violence and psychiatric disorder. *Canadian Journal of Psychiatry, 31,* 129–137.

Blood, R., Jr., & Wolfe, D. (1960). *Husbands and wives: The dynamics of married living.* Glencoe, IL: Free Press.

Blumstein, A., Cohen, J., & Nagin, D. (Eds.). (1978). Deterrence and incapacitation: *Estimating the effects of criminal sanctions on crime rates.* Washington, DC: National Academy of Sciences.

Bower, S. A., & Bower, G. H. (1976). *Asserting yourself: A practical guide for positive change.* Reading, MA: Addison-Wesley.

Bowker, L. H. (1983). *Beating wife beating.* Lexington, MA: Lexington Books.

Bowlby, J. (1969). *Attachment and loss: Vol. I. Attachment.* New York: Basic Books.

Bronfenbrenner, U. (1977). Toward an experimental ecology of human development. *American Psychologist, 32*(6), 513–531.

Bronfenbrenner, U. (1979). *The ecology of human development.* Cambridge, MA: Harvard University Press.

Browning, J. J. (1983). *Violence against intimates: Toward a profile of the wife assaulter.* Unpublished doctoral dissertation, University of British Columbia, Vancouver, B.C.

Browning, J. J. (1984). *Stopping the violence: Canadian programmes for assaultive men.* Ottawa: Health & Welfare Canada.

Browning, J. J., & Dutton, D. G. (1986). Assessment of wife assault with the conflict tactics scale: Using couple data to quantify the differential reporting effect. *Journal of Marriage and the Family, 48,* 375–379.

Bugenthal, M. D., Kahn, R. L., Andrews, F., & Head, K. B. (1972). *Justifying violence: Attitudes of American man.* Ann Arbor, MI: Institute for Social Research.

Bulman, R. J., & Wortman, C. (1977). Attributions of blame and coping in the "real world." Severe accident victims react to their lot. *Journal of Personality and Social Psychology, 35,* 351–363.

Bumpass, L. (1984). Children and marital disruption: A replication and update. *Demography, 21,* 7–82.

Burgess, R. (1978). Child abuse: A behavioral analysis. In B. Lakey & A. Kazdin (Eds.), *Advances in child clinical psychology.* New York: Plenum Press.

Burris, C. A., & Jaffe, P. (1983, July). Wife abuse as a crime: The impact of police laying charges. *Canadian Journal of Criminology,* 309–318.

Burt, M. R. (1980). Cultural myths and supports for rape. *Journal of Personality and Social Psychology, 38*(2), 217–230.

Buss, A. H., & Durkee, A. (1957). An inventory for assessing different kinds of hostility. *Journal of Consulting Psychology, 21,* 343–349.

Caine, T. M., Foulds, G. A., & Hope, K. (1967). *Manual of hostility and direction of hostility questionnaire (HDHQ).* London: University of London Press.

Campbell, D. T. (1969). Reforms as experiments. *American Psychologist, 24,* 409–429.

Campbell, J. C. (1987). *Making sense of the senseless: Woman's attributions about battering.* Paper presented at the Third National Family Violence Research Conference, Durham, NH.

Caplan, N., & Nelson, S. D. (1973, March). On being useful: The nature and consequences of psychological research on social problems. *American Psychologist, 28*(3), 199–211.

Caplan, P. (1984). The myth of women's masochism. *American Psychologist, 39*(2), 130–139.

Carroll, J. (1978). A psychological approach to deterrence: The evaluation of crime opportunities. *Journal of Personality and Social Psychology, 36*(12), 1512–1520.

Chambers, D. (1979). *Making fathers pay: The enforcement of child support.* Chicago: University of Chicago Press.

Clanton, G., & Smith, L. (1977). *Jealousy.* Englewood Cliffs, NJ: Prentice-Hall.

Cohn, E. S., & Giles-Sims, J. (1979). *Battered women: Whom did they blame?* Paper presented at the meeting of the Eastern Psychological Association, Philadelphia, PA.

Coleman, D. H., & Straus, M. A. (1985). *Marital power, conflict, and violence.* Paper presented at the meeting of the American Society of Criminology, San Diego, CA.

Conway, F., & Siegleman, J. (1978). *Snapping: America's epidemic of sudden personality change.* New York: Dell.

Crowne, D. P., & Marlowe, D. A. (1960). A new scale of social desirability independent of psychopathology. *Journal of Consulting Psychology, 24,* 349–354.

Daly, M. (1973). *Beyond god the father*. Toronto: Fitzhenry & Whiteside.

Daly, M. (1978). *Gyn/ecology: The metaethics of radical feminism*. Boston: Beacon Press.

Daly, M., Wilson, M., & Weghorst, S. J. (1982). Male sexual jealousy. *Ethology and Sociobiology, 3*, 11–27.

Darwin, C. (1871). *The descent of man and selection in relation to sex* (Vol. 1). London: John Murray.

Darwin, C. (1872). *The expression of emotion in man and animals*. London: John Murray.

Davidson, T. (1977). Wife beating: A recurring phenomenon throughout history. In M. Roy (Ed.), *Battered women: A psychosociological study of domestic violence*. New York: Van Nostrand.

Davidson, T. (1978). *Conjugal crime: Understanding and changing the wife beating pattern*. New York: Hawthorn Books.

de Reincourt, A. (1974). *Sex and power in history*. New York: Delta.

Deschner, J. (1984). *The hitting habit: Anger control for battering couples*. New York: Free Press.

Deutsch, H. (1944). *The psychology of women* (Vol. 1). New York: Grune & Stratton.

Diagnostic and Statistical Manual of the Mental Disorders (3rd ed.). (1981). Washington, DC: American Psychiatric Association.

Diener, E. (1976). Effects of prior destructive behavior, anonymity and group presence on deindividuation and aggression. *Journal of Personality and Social Psychology, 33*(5), 497–507.

Dixon, W. J., Brown, M. B., Engelman, L., Frane, J. W., Hill, M. A., Jennrich, R. J., & Joporek, J. D. (1981). *BMPD statistical software*. Berkeley: University of California Press.

Dobash, R. E., & Dobash, R. P. (1978). Wives: The appropriate victims of marital assault. *Victimology: An International Journal, 2*, 426–442.

Dobash, R. E., & Dobash, R. P. (1979). *Violence against wives: A case against the patriarchy*. New York: Free Press.

Dobash, R. E., & Dobash, R. P. (1984). The nature and antecedents of violent events. *British Journal of Criminology, 24*(31), 269–288.

Dobson, K. S., & Block, L. (1987). Historical and philosophical bases of the cognitive-behavioral therapies. In K. S. Dobson (Ed.), *Handbook of cognitive-behavioral therapies*. New York: Guilford Press.

Dooley, D. G., & Catalano, R. (1984). The epidemiology of economic stress. *American Journal of Community Psychology, 12*, 4, 387–409.

Douglas, M. A., & Perrin, S. (1987). *Recidivism and accuracy of self-reported violence and arrest in court ordered treatment to batters*. Paper presented at the Third National Family Violence Research Conference, Durham, NH.

Dutton, D. G. (1977). *Domestic dispute intervention by police. Proceedings of the United Way Symposium on Domestic Violence*, Vancouver, B.C.

Dutton, D. G. (1981a). *The criminal justice system response to wife assault*. Ottawa: Solicitor General of Canada, Research Division.

Dutton, D. G. (1981b). *A nested ecological theory of wife assault*. Paper presented at the Canadian Psychological Association, Toronto.

Dutton, D. G. (1981c). Training police officers to intervene in domestic violence. In R. B. Stuart (Ed.), *Violent behavior*. New York: Brunner/Mazel.

Dutton, D. G. (1983). *Masochism as an "explanation" for traumatic bonding: An example of the "fundamental attribution error."* Boston: American Orthopsychiatric Association.

Dutton, D. G. (1985). An ecologically nested theory of male violence towards intimates. *International Journal of Women's Studies, 8*(4), 404–413.

Dutton, D. G. (1986a). Wife assaulters' explanations for assault: The neutralization of self-punishment. *Canadian Journal of Behavioral Science, 18*(4), 381–390.

Dutton, D. G. (1986b). The public and the police: Training implications of the demand for a new model police officer. In J. Yuille (Ed.), *Police selection and training: The role of psychology.* Nijhoff: Amsterdam.

Dutton, D. G. (1987a). The outcome of court-mandated treatment for wife assault: A quasi-experimental evaluation. *Violence & Victims, 1*(3), (in press).

Dutton, D. G. (1987b). The criminal justice response to wife assault. *Law and Human Behavior, 11*(3), 189–206.

Dutton, D. G., & Aron, A. (in press). Romantic attraction and generalized liking for others who are sources of conflict-based arousal. *Canadian Journal of Behavioural Science.*

Dutton, D. G., & Browning, J. J. (1984). *Concern for power, fear of intimacy and aversive stimuli for wife assault.* Unpublished manuscript, University of British Columbia, Vancouver, B.C.

Dutton, D. G., & Browning, J. J. (1987). Power struggles and intimacy anxieties as causative factors of violence in intimate relationships. In G. Russell (Ed.), *Violence in intimate relationships.* New York: Sage.

Dutton, D. G., Fehr, B., & McEwen, H. (1982). Severe wife battering as deindividuated violence. *Victimology: An International Journal, 7*, 13–23.

Dutton, D. G., & Levens, B. R. (1977). Domestic crisis intervention: Attitude survey of trained and untrained police officers. *Canadian Police College Journal, 1*(2), 75–92.

Dutton, D. G., & Painter, S. L. (1980). *Male domestic violence and its effects on the victim.* Ottawa: Health and Welfare Canada.

Dutton, D. G., & Painter, S. L. (1981). Traumatic bonding: The development of emotional attachments in battered women and other relationships of intermittent abuse. *Victimology: An International Journal, 6*, 139–155.

Dutton, D. G., & Strachan, C. E. (1987a). *Motivational needs for power and dominance as differentiating variables of assaultive and non-assaultive male populations.* Unpublished manuscript.

Dutton, D. G., & Strachan, C. E. (1987b). *The prediction of recidivism in a population of wife assaulters.* Paper presented at the Third National Family Violence Conference, Durham, NH.

Easterbrook, J. (1959). The effect of emotion on the utilization and organization of behavior. *Psychological Review, 66*, 183–201.

Eddy, M. J., & Meyers, T. (1984). *Helping men who batter: A profile of programs in the U.S.* Texas Council on Family Violence, Arlington, Texas.

Edelson, J. L., & Grusznski, R. J. L. (in press). Treating men who batter: four years of outcome data from the Domestic Abuse Project. *Journal of Social Science Research.*

Edelson, J. L., Syers, M., & Brygger, M. P. (1987). *Comparative effectiveness of group treatment for men who batter.* Paper presented at the Third National Family Violence Conference, Durham, NH.

Ehreneich, B. (1983). *The hearts of men.* New York: Anchor Press/Doubleday.

Ehrlich, I. (1975). The deterrent effect of capital punishment: A question of life and death. *American Economic Review, 65*, 397–412.

Elias, N. (1978). The history of manners. New York: Pantheon.

Elliot, F. (1977). The neurology of explosive rage: The episodic dyscontrol syndrome. In M. Roy (Ed.), *Battered women: A psychosociological study of domestic violence.* New York: Van Nostrand.

Emerson, C. D. (1979, June). Family violence: A study by the L. A. County Sheriff's Department. *Police Chief,* 48–50.

Eysenck, H. (1969). *The effects of psychotherapy.* New York: Science House.

Fagan, J. (1987). Cessation of family violence: Deterrence and dissuasion. In *Crime and justice: An annual review of research.*

Fallaci, O. (1981). *A man.* New York: Simon & Schuster.

Farberow, N. (1980). *The many faces of suicide.* New York: McGraw-Hill.

Fasteau, M. F. (1974). *The male machine.* New York: McGraw-Hill.

Fattah, E. A. (1981). The victimization experience and its aftermath. *Victimology: An International Journal,* 6(1–4), 29–47.

Faulk, M. (1974). Men who assault their wives. *Medicine, Science and the Law, 14,* 180–183.

Felson, R., & Ribner, S. (1981). An attributional approach to accounts and sanctions for criminal violence. *Social Psychology Quarterly, 44,* 137–142.

Feshback, S. (1970). Aggression. In P. H. Mussen (Ed.), *Carmichael's manual of child psychology* (Vol. 2). New York: John Wiley & Sons.

Field, M. (1978). Wife beating: Government intervention policies and practices. In *Battered women: Issues of public policy.* U.S. Civil Rights Commission.

Fields, M., & Fields, H. (1973, June). Marital violence and the criminal process: Neither justice nor peace. *Social Service Review, 47,* 221–240.

Fincham, F., & Jaspars, J. (1980). Attribution of responsibility from man the scientist to man as lawyer. *Advances in Experimental Social Psychology, 13,* 81–138.

Fischer, A. E. (1955). *The effects of differential early treatment on the social and exploratory behavior of puppies.* Unpublished doctoral dissertation, Pennsylvania State University.

Fischer, C. (1982). *To dwell amongst friends: Personal networks in town and city.* Chicago: University of Chicago Press.

Fiske, D. W., & Maddi, A. R. (1961). A conceptual framework. In D. W. Fiske & S. R. Maddi (Eds.), *Functions of varied experience.* Homewood, IL: Dorsey Press.

Fleming, J. B. (1979). *Stopping wife abuse.* Garden City, NY: Anchor Books.

Flynn, E. E. (1986). Victims of terrorism: Dimensions of the victim experience. In E. Fattah (Ed.), *The plight of crime victims in modern society.* London: MacMillan.

Ford, D. A. (1987). *The impact of police officers' attitudes toward victims on the disinclination to arrest wife batterers.* Paper presented at the Third National Family Violence Conference, Durham, NH.

Freedman, J., Levey, A., & Price, J. (1972). Crowding and human aggressiveness. *Journal of Experimental Social Psychology, 8,* 528–548.

Freud, A. (1942). *The ego and the mechanisms of defense.* New York: International Universities Press.

Freud, S. (1938). Three contributions to the theory of sex. In A. A. Brill (Ed.), *The basic writings of Sigmund Freud.* New York: Random House.

Frieze, I. H. (1979). Perceptions of battered wives. In I. H. Frieze, D. Bar-Tal, & S. Carroll (Eds.), *New approaches to social problems.* San Francisco: Jossey-Bass, 1979.

Fromm, E. (1941). *Escape from freedom.* New York: Avon Books.

Fromm, E. (1973). *The anatomy of human destructiveness.* New York: Fawcett.

Ganley, A. (1980, March). *Interview: Whatcom County counseling and psychiatric center,* Bellingham, Washington.

Ganley, A. (1981). *Participant's manual: Court mandated therapy for men who batter: A three day workshop for professionals.* Washington, DC: Center for Women Policy Studies.

Ganley, A., & Harris, L. (1978). *Domestic violence: Issues in designing and implementing programs for male batterers.* Paper presented at the 86th annual convention of the American Psychological Association, Toronto.

Gaquin, D. A. (1977). Spouse abuse: Data from the National Crime Survey. *Victimology: An International Journal, 2*(3–4), 632–642.

Garbarino, J. (1977). The human ecology of child maltreatment: A conceptual model for research. *Journal of Marriage and the Family, 39,* 721–736.

Gayford, J. J. (1975). Wife battering: A preliminary survey of 100 cases. *British Medical Journal, 30*(1), 194–197.

Geen, R. J. (1970). Perceived suffering of the victim as an inhibitor of attack-induced aggression. *Journal of Social Psychology, 81,* 209–216.

Geen, R. J., Rakosky, J. J., & Pigg, R. (1972). Awareness of arousal and its relation to aggression. *British Journal of Social and Clinical Psychology, 11,* 115–121.

Gelles, R. J. (1972). *The violent home: A study of physical aggression between husbands and wives.* Beverly Hills: Sage.

Gelles, R. J. (1975). Violence and pregnancy: A note on the extent of the problem and needed services. *The Family Co-ordinator, 24,* 81–86.

Gelles, R. J. (1976). Abused wives: Why do they stay? *Journal of Marriage and the Family, 38,* 659–668.

Gelles, R. J. (1978). Violence towards children in the United States. *American Journal of Orthopsychiatry, 48,* 580–592.

Gelles, R. J., & Straus, M. A. (1979). Determinants of violence in the family: Toward a theoretical integration. In W. Burr, R. Hill, I. Nye, & I. Reiss (Eds.), *Contemporary theories about the family* (Vol. 1). New York: Free Press.

Gendreau, P., & Ross, R. (1980). Correctional potency: Treatment and deterrence on trial. In R. Roesch & R. Corrado (Eds.), *Evaluation and criminal justice policy.* Beverly Hills, CA: Sage.

Gibbs, G. (1985). Deterrence theory and research. *Nebraska Symposium on Motivation, 33,* 87–130.

Giles-Sims, J. (1983). *Wife battering: A systems theory approach.* New York: Guilford.

Goldman, P. (1978). *Violence against women in the family.* Unpublished master's thesis, McGill University, Faculty of Law.

Gondolf, E. W. (1985a). *Men who batter: An integrated approach for stopping wife abuse.* Holmes Beach, CA: Learning Publications.

Gondolf, E. W. (1985b). Anger and oppression in men who batter: Empiricist and feminist perspectives and their implications for research. *Victimology: An International Journal, 10*(1–4), 311–324.

Goode, W. G. J. (1971). Why men resist. *Dissent,* 181–193.

Gould, S. J. (1983, June). Genes on the brain. *New York Review of Books,* p. 5.

Greenglass, E. R. (1982). *A world of difference: Gender roles in perspective.* New York: John Wiley & Sons.

Greenhouse, S. W., & Geisser, G. (1959). On methods in the analysis of profile data. *Psychometrika, 24,* 95–112.

Groves, R. M., & Kahn, R. L. (1979). *Surveys by telephone: A national comparison with personal interviews.* New York: Academy Press.

Hamberger, L. K., & Hastings, J. E. (1986). *Characteristics of male spouse abusers: Is psychopathology part of the picture?* Paper presented at American Society of Criminology, Atlanta, GA.

Hare, R. D. (1965a). Psychopathy, fear, arousal, and anticipated pain. *Psychological Reports, 16,* 499–502.

Hare, R. D. (1965b). Temporal gradient of fear arousal in psychopaths. *Journal of Abnormal Psychology, 70,* 442–445.

Hare, R. D. (1968). Psychopathy, autonomic functioning and the orienting response. *Journal of Abnormal Psychology, 73.*

Harlow, H. F., & Harlow, M. (1971). Psychopathology in monkeys. In H. D. Kinnel (Ed.), *Experimental psychopathology.* New York: Academic Press.

Harris, R. J. (1975). *A primer of multivariate statistics.* New York: Academic Press.

Haynes, R. B. (1985). The predictive value of the clinical assessment for the diagnosis, prognosis and treatment response of patients. In C. Webster, M. Ben-Aron, & S. J. Hucker (Eds.), *Dangerousness: Probability and prediction, psychiatry and public policy.* Cambridge: Cambridge University Press.

Henderson, M., & Hewstone, M. (1984). Prison inmates' explanations for interpersonal violence: Accounts and attributions. *Journal of Consulting and Clinical Psychology, 52*(5), 789–794.

Hendrick, J. (1977, January 29). When television is a school for criminals. *TV Guide,* pp. 4–10.

Hetherington, E. M. (1965). A developmental study of the effects of sex of the dominant parent on sex-role preference, identification and imitation in children. *Journal of Personality and Social Psychology, 2,* 188–194.

Hilberman, E. (1980). Overview: The "wife beater's wife" reconsidered. *American Journal of Psychiatry, 137*(11), 1336–1347.

Hilberman, E., & Munson, K. (1977–78). Sixty battered women. *Victimology, 2,* 460–470.

Hogarth, J. (1980). *Battered wives and the justice system.* Unpublished manuscript. University of British Columbia, Faculty of Law.

Hokanson, J. E., Willers, K. R., & Koropsak, E. (1968). Modification of autonomic responses during aggressive interchange. *Journal of Personality, 36,* 386–404.

Holmes, T. H., & Rahe, R. H. (1967). The social readjustment rating scale. *Journal of Psychosomatic Research, 11,* 213–218.

Hood, R., & Sparks, R. (1970). *Key issues in criminology.* New York: McGraw-Hill.

Hunt, J. M., Cole, M. W., & Reis, E. E. A. (1958). Situational cues distinguishing anger, fear, and sorrow. *American Journal of Psychology, 71,* 136–151.

Hunt, M. (1959). *The natural history of love.* New York: Alfred A. Knopf.

Huxley, A. (1980). *The human situation.* Great Britain: Granada Publishing and Triad Paperbacks.

Izard, C. E., Dougherty, F. E., Bloxom, B. M., & Kotsch, W. E. (1974). *The differential emotions scale: A method of measuring the subjective experience of discrete emotions.* Nashville: Vanderbilt University.

Jacob, J. (1975). Family interaction in disturbed and normal families: A methodological and substantive review. *Psychological Bulletin, 82,* 33–65.

Jaffe, P. (1982, February). *Testimony before Standing Committee on Health, Welfare and Social Affairs* (pp. 27–15). Ottawa: House of Commons.

Jaffe, P., & Burris, C. A. (1982). *An integrated response to wife assault: A community model*. Ottawa: Research Report of the Solicitor General of Canada.

Jaffe, P., Wolfe, D. A., Telford, A., & Austin, G. (1986). The impact of police charges in incidents of wife abuse. *Journal of Family Violence*. 1(1), 37–49.

Jaffe, P., Wolfe, D., Wilson, S. K., & Zak, L. (1986a). Family violence and child adjustment: A comparative analysis of girls' and boys' behavioral symptoms. *American Journal of Psychiatry*, 143, 74–77.

Jaffe, P., Wolfe, D., Wilson, S., & Zak, L. (1986b). Similarities in behavioral and social maladjustment among child victims and witnesses to family violence. *American Journal of Orthopsychiatry*, 56(1), 142–146.

Janoff-Bulman, R. (1979). Characterological versus behavioral self-blame: Inquiries into depression and rape. *Journal of Personality and Social Psychology*, 37, 1798–1809.

Janoff-Bulman, R., & Lang-Gunn, L. (1985). Coping with disease and accidents: The role of self-blame attributions. In L. Y. Abramson (Ed.), *Social-personal influence in clinical psychology* (Vol. 5). Hillsdale, NJ: Erlbaum.

Johnson, E., & Tversky, A. (1983). Affect, generalization and the perception of risk. *Journal of Personality and Social Psychology*, 45(1), 20–31.

Jones, E. E., & Nisbett, R. E. (1971). The actor and the observer: Divergent perceptions of the causes of behavior. In E. E. Jones, D. Kanouse, H. H. Kelley, R. E. Nisbett, S. Valins, & B. Weiner, *Attribution: Perceiving the causes of behaviors*. Morristown, NJ: General Learning Press.

Joreskog, K. (1979). Statistical estimation of structural models in longitudinal development investigations. In J. Nesselroade & P. Baltes (Eds.), *Longitudinal research in the study of behavior and development*. New York: Academic Press.

Jorgenson, D. O., & Dukes, F. O. (1976). Deindividuation as a function of density and group membership. *Journal of Personality and Social Psychology*, 34(1), 24–29.

Kahneman, D. S., & Tversky, A. (1973). On the psychology of prediction. *Psychological Review*, 80, 237–251.

Kalmuss, D. S. (1984, February). The intergenerational transmission of marital aggression. *Journal of Marriage and the Family*, 46, 11–19.

Kalmuss, D. S., & Seltzer, J. A. (1986). Continuity of marital behavior in remarriage: The case of spouse abuse. *Journal of Marriage and the Family*, 48, 113–120.

Kalmuss, D. S., & Straus, M. A. (1982, May). Wife's marital dependency and wife abuse. *Journal of Marriage and the Family*, 44, 277–286.

Kardiner, S. H., & Fuller, M. (1970). Violence as a defense against intimacy. *Mental Hygiene*, 54(2), 310–315.

Kelley, H. H., & Stahelski, A. J. (1970). Errors in perception of intentions in a mixed-motive game. *Journal of Experimental Social Psychology*, 6, 379–400.

Kempe, R. S., & Kempe, C. H. (1978). *Child abuse*. Cambridge, MA: Harvard University Press.

Kendrick, D. J., & Cialdini, R. (1977). Romantic attraction: Misattribution vs. reinforcement explanations. *Journal of Personality and Social Psychology*, 36(6), 381–391.

Kennedy, L. W., & Dutton, D. G. (1987). *The incidence of family violence in Alberta*. Unpublished manuscript, Population Research Laboratory, University of Alberta, Edmonton, Alberta.

Kirk, R. E. (1968). *Experimental design: Procedure for the behavioral sciences*. Belmont, CA: Wadsworth Publishing Co.

Kitson, G. C. (1982, May). Attachment to the spouse in divorce: A scale and its application. *Journal of Marriage and the Family*, 44, 379–393.

Konecni, U. J. (1975). Annoyance, type and duration of postannoyance activity, and aggression: The "cathartic effect." *Journal of Experimental Psychology, 104*(1), 76–102.

Langer, E. (1983). *The psychology of control.* Beverly Hills, CA: Sage.

Lazarus, R. A., & Averill, J. R. (1972). Emotion and cognition: With special reference to anxiety. In C. D. Spielberger (Ed.), *Anxiety: Current trends in theory and research* (Vol. II). New York: Academic.

Lerman, L. G. (1981). *Prosecution of spouse abuse: Innovations in criminal justice response.* Center for Women Policy Studies, Washington, DC.

Lerner, M. (1977). The justice motive in social behavior. *Journal of Social Issues, 45,* 1–50.

Leuba, C. (1955). Toward some integration of learning theories: The concept of optimal stimulation. *Psychological Reports, 1,* 27–33.

Levens, B. R., & Dutton, D. G. (1977). Domestic crisis intervention: Citizens' requests for service and the Vancouver Police Department response. *Canadian Police College Journal, 1,* 29–50.

Levens, B. R., & Dutton, D. G. (1980). *The social service role of the police: Domestic Crisis Intervention.* Ottawa: Solicitor General of Canada.

Levenson, R. W., & Gottman, J. M. (1983). Marital interaction: Physiological linkage and affective exchange. *Journal of Personality and Social Psychology, 45,* 587–597.

Levinger, G. (1966). Sources of marital dissatisfaction among applicants for divorce. *American Journal of Orthopsychiatry, 36,* 803–807.

Lewin, K. (1951). *Field theory in social science.* New York: Harper & Row.

Lewin, K., Lippitt, R., & White, R. (1947). An experimental study of leadership and group life. In T. M. Newcombe & E. L. Hartley (Eds.), *Readings in social psychology.* New York: Holt, Rinehart & Winston.

Leyens, J. P., Camino, L., Parke, R. D., & Berkowitz, L. (1975). Effects of movie violence on aggression in a field setting as a function of group dominance and cohesion. *Journal of Personality and Social Psychology, 32,* 346–360.

Liebman, D. A., & Schwartz, J. A. (1973). Police programs in domestic crisis intervention: A review. In J. Snibbe & H. Snibbe (Eds.), *The urban policeman in transition.* Springfield, IL: Charles C Thomas.

Lion, J. (1977). Clinical aspects of wife battering. In M. Roy (Ed.), *Battered women: A psychosociological study of domestic violence.* New York: Van Nostrand Reinhold.

Lorenz, K. (1937). The companion in the bird's world. *Auti, 54,* 245–273.

Loving, N., & Farmer, M. (1980). *Police handling of spouse abuse and wife beating calls: A guide for police managers.* Police Executive Research Forum, Washington, DC.

Maccoby, E. E., & Jacklin, C. N. (1974). *The psychology of sex differences.* Stanford, CA: Stanford University Press.

MacLeod, L. (1980). *Wife battering in Canada: The vicious circle.* The Canadian Advisory Council on the Status of Women: Canadian Government Publishing Centre.

Mahoney, M. J., & Thoreson, C. E. (1979). *Self-control: Power to the person.* Monterey, CA: Brooks/Cole.

Maiuro, R. D., Cahn, T. S., Vitaliano, P. P., & Zegree, J. B. (1986). *Anger control treatment for men who engage in domestic violence: A controlled outcome study.* Paper presented at the annual convention of the Western Psychological Association, Seattle, WA.

Mandler, G. (1975). *Mind and emotion.* New York: John Wiley & Sons.

Marascuilo, L. A., & Levin, J. R. (1983). *Multivariate statistics in the social sciences: A researcher's guide.* Belmont, CA: Wadsworth.

Margolin, G. (1983). *Marital conflict: Intrapersonal and interpersonal factors.* Washington, DC: National Institute of Mental Health.

Margolin, G. (1984). *Interpersonal and intrapersonal factors associated with marital violence.* Paper presented at the Second National Family Violence Research Conference, Durham, NH.

Marlatt, G. A., & Rohsenow, D. J. (1981). The think-drink effect. *Psychology Today, 15*(12), 60.

Martin, D. (1977). *Battered wives.* New York: Kangaroo Paperbacks.

Maslach, C. (1974). Social and personal bases of deindividuation. *Journal of Personality and Social Psychology, 29*(3), 411–425.

McClelland, D. (1975). *Power: The inner experience.* New York: Halstead Press.

Megargee, E. (1970). The prediction of violence with psychological tests. In C. Speilberger (Ed.), *Current topics in clinical and community psychology.* New York: Academic Press.

Meichenbaum, D. (1977). *Cognitive behavior modification.* New York: Plenum Press.

Meyer, J. K., & Lorimer, T. D. (1979). Police intervention data and domestic violence: Exploratory development and validation of prediction models. National Institute of Mental Health, Kansas City, MO, Police Department.

Milgram, S. (1974). *Obedience to authority.* New York: Harper & Row.

Mill, J. S. (1970). *The subjection of women (1869),* introduction by Stanton Coit. London: Longmans, Green and Co.

Mishler, E. G., & Waxler, N. E. (1968). *Interaction in families: An experimental study of family processes and schizophrenia.* New York: John Wiley & Sons.

Monahan, J. (1976). The prevention of violence. In J. Monahan (Ed.), *Community mental health and the criminal justice system.* New York: Pergamon.

Muller, K., & Dutton, D. G. (1982). *A Vancouver court's response to domestic assault.* Unpublished manuscript, University of British Columbia, School of Social Work, Vancouver.

Murstein, B. I. (1978). *Exploring intimate lifestyles.* New York: Springer.

National Research Council, U.S. (1978). *Deterrence and incapacitation.* Washington, DC: National Academy of Sciences.

Neidig, P. H., & Friedman, D. H. (1984). *Spouse abuse: A treatment program for couples.* Champaign, IL: Research Press.

Neidig, P. H., Friedman, D. H., & Collins, B. S. (1986). Attitudinal characteristics of males who have engaged in spouse abuse. *Journal of Family Violence, 1*(3), 223–234.

Ng, S. H. (1980). *The social psychology of power.* New York: Academic Press.

Nielsen, J. M., Eberle, P., Thoennes, N., & Walker, L. (1979). *Why women stay in battering relationships: Preliminary results.* Paper presented at the annual meeting of the American Sociological Association, Boston.

Nisbet, R. T., & Ross, L. (1980). *Human inference: Strategies and shortcomings of social judgment.* Englewood Cliffs, NJ: Prentice-Hall.

Notarius, C. I., & Johnson, J. I. (1982). Emotional expression in husbands and wives. *Journal of Marriage and the Family, 44,* 483–492.

Novaco, R. (1975). *Anger control: The development and evaluation of an experimental treatment.* Lexington, MA: Lexington Books.

Novaco, R. (1976, October). The functions and regulation of the arousal of anger. *American Journal of Psychiatry, 133*(10), 1124–1128.

Okun, L. (1984). *Termination or resumption of cohabitation in women-battering relationships: A statistical study.* Paper presented at the Second National Family

Violence Research Conference, Durham, NH.

Orne, M. (1969). Demand characteristics and the concept of quasi-controls. In R. Rosenthal & R. Rosnow (Eds.), *Artifact in Behavioral Research*. New York: Academic Press.

Pagelow, M. (1984). *Family Violence*. New York: Praeger.

Painter, S. L. (1985). Why do battered women stay? Theoretical perspectives. *Highlights: Newsletter of the Canadian Psychological Association*.

Parke, R., & Collmer, C. (1975). Child abuse: An interdisciplinary review. In E. M. Hetherington (Ed.), *Review of child development research* (Vol. 5). Chicago: University of Chicago Press.

Parnas, R. I. (1972). The police response to domestic disturbance. In L. Radzinowicz & M. Wolfgang (Eds.), *The criminal in the arms of the law*. New York: Basic Books.

Parnas, R. I. (1973). Prosecutorial and judicial handling of family violence. *Criminal Law Bulletin, 9*, 733.

Patterson, G. R. (1976). The aggressive child: Victim and architect of a coercive system. In E. Mash, L. Hamerlynck, & L. Handy (Eds.), *Behavior modification and families: I. Theory and research*. New York: Brunner/Mazel.

Patterson, G. R. (1979). A performance theory for coercive family interactions. In R. Cairns (Ed.), *Social interaction: Methods, analysis, and illustrations*. Hillsdale, NJ: Lawrence Erlbaum.

Patterson, G. R. (1981). *Families of antisocial children: An interactional approach*. Eugene, OR: Castalia.

Patterson, G. R., Cobb, J. A., & Ray, R. S. (1972). A social engineering technology for retraining families of aggressive boys. In H. E. Adams & J. P. Unikel (Eds.), *Issues and trends in behavior therapy*. Springfield, IL: Charles C Thomas.

Patterson, G. R., Littman, R. A., & Brickner, W. (1967). Assertive behavior in children: A step toward a theory of aggression. *Monographs of the Society for Research in Child Development, 32*(5, Serial No. 133).

Patterson, M. L. (1976). An arousal model of interpersonal intimacy. *Psychological Review, 83*(3), 235–245.

Perlmuter, L. C., & Monty, R. A. (Eds.). (1979). *Choice and perceived control*. Hillsdale, NJ: Erlbaum.

Peters, E. (1985). *Torture*. New York: Blackwell.

Phillips, D. P., & Hensley, J. E. (1984, summer). When violence is rewarded or punished: The impact of mass media stories on homicide. *Journal of Communication, 34*(3), 101–116.

Pirog-Good, M. A., & Stets, J. Recidivism in programs for abusers. *Victimology: An International Journal* (in press).

Pizzey, E. (1974). *Scream quietly or the neighbours will hear*. London: Penguin Books.

Platt, J. (1973). Social traps. *American Psychologist, 28*, 641–651.

Pleck, J. H. (1981). *The myth of masculinity*. Cambridge, MA: M.I.T. Press.

Pollack, S., & Gilligan, C. (1982). Images of violence in thematic apperception test stories. *Journal of Personality and Social Psychology, 42*, 1, 159–167.

Porter, C. A. (1983). *Blame, depression and coping in battered women*. Unpublished doctoral dissertation, University of British Columbia.

Ptacek, J. (1984). *The clinical literature on men who batter: A review and critique*. Paper presented at the Second National Conference for Family Violence Research, University of New Hampshire, Durham, NH.

Rachman, S. J., & Wilson, G. T. (1980). *The effects of psychological therapy* (2nd ed.). Oxford: Pergamon Press.

Rajecki, P., Lamb, M., & Obmascher, P. (1978). Toward a general theory of infantile attachment: A comparative review of aspects of the social bond. *The Behavioral and Brain Sciences, 3,* 417–464.

Rathus, S. A. (1973). A 30 item schedule for assessing assertive behavior. *Behavior Therapy, 4,* 498–596.

Reid, J. B., & Patterson, G. R. (1976). The modification of aggression and stealing behavior of boys in the home setting. In E. Ribes-Inesta & A. Bandura (Eds.), *Analysis of delinquency and aggression.* Hillsdale, NJ: Erlbaum.

Reid, J. B., Patterson, G. R., & Loeber, R. (1981). The abused child: Victim, instigator or innocent bystander? In D. J. Bernstein (Ed.), *Response structure and motivation.* Nebraska Symposium on Motivation, Lincoln / London, University of Nebraska Press.

Repucci, N. D., & Clingempeel, W. G. (1978). Methodological issues in research with correctional populations. *Journal of Consulting and Clinical Psychology, 46,* 727–746.

Richter, H. (1974). *The family as patient.* New York: Farrar, Straus & Giroux.

Robins, L. N., Helzer, J. E., Croughan, J., Williams, J. B. W., & Spitzer, R. L. (1981). *The NIMH Diagnostic Interview Schedule, Version III.* Washington, DC: Public Health Service.

Rokeach, M., Miller, M. G., & Snyder, J. A. (1971). The value gap between police and policed. *Journal of Social Issues, 27*(2), 155–171.

Rosenbaum, A., & O'Leary, K. D. (1981). Marital violence: Characteristics of abusive couples. *Journal of Consulting and Clinical Psychology, 41,* 63.

Rosenbaum, M. E., & deCharms, R. (1960). Direct and vicarious reduction of hostility. *Journal of Abnormal and Social Psychology, 60,* 105–111.

Rosenthal, R. (1969). Interpersonal expectations: Effects of the experimenter's hypothesis. In R. Rosenthal & R. L. Rosnow (Eds.), *Artifact in behavioral research.* New York: Academic Press.

Rosenthal, R. (1983). Assessing the statistical and social importance of the effects of psychotherapy. *Journal of Consulting and Clinical Psychology, 51*(1), 4–13.

Ross, H. L. (1982). *Deterring the drinking driver: Legal policy and social control.* Toronto: Hextington.

Rounsaville, B. (1978). Theories in marital violence: Evidence from a study of battered women. *Victimology: An International Journal, 3*(1–2), 11–31.

Rounsaville, B., Lifton, N., & Bieber, M. (1979). The natural history of a psychotherapy group for battered wives. *Psychiatry, 42*(1), 63–78.

Roy, M. (1977). *Battered women: A psychosocial study of domestic violence.* New York: Van Nostrand.

Rule, B. G., & Leger, G. L. (1976). Pain cues and differing functions of aggression. *Canadian Journal of Behavioural Science, 8,* 213–233.

Rule, B. G., & Nesdale, A. R. (1976). Emotional arousal and aggressive behavior. *Psychological Bulletin, 83,* 851–863.

Russell, J., & Mehrabian, A. (1974). Distinguishing anger and anxiety in terms of emotional response factors. *Journal of Consulting and Clinical Psychology, 42,* 79–83.

Ryan, W. (1971). *Blaming the victim.* New York: Vintage.

Sage, W. (1976, October). The war on the cults. *Human Behavior,* 40–49.

Sales, E., Baum, M., & Shore, B. (1984). Victim readjustment following assault. *Journal of Social Issues, 40*(1), 117–136.

Sanders, G. A., & Baron, R. A. (1977). Pain cues and uncertainty as determinants of aggression in a situation involving repeated instigation. *Journal of Personality and Social Psychology, 32,* 495–502.

Saulnier, D., and Perlman, D. (1981). Inmates attributions: Their antecedents and effects on coping. *Criminal Justice and Behavior, 8,* 159–172.

Saunders, D. G., & Hanusa, D. R. (1984). *Cognitive-behavioral treatment for abusive husbands: The short term effects of group therapy.* Paper presented at the Second National Conference on Family Violence Research, Durham, NH.

Schachter, S., & Singer, J. (1962). Cognitive, social and physiological determinants of emotional state. *Psychological Review, 69,* 379–399.

Schein, E. (1971). *Coercive persuasion.* New York: Norton.

Scheppele, K. L., & Bart, P. B. (1983). Through women's eyes: Defining danger in the wake of sexual assault. *Journal of Social Issues, 39*(2), 63–81.

Schram, D. (1978). Rape. In R. Chapman & M. Gates (Eds.), *The victimization of women.* Beverly Hills, CA: Sage.

Schulman, M. (1979). *A survey of spousal violence against women in Kentucky.* Washington, DC: U.S. Department of Justice, Law Enforcement Assistance Administration.

Scott, J. P. (1963). The process of primary socialization in canine and human infants. *Monographs of the Society for Research in Child Development, 28.*

Sears, R. R., Maccoby, E. E., & Levin, H. (1957). *Patterns of child rearing.* Evanston, IL: Row, Peterson.

Seay, B., Alexander, B., & Harlow, H. F. (1964). Maternal behavior of socially deprived rhesus monkeys. *Journal of Abnormal and Social Psychology, 69,* 345–354.

Seligman, M. E. (1975). *On depression, development and death.* San Francisco: Freeman.

Shainess, N. (1977). Psychological aspects of wife battering. In M. Roy (Ed.), *Battered women: A psychosocial study of domestic violence.* New York: Van Nostrand.

Sheilds, N. M., & Hanneke, C. R. (1983). Attribution processes in violent relationships: Perceptions with violent husbands and their wives. *Journal of Applied Social Psychology, 13,* 515–527.

Shepard, M. (1987). *Interventions with men who batter: An evaluation of a domestic abuse program.* Paper presented at the Third National Family Violence Research Conference, Durham, NH.

Sherman, L. W., & Berk, R. A. (1984). The specific deterrent effects of arrest for domestic assault. *American Sociological Review, 49,* 261–272.

Shore, M., & Massimo, J. V. (1979). Fifteen years after treatment: A follow up study of comprehensive psychotherapy. *American Journal of Orthopsychiatry, 49*(2), 240–245.

Short, J. F., Jr. (Ed.). (1968). *Gang delinquency and delinquent subcultures.* New York: Harper & Row.

Shotland, L., & Straw, M. (1976). Bystander response to an assault: When a man attacks a woman. *Journal of Personality and Social Psychology, 34*(5), 990–999.

Silver, R. L., Boon, C., & Stones, M. L. (1983). Searching for meaning in misfortune: Making sense of incest. *Journal of Social Issues, 39*(2), 83–103.

Simeons, W. (1962). *Man's presumptuous brain.* New York: Dutton.

Slavin, M. (1972). *The theme of feminine evil: The image of women in male fantasy and its effects on attitudes and behavior.* Unpublished doctoral dissertation, Harvard University, MA.

Slovic, P., Fischoff, B., & Lichenstein, S. (1982). Facts versus fears: Understanding perceived risk. In D. Kahneman, P. Slovic, & A. Tversky (Eds.), *Judgement under uncertainty: Heuristics and biases.* Cambridge, England: Cambridge University Press.

Smart, M. S., Dewey, J. E., & Goodman, M. S. (1987). *A progress report on measuring recovery in abused women.* Paper presented at the Third National Family Violence Research Conference, Durham, NH.

Smith, D. A., & Klein, J. R. (1984). Police control of interpersonal disputes. *Social Problems, 31*(4), 468–481.

Smith, P., & Chalmers, D. L. (1984). *Does sheltering help abused women?* Paper presented at the annual meeting of the Canadian Sociology and Anthropology Association, Guelph, Ontario.

Snell, J. E., Rosenwald, P. J., & Robey, A. (1964). The wifebeater's wife. *Archives of General Psychiatry, 11,* 107–113.

Snyder, D. K., & Fruchtman, L. A. (1981). Differential patterns of wife abuse: A database typology. *Journal of Consulting and Clinical Psychology, 49,* 848–885.

Snyder, D. K., & Scheer, N. A. (1981). Predicting disposition following brief residence at a shelter for battered women. *American Journal of Community Psychology, 9,* 559–566.

Solicitor General of Canada (1985). Canadian Urban Victimization Survey. *Female Victims of Crime,* Bulletin #4, Ottawa.

Solomon, R. L. (1980). The opponent-process theory of acquired motivation: The costs of pleasure and the benefits of pain. *American Psychologist, 35*(8), 691–712.

Sonkin, D. J., & Durphy, M. (1982). *Learning to live without violence: A handbook for men.* San Francisco: Volcano Press.

Sonkin, D. J., Martin, D., & Walker, L. E. (1985). *The male batterer: a treatment approach.* New York: Springer.

Spanier, G. (1976). Measuring dyadic adjustment: New scales for assessing the quality of marriage and similar dyads. *Journal of Marriage and the Family, 38,* 15–28.

Spence, J. T., & Helmreich, R. L. (1978). *Masculinity and Femininity: The psychological dimensions, correlates and antecedents.* Austin: University of Texas Press.

Standing Committee on Health, Welfare, and Social Affairs (1982). *Report on violence in the family: Wife battering.* House of Commons, Ottawa.

Stark, E., Flitcraft, A., & Frazier, W. (1979). Medicine and patriarchal violence: The social construction of a private event. *International Journal of Health Services, 9*(3), 461–493.

Stark, R., & McEvoy, J. (1970). Middle class violence. *Psychology Today, 4*(6), 107–112.

Steiner, G. (1981). *The futility of family policy.* Washington, DC: Brookings Institute.

Steinmetz, S. K. (1977). *The cycle of violence: Assertive, aggressive and abusive family interaction.* New York: Praeger.

Stewart, A., & Rubin, Z. (1976). The power motive in the dating couple. *Journal of Personality and Social Psychology, 34,* 305–309.

Stone, A. A. (1985). A new legal standard of dangerousness: Fair in theory unfair in practice. In C. Webster, M. Ben-Aron, & A. J. Hucker (Eds.), *Dangerousness: Probability and prediction, psychiatry and public policy.* Cambridge: Cambridge University Press.

Straus, M. A. (1973). A general systems theory approach to a theory of violence between family members. *Social Science Information, 12*(3), 105–125.

Straus, M. A. (1976). Sexual inequality, cultural norm and wife beating. *Victimology, 1*, 54–76.

Straus, M. A. (1977a). Wife beating: How common and why? *Victimology, 2*(3–4), 443–459.

Straus, M. A. (1977b, March). Violence in the family: How widespread, why it occurs and some thoughts on prevention. In *Family Violence: Proceedings from Symposium, United Way of Greater Vancouver.*

Straus, M. A. (1977c). Societal morphogenesis and intrafamily violence in cross cultural perspective. *Annals of the New York Academy of Sciences, 285*, 718–730.

Straus, M. A. (1979). Measuring family conflict and violence: The conflict tactics scale. *Journal of Marriage and the Family, 41*, 75–88.

Straus, M. A. (1980). Victims and aggressors in marital violence. *American Behavioral Scientist, 23*(5), 681–704.

Straus, M. A. (1986). Domestic violence and homicide antecedants. *Bulletin of the N.Y. Academy of Medicine, 62*(5), 446–465.

Straus, M. A., & Gelles, R. J. (1985, November). *Is family violence increasing? A comparison of 1975 and 1985 national survey rates.* Paper presented at the American Society of Criminology, San Diego, CA.

Straus, M. A., & Gelles, R. J. (1986). Societal change in family violence from 1975 to 1985 as revealed by two national surveys. *Journal of Marriage and the Family, 48*, 465–479.

Straus, M. A., Gelles, R. J., & Steinmetz, S. (1980). *Behind closed doors: Violence in the American family.* Doubleday, NY: Anchor Press.

Strentz, T. (1979, April). Law enforcement policy and ego defenses of the hostage. *FBI Law Enforcement Bulletin,* p. 2.

Strube, M. J., & Barbour, L. S. (1983). The decision to leave an abusive relationship: Economic dependence and psychological commitment. *Journal of Marriage and the Family. 45*, 785–793.

Strube, M. J., & Barbour, L. S. (1984). Factors related to the decision to leave an abusive relationship. *Journal of Marriage and the Family, 46*(4), 837–844.

Summers, M. (1928). *Malleus Maleficarum.* London: Pushkin.

Symonds, M. (1975). Victims of violence: Psychological effects and after effects. *American Journal of Psychoanalysis, 35*, 19–26.

Symonds, M. (1980). "The 'second injury' to victims" and "Acute responses of victims to terror." *Evaluation & Change,* Special Issue, 36–41.

Symons, D. (1980). *The evolution of human sexuality.* Cambridge, MA: Cambridge University Press.

Symons, D. (1981). Personal communication.

Tannahill, R. (1980). *Sex in history.* New York: Stein and Day.

Tannenbaum, P., & Zillmann, D. (1975). Emotional arousal in the facilitation of aggression through communication. *Advances in Experimental Social Psychology, 8*, 150–188.

Taylor-Johnson Temperament Analysis Manual (1980). Los Angeles: Psychological Publications.

Taylor, G. R. (1954). *Sex in history.* New York: Vanguard Press.

Taylor, S. P., & Epstein, S. (1967). The measurement of autonomic arousal. *Psychosomatic*

Medicine, 29, 514–525.

Teske, R. H., & Parker, M. L. (1983). *Spouse abuse in Texas: A study of women's attitudes and experiences.* Huntsville, TX: Criminal Justice Center, Sam Houston State University.

Timmerman, J. (1981). *Prisoner without a name, cell without a number.* New York: Vintage.

Tinbergen, N. (1951). *The study of instinct.* London: Oxford University Press.

Toch, H. (1969). *Violent men: An inquiry into the psychology of violence.* Chicago: Aldine.

Tuchman, B. W. (1984). *The march of folly.* New York: Alfred A. Knopf.

Turner, C., Fenn, M., & Cole, A. (1981). A social psychological analysis of violent behavior. In R. B. Stuart (Ed.), *Violent behavior: Social learning approaches.* New York: Brunner/Mazel.

Tversky, A., & Kahneman, D. (1973). Availability: A heuristic for judging frequency and probability. *Cognitive Psychology, 5,* 207–232.

Ulbrich, P., & Huber, J. (1981). Observing parental aggression: Distribution and effects. *Journal of Marriage and the Family, 43,* 623–631.

U.S. Commission on Civil Rights. (1978). *Battered women: Issues of public policy.* Washington, DC: U.S. Government Printing Office.

U.S. Department of Justice (1980). Intimate victims: A study of violence among friends and relatives. Washington, DC: U.S. Government Printing Office.

Waaland, P., & Keeley, S. (1985). Police decision making in wife abuse: The impact of legal and extralegal factors. *Law and Human Behavior, 9*(4), 355–366.

Wahler, R. G. (1980). The multiply entrapped parent: Obstacles to change in parent child problems. In J. P. Vincent (Ed.), *Advances in family intervention, assessment and therapy.* Greenwich, CT: JAI Press.

Walker, L. (1978). *Psychotherapy and counseling with battered women.* Paper presented at the American Psychological Association.

Walker, L. E. (1979a). *The battered woman.* New York: Harper & Row.

Walker, L. E. (1979b). Treatment alternatives for battered spouses. In J. R. Chapman, & M. Gates (Eds.), *The victimization of women.* Beverly Hills, CA: Sage.

Walters, R. H., & Brown, M. (1963). Studies of reinforcement of aggression. III. Transfer of responses to an interpersonal situation. *Child Development, 34,* 563–571.

Watson, R. I. (1973). Investigation into deindividuation using a cross-cultural survey technique. *Journal of Personality and Social Psychology, 25*(3), 342–345.

Weisz, A. E., & Taylor, R. L. (1970). American presidential assassination. In D. N. Daniels, M. F. Gilula, & F. M. Ochberg (Eds.), *Violence and the struggle for existence.* Boston: Little, Brown.

White, G. L. (1980). Inducing jealousy: A power perspective. *Personality and Social Psychology Bulletin, 6,* 222–227.

Whitehurst, R. N. (1971). Violence potential in extramarital sexual resposes. *Journal of Marriage and the Family, 33,* 683–691.

Whitehurst, R. N. (1974). Violence in husband-wife interaction. In S. K. Steinmetz & M. A. Straus (Eds.), *Violence in the family.* New York: Harper & Row.

Widiger, T. A., Williams, J. B., Spitzer, R. L., & Frances, A. (1985). The MCMI as a measure of DSM-III. *Journal of Personality Assessment, 49*(4), 366–391.

Williams, K., & Carmody, D. (1987). Wife assault: Perceptions of sanctions and deterrence. Unpublished manuscript, Family Research Laboratory, University of New Hampshire.

Williams, K., & Hawkins, R. (1984). *Perceptual research on general deterrence: A critical review.* Paper presented at American Society for Criminology, Cincinnati, OH.

Wilson, E. O. (1975). *Sociobiology.* Cambridge: Harvard University Press.

Wilson, E. O. (1978). *On human nature.* Cambridge: Harvard University Press.

Wilson, J. Q. (1983). *Thinking about crime.* New York: Basic Books.

Wilt, G. M., & Breedlove, R. K. (1977). *Domestic violence and the police: Studies in Detroit and Kansas City.* Washington, DC: Police Foundation.

Winter, D. G. (1973). *The power motive.* New York: Free Press.

Wolfe, D., Jaffe, P., Wilson, S., & Zak, L. (1985). Children of battered women: The relation of child behavior to family violence and maternal stress. *Journal of Consulting and Clinical Psychology, 53,* 657–665.

Wolfgang, M. E., & Ferracuti, F. (1967). *The subculture of violence.* London: Tavistock.

Worden, R. E., & Pollitz, A. A. (1984). Police arrests in domestic disturbances: A further look. *Law & Society Review, 18*(1), 105–119.

Wortman, C. (1976). Causal attributions and personal control. *New Directions in Attribution Research, 1,* 23–52.

Wynne-Edwards, V. C. (1962). *Animal dispersion in relation to social behaviour.* Edinburgh & London: Oliver & Boyd.

Yalom, T. D. (1975). *The theory and practice of group psychotherapy.* New York: Basic Books.

Zacker, J., & Bard, M. (1977). Further findings on assaultiveness and alcohol use in interpersonal disputes. *American Journal of Community Psychology, 5*(4), 373–383.

Zimbardo, P. G. (1969). The human choice: Individuation, reason and order vs. deindividuation, impulse and chaos. *Nebraska Symposium on Motivation,* University of Nebraska Press.

Zimbardo, P. G., Haney, C., & Banks, W. C. (1972, April 8). A Pirandellian prison: The mind is a formidable jailer. *New York Times Magazine,* pp. 38–60.

Zimring, F. E., & Hawkins, G. J. (1973). *Deterrence: The legal threat in crime control.* Chicago: University of Chicago Press.

Zuckerman, M. (1979). *Sensation seeking: Beyond the optimal level of arousal.* Hillsdale, NJ: Erlbaum.

Zuckerman, M., Lubin, B., Vogel, L., & Valerius, E. (1964). Measurement of experimentally induced affects. *Journal of Consulting Psychology, 28*(5), 418–425.

Author Index

Subject Index